On the drive to New York City, Joe Castellucci brought up the life insurance policy that was rejected by Horace Mann Life Insurance.

Herb Schwartz perked up. "What insurance?"

Castellucci explained, "If Jon died, 50 percent would go to me, and 50 percent to Jon's wife. But that agreement was rejected."

They talked about revising the policy so that Planet 3 Films would be the beneficiary. "If Planet 3 is the beneficiary, the money stays in the business," Herb suggested.

Joe Thomas, who was sitting in the back seat, laughingly said, "Well, we could always bump Jon off and collect the insurance!"

They all laughed and recalled television shows, like *Alfred Hitchcock Presents,* where people committed the perfect murder and got away with it.

Dedicated to the Pownall family

"When we think about murder, we start off thinking about the immediate consequences. We may think about the husband taken away from his wife, the father taken from his children, the son taken from his parents. We think about a hole left in people's lives and hearts. What we don't think about is how quickly that person is stripped of everything but his victimhood. To the world, that's all the victim will ever be. Society doesn't know how to deal with the family members who must continue on, victims themselves. They may even be shunned, making a victim of a violent crime even worse."

—Thomas G. Pownall

The Art of Murder in the State of Maine

GOODBYE, FAT LARRY

The Murder of
Movie Director Jon Pownall

ELLY STEVENS

With Larry Cieslinski

Cover by Kate Rawlins, Fiverr

Back cover photo provided by the Pownall family.

Layout by Suzanne Blessing

Copyright ©2024 Elly Stevens

No part of this book may be reproduced in whole or in part without the written permission from the author, unless it is public record.

Printed in the United States of America

ISBN 979-8-218-50244-7

Library of Congress Control Number: 2024919205

https://www.authorellystevens.com

AUTHOR'S NOTES:

All suspects are presumed innocent until proven guilty in a court of law.

The spoken word came directly from statements to police, the court transcripts, newspaper articles, movie cast, or family. In a few cases during the investigation, when it was not provided, conversation was constructed to support fact.

Several news agencies were contacted for permission to print the photos and articles used in this book. No copyright infringement was intended on photos they could no longer locate for the purpose of permission or where the news agencies no longer exist.

Contents

	Page
List of chief "actors"	i
Introduction *by Elly Stevens*	v
The calling *by Larry Cieslinski*	viii

The Murder   1
(August 30 – October 27, 1973)

The crime scene	3
Who was Jon Pownall?	21
The evidence	31
Canvassing the area	34
Cause and manner of death	38
The gun sale	42
The wormdigger's find	45

The Movie   53
(March – August 1973)

The partnership	55
The Salem Six	62
The investors	69
Horace Mann life insurance policy	79
Car ride to New York City	83
Transamerica life insurance policy	85
Failed promises and restless natives	89
Letter to Attorney Reef	91
Corporation vs. film ownership	93
The countdown: The altered drinks	100
Negotiations intensify	105
Contract for murder	108
The white fedora and matchbook	122
The last goodbye	130
Jon's last few hours	135
A sinking heart	137
Larry's promise *by Larry Cieslinski*	140

	Page
Statements, Arrests, and Indictments (August 31, 1973 – February 14, 1975)	**143**
Police interview Nancy Payne	145
Detectives interrogate Castellucci	150
Jean Pownall tells PPD to follow the money	153
The knock on Schwartz' door	156
Warnings and threats	158
Breaking news across the nation	161
Shock and tears	162
Reef accompanies Schwartz to PPD	166
Castellucci questioned again	168
Lying low	171
The missing Volvo, the wallet, and a check for heroin	175
David W. Joy	175
Donald G. Joy	177
Bruce Littlejohn	178
Police bring in Dongo	183
Paul Turnage calls detectives	185
Jean Pownall's updates	190
The pressure is on	192
Mounting debts and insurance money	199
Dickerman's statement	203
Planet 3's option agreement	205
Visits to Schwartz and Doyle	207
Follow-up with Dongo at home	210
Bramhall Pub	213
Miranda rights read to Castellucci	218
Arrests and indictments for murder	220
Jailhouse snitch	222
Detectives connect the dots	227

	Page
The Trials **(May 12, 1975 – July 22, 1976)**	**233**
The judge and trial lawyers	235
Superior Court Judge, Harry P. Glassman	235
The Prosecution team	235
The Defense team	236
The jury	237
Jury considerations in the murder trial	238
A decision reached	265
Preparation for the conspiracy trial	268
The conspiracy trial	271
Preparation for the civil suits	273
Civil-suit deposition	274
Whatever happened to…?	**287**
Whatever happened to Herbert Schwartz?	289
Whatever happened to Truman Dongo?	291
Tammy Bonneau Walter	292
Lisa Morelli	300
Whatever happened to Joe Castellucci?	304
Whatever happened to *The Salem Six* cast?	309
Whatever happened to the gun?	312
Whatever happened to the Pownall family?	314
Author's thoughts *by Elly Stevens*	317
Epilogue *by Larry Cieslinski*	322
Acknowledgements	324
About Elly Stevens	328
About Larry Cieslinski	329
Sources	330

List of chief "actors"

Jon Pownall – Filmmaker and Director of *Goodbye, Fat Larry* and *The Salem Six*

Jean Pownall – Jon's wife and assistant in the Chicago Photographic Studio, mother of three

Lynda Pownall – Jon and Jean's daughter

Jon & Thomas Pownall – Jon and Jean's sons

Joseph Castellucci – Principal owner of Planet 3 Films and Producer of *The Salem Six*

Joseph Thomas – Director of the Portland Players, introduced Herbert Schwartz as an investor

Herbert Schwartz – Owner of Herbert R. Schwartz Associates interior design, and promoter of *The Salem Six*

Truman Dongo – Business owner, convicted felon, introduced by Herb Schwartz as a potential investor

Michael Doyle – Chapman & Drake insurance agent, investor, owned 2 percent of Planet 3 Films

Nancy Payne – Planet 3 secretary, talent coordinator, and Castellucci's lover

Stuart Lamont – Horace Mann Insurance agent and cohort of Castellucci

Nancy Phillips – Transamerica Insurance Company agent, Los Angeles, California

Felipe Fabregat – Estudios Churubusco Azteca, Mexico City

Jean Shepherd, Jr. – Scriptwriter and humorist

David Dickerman – Potential big investor from Boston who wanted ownership

Peter O'Donovan – Associate of Dongo

Planet 3's Film Crew:

    Bill Birch – Director of Photography

    Bill Wilson – Unit Manager, Chicago

    Irby Smith – Assistant Director to Jon Pownall, Los Angeles

    Bruce Littlejohn – Worked on the Conrak boards

    David W. Joy – Grip/Film Technician

Joe Emerton – Wormdigger and trial witness

Roland Dube – Dongo's cellmate in the Cumberland County Jail

Portland Police Department:

    Sergeant Kenneth Peterson – First officer on scene

    Sergeant Ronald Eccles – Responsible for crime scene evidence/photography

    Detective Peter Conley – Lead Homicide investigator on Pownall case

    Detective Clement Dodd – Homicide investigator on Pownall case

Maine State Police:

    Corporal William Manduca – Firearms examiner & ballistics expert

    Detective Martin Greeley – Investigative detective

    Deputy Willard Stuart – Sold gun

Doctor Charles F. Branch – Chief Medical Examiner for the State of Maine

Paul Baumgarten – New York attorney, specializing in corporate law

Planet 3 Films Attorneys:

> **Norman Reef** – Primary attorney for Planet 3 Films, pushed a Director's Contract
>
> **Daniel Mooers** – Worked on agreement

Richard A. Spencer – Jon Pownall's attorney; worked on contract negotiations

Alexander MacNichol – Joe Castellucci's attorney

Ralph I. Lancaster, Jr. – Transamerica Insurance Company attorney

Honorable Harry P. Glassman – Justice, Superior Court, State of Maine

Richard S. Cohen – Deputy Attorney General for the State of Maine, Prosecutor

Vernon E. Arey – Assistant Attorney General for the State of Maine, Prosecutor

Daniel G. Lilley – Defense attorney for T. Dongo

Jack Simmons – Defense attorney for H. Schwartz

Terms:

Conrak Boards – "Day-to-day" film shooting: who/what is needed. Today it would be called a "stripboard."

The Books – Script, pictures of the children on location, the completed budget, and the Conrak boards.

Introduction

By Elly Stevens

Goodbye, Fat Larry is a true crime, based on facts—evidence, depositions, and court transcripts after the murder of Jon Pownall on August 30, 1973. The story has been an obsession of Jon's first son-in-law, Larry Cieslinski.

Why was Larry so adamant that I write about a murder that happened over 50 years ago? Because he is a medium and Jon Pownall speaks to him from the afterlife, directing Larry to have his story told. However, this is not a story of Larry's psychic ability; it is a story of a creative man whose lifelong dream to direct a full-length film was destroyed by greed, and whose loved ones were left without a husband/father/son/brother.

I met Larry in kindergarten at Our Lady of Perpetual Help grammar school and church in Rochester, New York, in the fall of 1953. As children, we observed our classmates, but rarely interacted with the opposite sex. I don't remember talking to Larry, or Larry talking to me, in nine years. He always sat near the front of class due to his small stature. His dark hair always fell on his forehead, and he seemed anxious and unable to sit still, but he was smart. I always sat in the second vertical row of girls, in alphabetical order.

Larry and I graduated together from eighth grade in 1962. Larry went on to attend the first class of Bishop Kearney High School in the nearby suburb of Irondequoit. I went to an all-girls school, Nazareth Academy. We didn't see each other again for decades.

It wasn't until our mutual grade-school classmate, Irene, decided to have an informal class reunion in 2013 at Bill Gray's restaurant in Irondequoit that we met again. Larry and I hugged, and we were happy to see each other, but there wasn't a lot of time to dig into each other's past. After a second reunion in 2015, we became Facebook friends. We both liked cats, and that was how we bonded. Until April 16, 2020.

For about two weeks, Larry had been on my mind. He seemed to have experienced a great deal over the years—jamming with major musicians and bands and owning a foreign car automotive repair business and junkyard. I found myself wondering, *Who is Larry really? I want to know.* So, on one of his posts about a Steppenwolf concert, I said, "I'd like to hear about your life sometime, Larry. We'll have to chat."

I never expected such an immediate response: "We need to write a book. We can start today!" I was taken aback as it was so sudden and so imperative; also, I was already in the middle of writing a mystery novel; and lastly, because it was my birthday, and I was spending my time during the COVID-19 pandemic thanking online friends for their wishes and answering texts and phone calls.

Larry began to send me notes about the story he needed to tell, and that I was the chosen one to write this book. He called me "the hero." He couldn't rest until Jon Pownall's story was out there.

GOODBYE, FAT LARRY

Jon Pownall was messaging Larry that "It is time." And so it was.

I began researching, forming a storyboard, and putting words on paper.

Larry and I traveled to Portland, Maine, twice, to do research and visit the key locations in the story. We saw the haunts of the alleged conspirators, the building where the murder was committed, the place where the murder weapon was found, and Jon Pownall's final resting place. On our second trip, we met with the Portland Police Department's Attorney Jen Thompson (courtesy of Detective Robert Martin), who allowed us to copy whatever we needed from the case files.

"Once you kill a man, it's a lot easier the second time..."

The calling

By Larry Cieslinski

My name is Larry and I've been talking to dead people since I was four, just before kindergarten. They didn't think I'd be alive when I was 17. I fooled them.

The voices come in one ear and go back out the other. They don't like that.

Even though I have a 148+ I.Q., I didn't complete high school, and it took me 36 years to get my GED. I couldn't sit still. I had a couple of teachers who liked me, but I was often asked to step outside of class by a few other teachers. Sometimes I just come off as annoying. Maybe I'm a little bi-polar.

I always loved cars. When I was 17, General Motors recruited me to talk to their engineers about fuel injection.

Ten years after Jon Pownall hit the floor, dead, I was in Maine, stirring around the dust. Since I owned a junkyard, every time I went to Portland, it was in a different car.

And I was blinded either by love or the adventure. From the moment I met her (Jon's daughter Lynda) at my business in Rochester, New York, in 1981, I knew my life would never be the same.

I was playing old records on a Victrola that my mother had given me. The music came to a complete stop when the woman began speaking to me.

GOODBYE, FAT LARRY

Something was happening. I couldn't figure out what. Her name was Lynda. Lynda Pownall.

She had an unusual accent and drove a blue Saab that needed to have a door replaced. We started to chat. I needed to know everything about her. She told me where she lived, and it was just around the corner from me. Yes, I was in a serious relationship with two children at home, but I was captivated with Lynda.

When Lynda came to pick up her car, she told me that we had replaced the wrong door. I got out a bottle of Jim Beam and we had a shot.

One night after the correct car door was installed, I delivered her Saab, and we talked. Lynda said that her father had been murdered. She brought out a scrapbook filled with pictures and newspaper clippings dealing with her father's death on August 30, 1973—her own Murder Book. It was a bizarre, disturbing story that kept me up at night.

Back in 1973, inflation forced higher wages and higher gas prices; Japanese car manufacturers began to make an impact on the buying public; corporations were growing and hiring; Automatic Teller Machines (ATMs) made an appearance as well as desktop IBM computers; and Steve Sassone, the inventor of the digital camera, went to work for Kodak. The U.S. made abortion a constitutional right; the Watergate proceedings began; Spiro Agnew resigned as Vice-President; and Skylab was launched into space. Music was changing from rock and roll and folk to disco, and fashion was transitioning from the casual hippie look to three-piece suits, wide collars, and classic bell bottoms. Organized crime (and unorganized crime) was alive and well throughout the U.S.

ELLY STEVENS

And Jon Pownall was murdered.

I had a million thoughts going through my head. I finally understood why it was important for Lynda and me to meet. Jon Pownall needed to talk to me.

Lynda introduced her mother to me. I heard their whispered conversation in the kitchen as I sat on the living room couch. Jean Pownall was asking with disdain in her voice, "What is it you see in him?" It stung, but I knew Lynda and I were meant for each other.

Jean was Jon's "Best Girl," a filmmaker's term for his female assistant, gofer, someone who handles the lighting, electrical, costuming, model positioning, hair, makeup, and more. While Jon photographed the models, Jean took care of everything else under his direction. Plus, she made sure the models had a place to rest and fed them and the crew during shooting and mixed their drinks.

I was hooked on Jon's story, and it wasn't long before Lynda, her mother, and I headed to Maine so that I could "meet" Jon and get a glimpse of the men who killed him.

On the way out of Rochester, we stopped where I got a reading from a seer. She sat across from me and in her matter-of-fact voice advised, "Once you kill a man, it's a lot easier the second time..." I had been told that many times by different men and one dangerous woman. When you hear that from someone you're with, your blood runs cold.

The seer also told me, "You cannot write this story until everyone is dead. Then it will be safe to continue. You can do it. But it has to be through your eyes." So,

I put the story "in my back pocket." Always at my fingertips; never forgotten.

As we were reaching our destination, Jon's voice was strong, pushing me forward. I was meant to be there to learn all I could about his murder to tell the story to anyone who would listen.

It was my first trip to Portland, but it wouldn't be the last.

On another trip to Portland, Lynda and I met with the attorney for the insurance company and Detectives Conley and Dodd, the lead Homicide detectives in the case.

When we asked questions around town, no one wanted to talk to a New Yorker; they would give you the cold shoulder. I was just following the directions given to me by a dead man.

A Portland news reporter showed up and wrote an article about Lynda and me, "drinking cheap champagne from Styrofoam cups, celebrating an unusual anniversary—the death of Jon Pownall." My Rambler's windshield was cracked by uncorking the bottle of champagne.

In 1986, Lynda and I were married by the Brighton Justice of the Peace in New York. I was officially part of the Pownall family, and it wasn't coincidence or chance. Not when I talk to dead people. I was on a mission to find out what really happened to my father-in-law.

Lynda and I drove to Portland that December and stayed at Jon's "camp." I saw a moose swimming across the pond. It must have weighed 2,000 pounds. It was as big as a small car.

We could see daylight through the walls of the house and slept in a sleeping bag with the fireplace blazing.

On August 10, 1986, Lynda gave birth to our beautiful little girl, Erin. And at the end of that same month, the three of us were on our way back to Sanford, Maine, in an orange 1973 VW camper van. A couple of neighborhood kids (brothers) also came along for the ride.

It was just a few miles down the road when the van slowed down. I heard the rod bearing start to rattle and realized that the engine was about to go. I took the first left...

We were at the top of a hill. People sing about Jesus taking the wheel, but on this night, Jon took the wheel, and the bus glided down the hill for what seemed like hours and miles, sometimes reaching over 50 miles an hour. We went through a couple of red lights where there was no traffic, thankfully.

Finally, I was able to pull the VW camper into a strip-mall parking lot at the corner of Sandusky Boulevard in Utica, New York. We could go no further, and I was exhausted. We packed enough food and drinks to be comfortable for the night.

The next day, I found a 1976 Pontiac convertible for sale, bought it, and continued to Portland. Lynda had taken the wheel, and I went to sleep. Suddenly, Jon woke me up...and I yelled to Lynda to "stop the car!" She was doing 50 mph and, as I yelled, I caught a glimpse of a "Road Ends" sign. If it weren't for Jon waking me up, we would have wrecked the car, or worse.

GOODBYE, FAT LARRY

On August 30, 2023, it was 50 years since Jon was murdered and the mystery remains.

My author friend Elly Stevens and I will take you back to 1973 and tell you what happened to Jon Pownall.

The Murder

(August 30 – October 27, 1973)

"No one here gets out alive." — Jim Morrison

The crime scene

Portland, Maine

August 30, 1973

Gunshots rang out on Congress Street across from Monument Square in the Arts section of the city. Pigeons, nestled on the Soldiers and Sailors Monument, were startled by the loud sounds and flew out frantically to find a safer spot some distance away until it was safe to return. The digital readout above the historic Time and Temperature Building flashed the time at 11:11 p.m. The silent street and buildings were empty at that hour. Other than the pigeons, no one heard the shots.

A cassette tape of a John Denver album was heard through an open upper window of the Maine National Bank.

The square, which was under renovation, housed various construction vehicles and trailers, and Congress Street itself was torn up for new utilities and a new traffic pattern. Most of the usual parking spots were empty...except for an orange-and-white Volkswagen bus and one or two other vehicles parked along the square.

August 17, 1973 "Monument Square, 1973." *Street Scenes – Portland Press Herald Still Film Negatives.*

Planet 3 Films' President Joseph Castellucci was nervous. He had gone to the house of his secretary, Nancy Payne, around midnight, concerned that Jon Pownall was not answering his phone. Nancy tried calling the office herself. Perhaps Jon had stepped out for something to eat. Perhaps he was sleeping or using the third-floor restroom. Joe convinced Nancy that they needed to go to their office and make sure Jon was okay.

GOODBYE, FAT LARRY

Castellucci drove past Jon's VW Bus and parked. Joe and Nancy entered the side entrance to the Maine National Bank and went to the mezzanine level where the office was located. They saw that the glass door to the office was open. Joe nudged Nancy to walk in front of him as they entered the office and headed down the carpeted hallway.

Just after 12:40 a.m., the secretary walked into the office of movie director Jon Pownall and found him slumped over the edge of a couch...

...Dead.

Nancy raised her trembling hands to cover her mouth and gasped.

She rushed to her desk, picked up the phone receiver, and dialed the number for the police, but Joe took the receiver from her and told the police that they had discovered a body on the mezzanine of the Maine Bank inside Planet 3 Films, 465 Congress Street.

* * * * *

Sergeant Kenneth Peterson of the Portland Police Department (PPD) was at the scene of a fire when he was dispatched to 465 Congress Street. Someone had found a dead body in the offices above the Maine National Bank. He raced to the scene in his vehicle, Code 3 (lights and sirens). At approximately 12:55 a.m., Peterson pulled up to the bank entrance where a man and a woman stood on the sidewalk. He radioed in his arrival at the scene of a reported 10-44 (fatality) and requested assistance. Nancy Payne told Peterson that she was the secretary at Planet 3 Films and that she had seen "a foot" on the floor in one of their offices. The tall, balding male with Nancy gave the name

Joseph Castellucci. Castellucci claimed that he was the President of Planet 3 Films. He seemed nervous and allowed Miss Payne to do all the talking.

There were two elevators inside the entry, but they took the stairway up to the mezzanine. The door to Planet 3 was ajar, and popular music was coming from a tape deck inside the office. They went in.

Maine National Bank back entrance, stairway to the mezzanine, and elevators.

Photo ©Elly Stevens, 2021

Payne and Castellucci led Peterson to Jon Pownall's office. There, in the first room on the left, on the west end of the building, he saw a rather heavyset man with long, dirty-blond hair tied with a ribbon in a ponytail, slumped on a couch, face down in a pool of blood. Peterson touched the victim's wrist to check for a pulse. There was none, and the man was cool. He was dead, but not yet in rigor.

The victim was in a kneeling position on the floor, with his left foot under his buttocks and his right foot off to the right. His right hand and head were resting on top of the green-and-yellow striped couch cushion and, under his head, near the forehead, were a pair of wire-rimmed "granny glasses," somewhat askew. His left arm was dangling. He was wearing a long-sleeved denim shirt and blue-and-white striped pants. Peterson noticed a significant amount of dark red blood (about three inches below the collar of the blue shirt) that had spread downwards. There was also blood coming from his nose.

Castellucci asked, "Is he dead?"

"Yes, sir. I am sorry; he has expired," the sergeant replied.

Although the pair were nervous up to that point, they seemed to relax and accept that the man was dead.

At that moment, they heard someone knocking on the outside door to the building. Nancy went down to let in Officer Robert Miles. She identified herself and led him up the stairs to the mezzanine. Miles then took charge of the Planet 3 Films offices.

Officer Miles ordered Nancy and Joe to sit on the couch in the reception area, not to go anywhere, or touch anything. as he and Peterson began to clear the rest of the space.

The Planet 3 Film reception area was at the far-left end of their offices. Turning to the right, the officers went through an area closest to Preble Street where they came to a hallway going in two directions.

They entered the office where the dead man was slumped on the couch. Miles and Peterson glanced around the room for a weapon, but saw none, ruling out suicide in their minds. Inside the room were two tables, two chairs, a desk, a couch, and a radiator against the wall.

Soon, the scene would be busy with investigators, each fulfilling their part of the process, so Miles mentally observed everything around the office and especially around the victim so he could write an accurate report.

Despite the victim's suspicious death, there were no signs of a struggle in any of the offices. No lamps overturned, no files rummaged through, no pockets turned inside out.

Still armed and ready, Miles and Peterson continued down the hallway to an open door and cleared the last room—a conference room with a long table and several chairs. On the table was a man's wallet. Peterson went through the wallet, finding a receipt for the Stagecoach Restaurant for $15.75, $4.02 in cash, photos of kids, and a license belonging to Jon Pownall. That matched the identification he was given by Miss Payne. Peterson picked up an envelope with a folded piece of paper—reservations for a plane trip to California that same day. He wondered if the trip had anything to do with the murder. They left the evidence where they found it and planned to point out everything to the Homicide detectives.

Meanwhile, in the reception area, Nancy was still in shock and distress, and Joe was nervous and restless. They had given a brief description of when and how they found the body, and Miles took notes.

When Peterson returned to where they were seated, he picked up the desk phone and called his supervisor, Lieutenant Quirk, and asked for assistance from Homicide and the Maine State Police.

A minute later, the telephone rang, and everyone stared at it.

Sergeant Peterson answered the call. It was a woman who pressed for answers.

"This is Mrs. Pownall. Where is my husband? Who are you and why are you there?" she challenged.

He replied, "This is Sergeant Peterson of the Portland Police Department. I'm sorry, Ma'am. I'm not at liberty to discuss the matter."

"What 'matter'?" she asked with rising fear in her voice. Shaken, she demanded to speak to Joe Castellucci. Peterson handed the phone receiver to him.

"Jeannie, he's been shot," Joe said with as much sympathy as he could muster.

Then Nancy took the phone receiver.

Nancy heard Jeannie ask, "Is he dead?"

"Oh my God, yes, he's dead."

Jean matter-of-factly asked Nancy, "Was it a shotgun blast to the face?"

Bewildered, Nancy said no.

Jean then asked, "To his heart?"

Nancy wasn't sure and told Jean that. After she expressed her condolences, she told Jean Pownall that she would call her later.

Peterson looked at the witnesses. There was something odd about Castellucci's comment to the victim's wife. He had not told Castellucci anything about the cause of death.

Peterson asked Miles to call the janitor to find out who entered or left the building that night. Shortly thereafter, Alfie J. Oaks arrived, dressed in work gear.

"We need to ask you a few questions," Miles informed him.

Oaks nodded.

"When do you get on duty?"

"I work the day shift, so I get in just before 9 a.m."

"Do you lock up?"

"Yes, sir. Every night, the main entrance is locked at 6 o'clock sharp."

"So, you locked up last night?"

"Yes, sir. I remember locking the door."

"How would someone get inside after the door is locked?"

"If they had a key, they could get in. They just need to close the door tight. It locks itself."

"What time did you leave?"

"At 6:58 p.m."

"Did you see anyone enter the building last night?"

"Around 6:30, a young man about 25 came, carrying a yellow envelope, asking if he could be let into the Planet 3 office on the mezzanine."

"Oh? Can you describe him?"

"He was white, but dark complexioned. He stood about five-foot-seven, maybe 165 pounds. Medium long, straight, black hair."

"Did you let him into the Planet 3 office?"

"No, sir. I told him I didn't have a key. He had to call the head cleaning lady, Mrs. Voisine. I gave him her telephone number." He explained that there were four cleaning women, but only Mrs. Voisine had the keys.

"Did anyone else show up here last night?"

"Just the night janitor, Bradley Hall. He leaves at 10:20 p.m."

"Can we check your timecards?"

"Sure. They're in the basement." Peterson followed him there. Everything seemed to be in order. Peterson returned to the mezzanine and later reported his findings to Detective Conley, Homicide.

Around 1:55 a.m., Lieutenant Quirk arrived with Evidence Technician Paul Lewis. Quirk called Patrol Car 1, Carl McAffee, to assist searching inside the entire building. Officers McAffee and Miles cleared the basement, the first floor including the Bank, mezzanine, and second and third floors, checking all the doors to make sure they were locked. Results were negative. McAffee went back on patrol.

Ignored by the team working around them, Joe and Nancy remained seated on the couch in the waiting room.

* * * * *

At the time of Jon's death, homicides were the responsibility of Maine's Attorney General's office by law. Previously, overall homicide investigations had been assigned to the State Police Homicide Team, but they worked together with the local departments and detectives.

Deputy Attorney General Richard Cohen was in charge of the Criminal Division at the Attorney General's office, and the Portland Police and Maine State Police detectives reported to him throughout all investigations.

Detective Peter Conley of the PPD, who had been a police officer for four years and a detective for seven months, was assigned to this case as lead investigator, as well as Lieutenant Clement Dodd.

The side entry of the Maine Bank Building was taped off when Lieutenant Dodd and Detective Conley arrived at 465 Congress Street. They were let in, along with State Police Detective Bickford, Legal Advisor William Gore, and Mr. Berry, a representative from the County Attorney General's office. Two photographers from the Maine State Police also arrived and began taking pictures, starting with the exterior and then the more intense job of the interior.

A patrol officer lifted the crime-scene tape as Dodd and Conley bent their heads to go under it. "What do we have?" Conley asked the officer out front.

"Man dead on the mezzanine. Watch your step."

Dodd nodded in response, and they headed inside.

Instead of using the elevator, Dodd and Conley chose the open staircase to go up one flight.

It was somewhat chaotic inside Planet 3 Films. Evidence Tech Lewis was hard at work, fingerprinting and taking black-and-white and color photographs of the crime scene. There were also blood droplets and smears where someone had obviously transferred the blood onto their shoes from the murder scene.

Peterson ushered in the two Homicide detectives and allowed them to take command of the scene. He led them to the deceased.

Conley began his report. There, slumped halfway on the couch, face down, was a man, perhaps in his late 30s, with a gaping hole in the back of the head and another in his upper back near his neck. His long hair was covered in dark red blood. He bent over to examine the wounds without disturbing the evidence and identified two shots in the back without stippling. That meant he was shot from at least six inches away or more. Either the victim was ambushed, or the assailant chased him into that room, and he had nowhere to run.

Conley inquired, "Any weapon found?"

"No, sir," answered Miles. "And no spent shell casings." That indicated a revolver had been used.

Someone had speculated that it might have been a suicide. Conley knew that was not possible. If it had been a suicide, the gun would have been near the body and there would have been only one gunshot wound, not two. This was, no doubt, a murder, and the weapon had been removed by the assailant or assailants. To Conley, it looked like a well-planned, professional hit.

"Lieutenant, look at this!" Conley said to Dodd.

Dodd walked over as Conley carefully lifted the head.

"Throat's cut! Somebody wanted him dead, now didn't they?" Dodd remarked.

"Get a picture of this!" he ordered, looking at his forensic team. A photographer ran over to the body, aimed, pressed the camera's button, and the flash went off.

Detective Conley stood aside, as he considered the facts. Two bullet wounds—one to the back of his head and one to his spine—and a knife wound on his throat. No weapons found. It was a possibility that there had been more than one perpetrator—a shooter and someone else handy with a blade. That person would likely have blood on their hands, clothing, and shoes. Perhaps a hand injury. He made a note to check all suspects.

Conley knew that it was not Homicide's job to determine *why* this man was murdered; only to build a case for the district attorney. It was the D.A.'s job to figure out the motive. To build the case, however, he had to find out everything about this man. What did he do for a living? Who were his associates and his enemies? What was he doing at the time and why at such a late hour? Determining the "what" would lead to the "why."

He looked around the room carefully, making notes on his pad. He wanted to make sure photos were taken from every angle, not only of the dead man and the blood, but also his surroundings—the desk, window, carpet, chairs, doors and locks, ceiling, trace evidence, and so on. Long after tonight, they could examine the photos and see exactly how everything was placed, where there was blood evidence, handprints or fingerprints, and determine the distance and angle of the shots. Where did the perpetrator stand, aim, and shoot? Not only would the photos be helpful in the investigation, but also as evidence in the courtroom.

"Do we know who the guy is?" Conley asked.

Sergeant Peterson replied, "The owner of Planet 3 identified him as Jon Pownall."

He nodded.

The sergeant led the detectives to the conference room where the contents of the victim's wallet was checked. Four dollar bills were found. No apparent robbery. The lieutenant pulled out the driver's license.

GOODBYE, FAT LARRY

"Jon Robert Pownall, Shapleigh, Maine." He found a few business cards. "Movie director."

Peterson filled him in. "Heard he was here to direct the movie, *The Salem Six.*"

"What's that? Another witch-trial movie?"

"They're making some kind of environmental movie with kids. One of the witnesses told me that the Press was here yesterday."

"Who are the witnesses?" Conley asked Officer Miles, who was nearby keeping notes.

"The secretary, Nancy Payne, came in with the owner of the film company, a Mr. Joseph Castellucci. She discovered the body and called the police."

"What did he do after she discovered the body?"

"He instructed her to go outside and wait for the police by the front door of the bank. He went with her."

"We need to talk to them. I'll let you know when you can take them to Headquarters for their formal statements." He continued, "Do we know who else came here tonight, how they got in, and if they were seen leaving?"

"Yes, sir. We have statements from the janitor and cleaning lady, and we know there were at least two others who were working on upper floors at that hour. No one was aware of any suspicious people or activity."

Conley interrupted. "Eccles is on his way. I want him and McCarthy to go to the autopsy. As soon as everyone's out, have them seal the door."

"Will do," replied Peterson.

Conley turned to Dodd, "I was hoping we'd get a good lead."

"Maybe those two who found the body."

"Let's find out why they showed up when they did."

Dodd pulled Nancy Payne aside and asked what brought her to Planet 3 on this night and to run down events in her own words.

Meanwhile, Conley interviewed Joe Castellucci with similar questions and asked if Pownall had any enemies. Joe recalled a falling-out between Jon and his film crew. He said they "quit" and returned to Chicago. This was a bit of a stretch as the crew was based in Chicago and, although one crew member demanded some answers, Jon had proceeded with his film project. Then Joe explained Jon's trip to L.A., and that Jon wanted to borrow some money from him for the trip.

During a phone call that Joe made in earshot of Dodd, he told someone that it wasn't a robbery, pointing out that neither the victim's wallet nor cash had been taken. Dodd wrote in his report that Castellucci would have no way of knowing this, as the wallet was in the Conference Room down the hall, and Castellucci had claimed that he never went in there that night.

Detective Martin Greeley from the Maine State Police arrived with Sergeant Ronald Eccles and Corporal Peter McCarthy. While Greeley and McCarthy took over the interviews of Nancy and Joe, Eccles collected and bagged evidence from the scene, including Jon's business cards, credit cards, Selective Service Card, verification of Voter Registration, and receipts.

At 3:30 a.m. Detective Lieutenant Charles Bruton showed up to take measurements and pictures. He was required to notify the Attorney General's office in

Augusta about the situation, since they prosecuted all murders and some drug offenses in the State of Maine. Bruton then went back to the station.

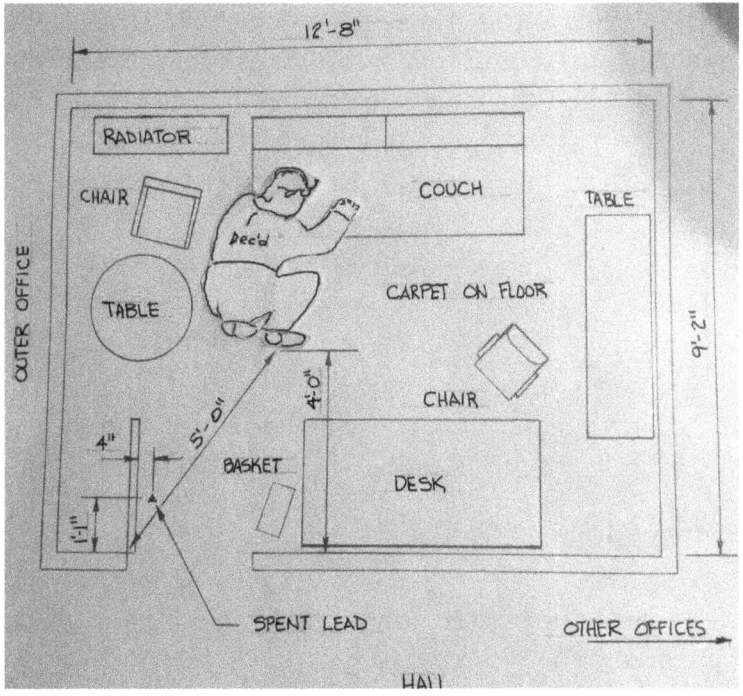

Redrawn sketch with measurements.

The repeating music from the tape deck was finally turned off, much to everyone's relief.

Greeley had been asked by Bruton to phone the state coroner to alert him about the incoming victim for autopsy. Bruton also left orders with his team to remeasure the crime scene, complete their notes, and make a thorough search of the area.

Paul Lewis and Eccles noticed a piece of lead on the carpet by Pownall's office door. As they scanned the walls and window along the Preble Street side of the room, they found a small indentation in the plaster over the window as if a bullet had skimmed it or ricocheted off. Then, on the wall between two inner offices, they found a similar indentation. The scene was measured and roughly diagrammed by Lewis. Eccles bagged the slug as evidence.

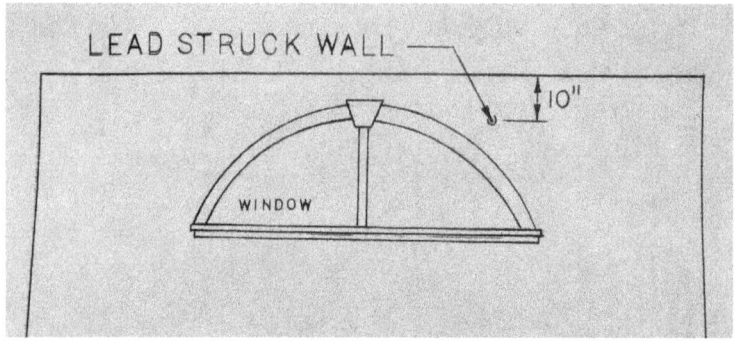

Redrawn diagram.

In Jon's typewriter, there was a release form which appeared to be interrupted.

Joe Castellucci had inferred that someone might still be on the third floor since an elevator was stuck on "3." The State Police obtained keys from Mrs. Voisine and, this time, they checked the lavatories and the interiors of all offices in the building.

Conley ordered Peterson, "Canvass the area. See if anyone saw something, heard something."

"We have two men out there now. Mostly everything's closed at this hour, but we'll keep trying." Peterson radioed a patrol officer to check the area for a possible 10-32 (person with weapon). He then returned to headquarters to make phone calls to individuals and law enforcement agencies, and to answer a stream of phone calls coming into their department from reporters who got wind of the murder. But once that was done, his job was finished on this case.

Dodd called Dispatch to arrange for the removal of the body. Greeley left, and around 4 a.m., Conley and Dodd went back to Headquarters with Nancy Payne for her recorded statement. Officer Miles remained with the body and continued to take notes for the report.

At 5 a.m., Dr. Leighton from the Medical Examiner's office arrived at Planet 3. Leighton followed Officer Miles to the deceased and did an initial exam of the body. After a quick probe, his estimation of the time of death was between 11 p.m. and the discovery of the body by the witnesses just after midnight, since the temperature of the body had not notably decreased, as well as the degree of rigor. That agreed with Detective Conley's findings, as the pooling blood had appeared somewhat fresh.

At 5:10 a.m. Leighton pronounced Jon Pownall dead.

The funeral director from the Hay & Peabody Funeral Home arrived and Leighton directed him to take the body to the Maine Medical Center for autopsy.

Joe Castellucci did not want to sit in the reception area of Planet 3 and watch them roll out Jon's body, so Officer Miles moved him into an empty office.

The body was lifted onto a gurney, covered in sheets and taken to the elevators. The funeral home van was parked on Congress Street, and it would transport the body to the Medical Center in Augusta,

Maine, for a complete postmortem by the Chief Medical Examiner.

Eccles and McCarthy followed the body to the morgue to witness the autopsy.

At 5:50 a.m., Greeley transported Castellucci to Police Headquarters for his formal statement.

Officer Miles continued to write notes, and he took over Conley's duties until all the technicians and State Police were done with their jobs.

Then the door to Planet 3 Films was shut and sealed.

"The world needs dreamers and the world needs doers. But above all, the world needs dreamers who do."
— Sarah Ban Breathnach

Who was Jon Pownall?

Sanford High School senior picture.

Jon Pownall celebrated his thirty-nineth birthday two weeks before his murder on August 30, 1973. He was born "John" Pownall in Cumberland, Maryland, on August 12, 1934, to Germaine R. (Mailhot) and Alfred A. Pownall during The Great Depression. He later changed his name to "Jon."

Jon's father, Alfred, was born on March 17, 1901, in West Virginia, into a family of grist millers, and his ancestral tree can be traced back to Humphrey Pownall, a Tudor gentleman from Cheshire, England. In 1682, Jon's seventh great grandfather, George Pownall, emigrated from Laycock, Cheshire, England, to Philadelphia, Pennsylvania, arriving on *The*

Friends' Adventure, commanded by Captain Thomas Wall. As part of William Penn's Pennsylvania Settlers Community, George and his family and three servants then settled in Buck's County where he owned one thousand acres of land in Solebury Township until his death—by a falling tree. His was the first recorded death in Buck's County the same year he arrived—on August 30 (coincidentally, the same month and day as Jon's death), and just two weeks before the birth of his son, George, Jr.

Jon's mother, Germaine, was born in Quebec, Canada, February 19, 1912. Her deep French-Canadian roots go back on current records to the early 1800s. Jon spoke French from the time of his birth thanks to his mother and the grandmother who watched him while Germaine worked. He learned English when he went to school.

The trademark of the Pownalls is the cleft chin, a genetic trait that appears in both the men and women in the family. Jon also had an unmistakable laugh, called "the strangest ever" by journalist Mike Scanlon. "It surged forth in an electric, quavering bellow on spontaneity, again and again. It broke and pulsated upon the air, fading begrudgingly. You couldn't forget it; you were compelled to join it."

Two weeks after Jon's birth, Alfred moved his family into a modest home on Sherburne Street in Sanford, Maine. Jon had one sibling, a brother, Richard. Alfred had been hired as a shipper of goods for one of several shoe manufacturing companies located in the Village of Springvale, a suburb of Sanford. Alfred's son Richard also went into the shoe business in Texas.

GOODBYE, FAT LARRY

Alfred became active in Republican politics in York County, Maine, influencing Jon's upbringing.

Jon's early life was stable and full of promise. One year, when his *mére* Germaine gave him a KODAK BROWNIE Camera for his birthday, he started taking pictures, experimenting with existing light and different exposures. Jon read everything he could on photography and practiced his art during every free moment. He and his camera were inseparable. He knew at a young age what he wanted to do with his life. It was a vision he acted upon with ambition and passion.

After graduating high school, Jon moved to Rochester, New York, and attended Rochester Institute of Technology (RIT) where he majored in Color Illustration and Color Processes and was a member of Gamma Phi, the Student Council, Camera Club, and the Photographic Society of America.

Jon met Jean Flanagan in classes at RIT where Jean studied Studio Arts to become a sculptor. They both graduated with associate degrees in 1954.

They fell in love and married that September, "a team—partners for life."

He and Jean had three children, Lynda Lee, Jon Richard, and Thomas Grenable.

Lynda Pownall-Carlson recalled, "My dad was a family man with a magnetic personality and the connecting chemistry that held our small family together. He directed us into his big dreams and ambitious endeavors with a hearty laugh that captured the room.

"My parents knew that, to make it in the photographic and film world, they needed to live in a large, progressive city, like Chicago," Lynda explained. After completing his education at the Art Institute of Chicago, Jon opened his first studio on LaSalle Street in that city in 1957.

"I used to love drawing on 12-foot-wide rolls of paper, which had functioned as the backdrops of whatever project they were shooting," Lynda added. "My brother Ricky and I were cast for many of the ads in magazines and, later, commercials. It was good to keep the money in the family!

"My dad started as a still photographer, freelancing for magazines, such as *Life* and *Playboy*," she went on to say.

Jean was right by his side, doing makeup, obtaining props for each shoot, and even cooking for their clients.

Playboy Magazine's January 1963 issue featured a centerfold (Avis Kimble) and photo layout by Jon Pownall. Avis was one of three finalists for that year's Playmate of the Year, and one of the Editors' choices for the top ten Playmates of all time during Playboy's 10-year anniversary celebration.

Jon also shot centerfolds for *Rogue* magazine (Evanston, Illinois).

Lynda continued, "In the late 60s, my parents bought, gutted, and renovated an 8500 square foot factory building at 918 West Armitage Avenue in Chicago for his expanded business. On the first floor were four offices, a large space to make commercials, and a loading dock with a conveyor belt that went down to the basement. The second floor space was utilized for entertaining advertising agents to get commercial jobs. It had a full kitchen, a 12-foot round

GOODBYE, FAT LARRY

Herman Miller table, chairs, and living room set. The third floor was family space, and the basement was converted into a small theater for showing commercials, and a sound room."

In 1967, Jon and Jacques Veinat opened Pownall & Veinat Cinematography in Chicago, specializing in television commercials and industrial films. Jacques, a specialist in communications, had formerly been with Fred A. Niles Communications Center, Inc., Chicago, and La Comete, Paris, France. Some of the 400 commercials and ads they produced were for McDonald's, Alka-Seltzer, Bell & Howell, and Pabst Blue Ribbon beer.

One of Jon's most adventurous shoots was from the seat of a helicopter. A television commercial was created by Stern, Walters, & Simmons for the Chicagoland Oldsmobile Dealers Association and highlighted in an article written by Allan Jaklich in the *Chicago Tribune* in April 1970. "Son of Helicopter" featured an "Olds flying over Lake Michigan and was aimed at boosting sales of the Olds Cutlass. It was filmed with two helicopters; Pownall filming from one, while the Olds was suspended then dropped onto a cornfield from the other. Pownall's studio was chosen because 'he's crazy,' meaning he liked to film the unusual, and even the dangerous." It had to be filmed right the first time, so Jon Pownall used four cameras simultaneously to shoot the car drop.

Larry Postaer from Stern, Walters, & Simmons recalled, "I was there on that shoot; I wrote the spot. I remember worrying that the prop car they were releasing (talk about a windfall!) would crash into a grammar school not far from our drop site in a fallow cornfield. Three cameras, one car, one take. Oh, and the school decided to let all the kids out to watch the movie excitement. What was I thinking! And what was Jon's location scout thinking?"

Jon Pownall shooting the "Son of Helicopter" commercial created by Stern, Walters, and Simmons (1970).

Photo courtesy of Thomas G. Pownall.

GOODBYE, FAT LARRY

The experience Jon gained over the years led him to bigger and better things—filmmaking and the desire to direct a movie for the big screen.

Jon's first filmmaking endeavor was a documentary called *Goodbye, Fat Larry*, which he also directed. According to Lynda Pownall, "It's a 1970s story about a young woman who is tired of the big city, the harassment from her landlord (Fat Larry who lives next door), and the lifestyle she's stuck in. She rents a Hertz truck and heads West."

Good-By Fat Larry poster.

Author's note: This poster is the only place where Bye is spelled differently, putting the word "By" near her eye as a clever extension of the word.

In 1971, Bryon Grush produced a short film called *"Lonely"* for Pownall Cine, with a mix of still and moving images, as well as animated clips. The backgrounds were psychedelic, with bright colors and patterns of mushrooms and the phrase *Goodbye, Fat*

Larry, and a tiny truck. The soundtrack was folk music.

"My parents learned from their experiences on *Goodbye, Fat Larry* that they never wanted to produce, direct, *and* keep tabs on the commercial photography business," recalls Lynda. "At one time, they employed nine people, but that business was neglected during filming. My uncle, Felipe Fabregat, was in business with my parents and things didn't fall together as they should, with my father's attention elsewhere. It was a financial disaster, and my parents filed for bankruptcy. This hit them hard—and then my father was robbed at gunpoint."

After Jon was mugged, he felt it was too dangerous to raise his three children in Chicago. The decision was made to move the family to his hometown of Sanford, Maine, where his mother still lived and where crimes rarely occurred.

Lynda loved Maine when she visited her grandmother Germaine every summer. "She was the nicest person, kind to everyone and never spoke an ill word about anyone. She taught me to sew and make strawberry rhubarb pie, apple delight, and cookies. But at the end of summer 1971, we did not go home to Chicago. I was heartbroken. And an angry artistic teen. Now I was a sophomore in a new school where all the kids knew each other for years. I was an outsider."

Her brother Ricky (Jon) was "Mr. Adventure." And her other brother TG (Thomas) was an inventor, who hung out with the electrician at the Chicago studio and, at the age of 5, had the skill to change a DC motor to an AC motor.

GOODBYE, FAT LARRY

Initially, to support his family, Jon found a job at Bayside for Kids, teaching teenagers how to film, while he planned how to make his next film and distribute *Goodbye, Fat Larry*.

He had an ambitious goal—setting up a film company in Portland, Maine, and filming and directing a full-length movie of his own creation. He began searching for someone to work with to produce his film while he directed. This person would raise the money, pay the crews and actors, and take care of the business details.

In March 1973, at an advertising meeting for the Miss Maine Pageant, Jon was introduced to Joseph A. Castellucci, who impressed him with his apparent ability to raise funds. Jon proposed that Joe become his film producer.

Jean Pownall came up with the name, and Planet 3 Films was born.

Jon's official residence was in Shapleigh, Maine, about 13 miles out of Sanford, and 42 miles away from Portland and his new office. He also rented a small space on Monument Square for his photographic studio.

It was the beginning of a very exciting time for Jon, as his dreams were unfolding. There was a great deal for Jon and Joe to do—set up the office, hire a secretary, get a screenplay written, find investors, sign big-name actors, and all the other movie production tasks, many of which fell on Castellucci's shoulders. Jon wanted to focus on directing the film, while Joe handled the finances.

Jon had plans to fly to Hollywood on Friday, August 31, to sign acting contracts, but that meeting never took place.

The evening before, when everyone else in the office had gone home, he had one more appointment with Joe Castellucci...

"You had ONE job to do..." — *Ocean's 11*

The evidence

Sergeant Ronald Eccles of the Maine State Police was notified by Lieutenant Charles Bruton about the crime scene at 465 Congress Street. The lieutenant wanted Eccles to process and photograph the scene, collect all the evidence, and deliver it to State Police Headquarters in Augusta for testing. Eccles arrived at the Maine Bank Building in his black-and-white cruiser at approximately 3:30 a.m. on August 31 and took the stairs to the mezzanine level.

The *Portland Sunday Telegram* reported that it was a "beehive of activity as state and local detectives hustled in and out of the office and, at times, questioned witnesses in interrogation rooms."

Sergeant Eccles began processing the crime scene immediately, photographing everything to record the scene before anything was moved, fingerprinting, and collecting evidence.

"I retrieved an envelope which was underneath the table in the office in which the body was found, and also a spent bullet," Eccles reported. The slug was found at approximately 5:05 a.m., "right by the door, which was open at a 90-degree angle to the room where the deceased was found." He took a photograph of the slug at the scene, picked it up, and put it into a plastic container, which he then wrapped and kept in his possession.

Shortly after finding the slug, Eccles was told that the body was ready to be taken to the morgue.

But there was a problem. The coroner's team realized that their gurney would not fit in the tiny elevator. They had wrapped the body not in a bag or tarp, but in sheets. This resulted in a dripping blood trail throughout the Planet 3 Films' offices, down the hallway to the elevator, inside the elevator, and out to the Medical Examiner's vehicle. Fortunately, Eccles and the forensic team had already done their jobs.

Eccles and Corporal Peter McCarthy of the State Police accompanied the corpse of Jon Pownall to the morgue and remained present to witness the entire autopsy where the evidence was preserved and marked accordingly—the bloody clothes, fingernail scrapings, hair samples, fingerprints, bullet fragments, stomach contents, urine, bile, and a blood sample.

As Dr. Branch removed the first bullet from the brain of Jon Pownall, he dropped the butt into a glass vial, followed by three or four fragments. The same process was followed for the second bullet, but there was not much left except for some fragments. Because Dr. Branch was focused on the job at hand, he wasn't sure if he handed the sealed vial off to Eccles or McCarthy. Later, Eccles said that he put the vial in his pocket. At that time, McCarthy temporarily took possession of the bloody clothing in an evidence bag.

After the autopsy, numerous people handled the evidence. This hand-off occurred over several days and resulted in some confusion and misconception of what was being transported.

According to Sergeant Eccles, he didn't go to State Police Headquarters until around 2 p.m. on September 4, after another homicide on August 31 (a stabbing) plus his time off during the Labor Day holiday. He put an identification mark on the plastic container holding the slug from the carpet of Planet 3, locked it (as well as the vial with the bullet and fragments removed from the victim) in his evidence locker for Corporal William Manduca, the ballistics expert, to give to him for examination as soon as he could.

When he did so, Eccles was under the assumption that the vial in his possession held only the butt end of the first bullet, the one to the head, that he was handing over. He didn't look for fragments from either the first or second bullet and could not confirm that the fragments were or were not included. He also handed over the plastic container with the slug from the carpet in the Planet 3 offices.

Likewise, Corporal Manduca never saw any fragments in the vial given to him by Sergeant Eccles.

"Thinking something does not make it true. Wanting something does not make it real." — Michelle Hodkin

Canvassing the area

Two Portland Police Department officers were directed by Sergeant Peterson to canvass the downtown area for possible witnesses. It was a long process of knocking on doors and talking to people—a lot of work and paperwork for a crew of investigators.

During the early hours of August 31, Monument Square was mostly quiet except for a single man who stood outside the Plaza Hotel on Preble Street, on the side of the Maine National Bank building where the crime was committed.

Leonard Rupard, the Plaza Hotel Manager, lingered outside from 9 p.m. to 1 a.m. until the bar inside the hotel closed for the night, greeting customers and telling them to "have a good night" as they left. Earlier, there had been a band playing and the music had drifted out into the street. It was a slow night, but he didn't mind the peace and quiet of his post, and he was getting paid to be there.

Rupard told one of the canvassing officers that, about 11:45 p.m. on August 30, he saw a motorcycle approaching where he stood on Preble Street, then passing by, heading for Congress Street. At that point he heard it backfire. Then about 30 seconds later, he heard it backfire a second and third time. Immediately, the officer took down the report, as it was the approximate time shots were fired inside the Maine Bank building at 465 Congress.

Leonard was sure it was the motorcycle, not anything else, but was asked to make a statement, nevertheless.

465 Congress Street, Portland, Maine.

Photo ©Elly Stevens, 2021

Detective Joseph Pelletier and Detective Sergeant Arthur Murdock re-interviewed the head cleaning lady, Mrs. Voisine, who took them to the fourth floor of the Maine Bank building to view the corner of Preble and Congress Streets from above. They also talked to the day janitor, Alfie Oaks, again, who added that there were auditors working on the seventh and eighth floors when he left the building at 6:58 p.m. He didn't know their names, but they were in the offices of Mitchell & Maverick Company. Pelletier had to wait until morning to interview them.

They also re-interviewed the night janitor, Bradley Hall. Hall indicated that he was usually the last person out of the building, leaving at 10:20 p.m. on Thursday night. He had been cleaning the vault area of the bank. Shortly after 10 p.m., he could hear two men in a normal conversation, but he didn't hear what they were saying. One man had on a light-colored shirt and was sitting in one of the lounge chairs.

Hall also said that, while he was cleaning the third floor and later securing the building, a man he assumed to be a lawyer from the 300 suite of Drummond, Westcott, & Woodsum was present. After Hall left the Maine Bank building, he looked up and noticed the lights on in the mezzanine.

All the taxicab drivers were asked if they had seen anything or anyone unusual in the Monument Square vicinity between 11 p.m. and midnight. They hadn't.

Detective Conley contacted the Public Works Sewer Department and arranged to pump and rake the catch basins in Monument Square and check for any weapons—guns or knives—they might find.

Another lead police needed to follow was the recent arrest of a career criminal, Donald Henry McInniss. He was well known to police for breaking and entering and larceny, as well as numerous parole violations. He had been arrested just that Friday morning in the vicinity of the murder and volunteered information which resulted in a large recovery of stolen items. McInniss' former girlfriend, Betty Brown, used to work at 465 Congress Street, and police tried to confirm a "romantic" link between Brown and Jon Pownall, but determined it was rumor.

GOODBYE, FAT LARRY

A call came in from a Mr. McGorrill who stated that he had given police a list of *The Salem Six* cast members. Afterwards, it dawned on McGorrill that there was a man named Stump whose 8-year-old son had been removed from the cast by Pownall. McGorrill had heard Mr. Stump speak "slanderously" about Pownall and was very angry and bitter. Police had to follow up on the lead to determine if there was any merit. After interviewing Stump, they eliminated him from their suspect list.

The detectives began the time-consuming task of checking into the background of each person of interest, including their financial status, alibis, and possible motives.

In 1973, it meant face-to-face interviews, calling on the phone for information, and sometimes waiting for mail to arrive. There was no video surveillance to view, no cell phone records to check, no DNA to test, and no national database to match DNA to convicted felons, such as we have today in CODIS (Combined DNA Index System). They had to rely on evidence such as weapons, ballistics, blood type, fingerprinting, and witness testimony.

"*Every man's life ends the same way. It is only the details of how he lived and how he died that distinguish one man from another.*" — Ernest Hemingway

Cause and manner of death

Dr. Charles F. Branch, Chief Medical Examiner for the State of Maine and a pathologist, handled the autopsy of Jon Pownall, as he often did for high-profile cases.

In the State of Maine, the Chief Medical Examiner is appointed by the Governor for a term of seven years. The Medical Examiner and staff are responsible to determine the cause and manner of death when related to trauma, poisoning, and unexplained deaths in unusual and suspicious circumstances. Dr. Branch had many years of experience in pathology and was well respected.

Once the body was removed from the scene at 465 Congress Street, it was transported to the Maine Medical Center in Augusta. Dr. Branch had not been at the crime scene, so his first viewing of the subject was on the "carriage" (gurney) as it was rolled into the morgue at about 9 a.m. on August 31, 1973.

After the deceased had been identified to him by Corporal Peter McCarthy and Sergeant Ronald Eccles of the Maine State Police, Branch observed the victim's heavily blood-stained shirt and pants. He also noted that the deceased was short (five foot, eight inches tall) and extremely stocky, "a bull-necked" individual. Pownall had heavy sideburns and mustache, all matted with blood. There were no powder burns from the gun, so the shooter had to be at least six inches away from the victim, if not more.

The clothes were then removed and marked for evidence, and his initial inspection of the body began.

Turning the body over, Branch immediately noticed a bullet hole at the base of Pownall's skull at the hairline. There was a second, identical, bullet entry a little lower, in the midline of his spinal column.

In manipulating the body and visually scanning for other wounds or evidence of trauma, Dr. Branch moved the head and noticed a small spurt of blood coming from the victim's neck. In closer examination, it looked like a stab wound near the Adam's apple.

There was no other evidence of injury except a blue mark over the area of the left eye.

It was then time to examine the brain, "which had the most significant part of the damage." To do that, the skull had to be opened.

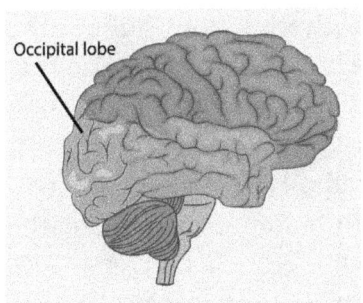

Branch recorded that the first bullet entered the base of the skull in the occipital area, on the left side of the neck, and proceeded anteriorly so that it came up and bounced off the left frontal area, destroying the entire brain hemisphere. As it came back into the eye area, it flanged off into the sinuses, leaving a bruise on the skin above the eye, but not exiting the skull.

The occipital lobes of the brain sit at the back of the head for visual perception, distance and depth perception, color, object and face recognition, and memory formation.

The M.E. removed the bullet from Jon's brain, dropped it into a glass vial along with three or four bullet fragments, and remanded it over to one of the state police officers standing nearby (Eccles and McCarthy) for definition by their ballistics expert. The brain itself was carefully lifted out from the skull and preserved as evidence.

Next, Branch shifted his attention to the second bullet hole in the victim's back. He noted that, at the point of the bullet's entry, the body was already falling forward, with the head tilted down. The bullet entered the fourth cervical vertebra, destroying it, went into the spinal canal and traveled upwards, racking the bones on either side. As with the first bullet, the second bullet did not exit the body. But unlike the first bullet, the second bullet left only specks of lead—no large pieces to be tested by a ballistics expert. Nevertheless, Branch removed all the specks, putting them in the same vial as the bullet, and handed the vial to the officer.

The body was turned over so that the M.E. could examine the injury near the deceased's Adam's apple. The wound was only a centimeter in width, and it went straight back through the bottom part of the cartilage into the trachea, nicking the esophagus. The aorta was intact and received no damage. In Branch's opinion, the injury was caused by a narrow, stiff-bladed instrument, similar to a stiletto blade.

Months later during the trial, Dr. Branch testified, "It is fair to assume that this was a coup de grâce wound after death. The heart was no longer beating."

Dr. Branch's autopsy continued and, after toxicology results were in, it was determined that there was no evidence of drugs or alcohol in Jon Pownall's blood.

He reported that Jon Pownall's death was immediate, caused by the first bullet, although the second bullet would have also been fatal had he survived the first bullet.

Cause of death was ruled gunshot wounds, and the manner of death, homicide.

"Fear and greed are potent motivators. When both of these forces push in the same direction, virtually no human being can resist." — Andrew Weil

The gun sale

On April 26, 1971, Willard Herman Stuart purchased a 5-shot revolver as an off-duty part-time deputy for the York County Sheriff's Department at Carl's Sporting Goods Store in Portland. The salesman and owner, Carl Lonstein, filled out the Federal Form 4473 for the Smith & Wesson revolver, Model 36, a .38 caliber special, serial number 9J3929, and Willard Stuart signed it.

It wasn't Stuart's only gun; he also owned a 6-shot, police/military special, and a 6-shot snub-nose revolver.

At the time of the gun purchase, Stuart was also a traveling salesman for Diagraph Bradley of New England that handled shipping-room supplies. Stuart's third job was running an automotive transmission repair business and selling his services to other repair shops in the area.

After a few months went by, Stuart decided he wanted a different gun model and offered the 5-shot for sale to several people including Police Officer David Kearns in Gorham, Maine. There were no takers.

Then, one morning in mid-August of the same year, Stuart went to breakfast, as usual, at Edna's Restaurant in Portland, with several other salesmen. His friend, Truman Dongo, almost always attended the traditional breakfast, as he was in the fender-cover business, and they often talked about cars. The subject of the .38 came up in their conversation, and Truman expressed an interest in buying it.

"I'd like to keep a gun in my truck with all the large amounts of money I carry," Dongo explained.

Stuart pointed in the direction of the parking lot and responded, "It's under the seat of my car, if you want to go look at it. It's in immaculate condition. The car's unlocked." Truman left the group and went out to Stuart's car.

"Do you like it?" Stuart asked when Truman returned.

"I do," Truman said, "but I don't have the money with me."

Stuart offered, "Well, go ahead and take it with you. I'm sure you're good for it." After all, Truman had been a good friend for four or five years.

A few days later at breakfast, Willard Stuart received $75 in cash from Truman Dongo.

A couple of years later, Willard Stuart received a phone call from Detective Pelletier of the Portland Police Department. He was asked if he could identify the gun.

"Not the serial number," Stuart replied, "but physically."

Pelletier asked, "When was the last time the gun was in your possession?"

Stuart said he wasn't quite sure. He thought to himself, *I need to be careful about my reply,* since he knew Truman was a felon.

He replied that he didn't know, offhand.

If Truman Dongo had taken it that day at Edna's, Stuart hadn't checked under his seat right away. He did notice it was gone a couple of days later when he felt under his seat. He had never seen Dongo hold the gun or take the gun. But Dongo did pay him $75, he assumed, for the gun.

Deputy Sheriff Stuart had knowingly sold a gun to a felon. He did not return the money to Dongo nor demand that the gun be returned. He just hoped the sale would never come to light.

"Follow the evidence, wherever it leads." — David Hoffman

The wormdigger's find

It was a cold and cloudy early morning on October 27, 1973, when old Joe Emerton, clad in a warm jacket and his rubber boots, and carrying a metal bucket and tubular clam holer, went to the mudflat at the end of Commercial Street in Portland near Long Wharf to dig for sea worms. Above him, on the wharf, was DiMillo's Restaurant parking lot and a second lot for Boone's.

When it was high tide in that area, it was covered in eight to twelve feet of water, but that morning the experienced wormdigger arrived within a half hour of the low tide. He had been digging for worms for several years, always during smelt season, and knew the tides well.

Joe was in between two wharves by the pilings of old, abandoned docks and had already dug up several worms when he came upon a small gun barrel sticking out of the sand. He wasn't sure it was a *real* gun, so he dug it out and picked it up. Emerton looked at the gun briefly, noting a little bit of rust on the outside and peeking down the barrel to see what appeared to be ammunition. He then placed it back on top of the sand until he dug up all the worms he needed for smelting. After he washed off his boots and clam holer, he also washed off the gun and realized that it was, indeed, a real gun. Joe, being a felon himself, knew that he couldn't keep it and had to turn it in. He carried it right to the Portland Police Department.

At 7:15 a.m., Joe walked into the Police Department with the gun in his hand. No one was alarmed nor did they stop him or question him.

"I found this here gun," Joe told the officer, placing the gun on the desk, "in the sand by Long Wharf."

The Information Officer, Peter Burbank, looked at the old man suspiciously then picked up the gun to examine it. It was a 5-shot, 2-inch, Smith & Wesson .38 caliber Chief's Special—a police officer's revolver. He broke open the cylinder for safety precautions, finding quite a lot of wet sand still inside. He spun the cylinder counterclockwise. There were three live bullets and one expended cartridge in the cylinder which he removed onto the desktop. He did not identify or mark the cylinders in any way. Under the firing pin, there was a second expended round.

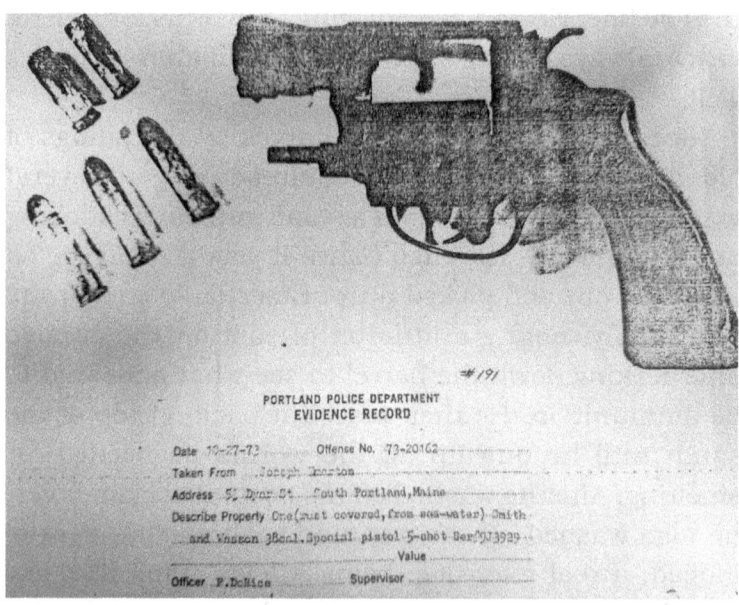

GOODBYE, FAT LARRY

Officer Burbank called another officer who took down Joe's name and address. Then Burbank told Joe that he was going to turn the gun over to the detectives' unit and that someone may or may not call on him. After making his statement to police, Joe Emerton never heard another thing until he received a subpoena in the Jon Pownall murder trial.

About forty-five minutes before Officer Peter DeRice (the Day Evidence Technician) came in, Officer Burbank began his report, writing down the serial number of the gun (9J3929), the number of spent cartridges and live ammunition, and the gun's description. At 8 a.m., he handed everything over to Officer DeRice, with a brief history on the gun's discovery, but without marking the gun for identification, which he left up to DeRice.

DeRice examined the weapon immediately. Then he placed the ammunition and spent shells in a plastic bag which he took to the police darkroom along with the muddy revolver. In 1973, the darkroom was in an older building on Federal Street. There, he took one photograph of the weapon, live rounds, and cartridge cases, and placed them in an evidence bag with a pink tag on the weapon, which he turned over to Sergeant Edward Welch shortly before 10 a.m. that same day.

A few nights later, Officer DeRice was substituting for another officer on patrol duty and answered a call from a woman on Baxter Boulevard about kids who were painting graffiti on a building. In his conversation with her, he mentioned that the gun in the Jon Pownall murder had been found and revealed that it was a "real break in the case," something he should have kept confidential. At this point, there was no proof that this was the gun used in the murder. However, the Portland PD suspected that it was evidence from the Pownall case, but *any* turned-in .38 caliber revolvers would have been marked for testing in the case.

Sergeant Edward Welch, the recipient of the gun and ammunition on October 27, put everything in his evidence locker. At approximately 11:50 p.m., he turned the evidence bag over to Detective Conley, who was in charge of the Pownall case and who had been at the crime scene.

Detective Conley received the sealed evidence bag, which he never opened. The next day, October 28, Conley met with Corporal William Manduca of the Maine State Police, whose office was in the Detective Bureau inside the PPD, and turned over the bag containing the gun for firearms identification. With his extensive training, Manduca was an expert at determining whether a bullet or cartridge casing had been fired from a particular weapon. Manduca opened the bag in Conley's presence and confirmed the contents.

With the evidence in his possession, Manduca marked each of the bullets with a W (with a line over it). He examined the revolver and observed its somewhat rusty condition. He rubbed gun oil all over it and wiped it with a rag, which he knew would not affect ballistics testing.

He then took all the evidence back to the State lab in Augusta, putting it under lock and key until he could do a ballistics test. The next day, October 29, he disassembled the weapon to soak the parts and remove any foreign material, including the sand. Cleaning the muzzle was done with a soft cotton cleaning patch, pushed through the muzzle with a metal rod. This process re-conditioned the weapon and its firing ability to a certain degree. However, there was still some pitting on the metal, both inside the barrel and outside, but the sand protected the surface of the barrel from getting totally rusty.

Corporal Manduca now had the revolver with three live rounds and two spent cartridges, and two spent bullets in a box from Sergeant Ronald Eccles, one of which came in a vial from the Medical Examiner after the autopsy of Jon Pownall and one in a plastic container from the floor of Planet 3 Films with Eccles' marking. Now his job was to compare the ammunition and identify it as coming from a specific weapon.

He set up a piece of stove pipe filled with soft cotton into which he could fire a gun. The Corporal put on ear and eye protection. Then he loaded the .38 caliber revolver with four live rounds, shooting them into the cotton, and retrieving the slugs. Manduca then took the marked slug from the autopsy and compared both spent casings under a two-stage microscope at the same time with a single eyepiece. Under the microscope, he examined the firing pin impressions and the breach base on the cartridge case, lining them up. If the striations matched, he had a match to the murder weapon.

When a gun comes off the assembly line, the machine tooling leaves unique characteristics (lands and grooves, firing pin impressions, ejector extractor marks) inside the barrel that a ballistics expert can identify under a microscope. The lands and grooves are created when the metal has been drilled out of a steel bar in a twisting motion. The purpose is to keep the bullet in "true flight" rather than tumbling through the air. Every gun barrel is slightly different from another because the machine itself keeps changing. The person comparing casings under a microscope needs training and expertise to reach a conclusion and determine if there is a match or not to a particular weapon.

By observing the lands and grooves and the weight of the two test bullets, Manduca positively confirmed both bullets were .38 caliber. Other than confirming both bullets came from a .38 caliber gun, he was unable to match the test bullet to the first autopsy bullet, which had sustained damage in Jon Pownall's skull. That bullet had struck "an object" and that object scarred the surface of it. Manduca could not testify that both bullets positively came from the same gun, although it was possible. Nevertheless, he couldn't prove it.

There was nothing to test from the second autopsy bullet which had disintegrated as it traveled in Jon Pownall's spine.

Manduca moved on to the mushroomed bullet that had been found on the floor at the Planet 3 offices. Under the microscope, he lined up the striations of the Planet 3 bullet with that of the test bullet and they matched perfectly. His conclusion was that both bullets were, without question, fired from the same gun. Admittedly, he did not take pictures of the comparison.

When the testing was completed, he placed everything, including his November 1 report labeled

"Jon Pownall Homicide" and his conclusions, inside his evidence locker, which stood seven feet high and two or three feet wide and two feet deep, and housed evidence from other crimes, including another .38 caliber bullet and three pieces of lead in a glass bottle from a September 5 case headed by Sergeant Baston. Since Baston just asked Manduca to hold them in his locker for him, Manduca did not put his mark on the bullet. However, Corporal Manduca did compare Baston's bullet to the bullets supplied by Sergeant Eccles on September 4, 1973. They did not match.

On October 11 of that same year, another .38 caliber gun (Serial No. 737949) had been sent to him from the Gorham Police Department for testing. Manduca compared the slugs from that gun under the microscope and did not find any matches to the Eccles bullet from the Pownall case.

Then, on October 28, Manduca compared the Smith & Wesson .38 caliber revolver found by the wormdigger (Serial No. 9J3929) to the Smith & Wesson .38 caliber revolver (Serial No. 185144) from Sergeant Baston's case. Both guns were test fired and the bullets were examined in conjunction with the two bullets that were remanded to him by Sergeant Eccles. The bullet comparisons showed that they had different markings under the microscope. *Only the gun found by the wormdigger left the exact striations on the test bullet to the slug in evidence from the carpet during Jon Pownall's murder.*

As to the gun (Serial No. 9J3929) itself, it was registered to Retired Captain R. Jordan of the Maine State Police.

Manduca studied microscopic analysis under Emery R. Jordan, so he contacted him to see if he could identify the weapon. After Manduca had completed his ballistic testing, Jordan came in and test-fired the gun. He said that it was, indeed, the gun he had once owned but sold to a dealer.

The Movie

(March – August 1973)

"Drama does not just walk into your life. Either you create it, invite it, or associate with it." — Sermons Online

The partnership

Joseph Castellucci, like Jon, was an ambitious man who loved Maine. While growing up, he spent summers in Bar Harbor with his family, who still had a place there in 1973. He and his wife Leslie were living in the town of Scarborough, Maine, as he collaborated with Jon and others at Planet 3 Films, where he was the principal owner and film producer.

But unlike Jon, there were unfavorable names associated with Joe Castellucci. In the forthcoming months, he was called shifty, a liar, a forger, a thief, a sharp operator, a big crook, a coward, and an adulterer.

Castellucci held 11 or 12 jobs since graduation from college, none of which gave him the income he desired. Before, and a little while after college ended, he was working as an industrial engineer at Ford Motor Company, but that lasted less than a year. Then he was in training for stockbroker Hayden Stone in New Jersey but was forced out of that job. He left New Jersey in 1971 for a new job in New York City selling ad placements for the *New York Daily News*. There he met Lawrence Ofiaro, and they started an advertising business, which lasted five months. Then Joe became involved in raising money for three psychologists to do testing for companies that hired or fired personnel, but it was not satisfying. After that, he had some interest in an inventor and patents in New York and worked with Messrs. Stanley Ruth and Henry Burbig. While he was in college, Castellucci had worked for the J. H. Butterfield Company and went back to them for a short time. Then, Joe decided to go back to Maine and was hired as a partner at Bar Harbor Candles, where he met co-worker Stuart Lamont. He was voted out (fired) after only nine months. Mr. Lamont was also fired.

A month later, Joe became a salesman for Phillips Maine Corp., a plastics company in Ashland, Massachusetts—mostly the giftware end—again with Stuart Lamont. The two snake-oil salesmen put their heads together to make their biggest pitch.

Phillip Dunham ran Phillips Maine before Stu and Joe were hired. At the time of their employment, Stu and Joe stayed at the Saco Motel in Maine from October through December of that year, then they "disappeared" from their jobs. In February, Stu somehow convinced the major stockholder, a man named Lindstrom, to get rid of Dunham and put him (Stu) in charge of the company! Dunham left the company, saying he had had enough. He described Stu and Joe as "two of the biggest crooks" he had ever met—"real sharp operators."

Unfortunately, the IRS locked the doors on Phillips Maine in May 1972, and Joe was on the job hunt again.

A short time later, Joe met George Garnache from Biddeford, Maine, who owned a large parcel of land and wanted to put up 42 single homes. As part of the Garnache real estate project, Joe worked again with Stuart Lamont. Joe's father-in-law, Elliott Stern, who

GOODBYE, FAT LARRY

owned Globe Photo in New York, had a neighbor, Sal Cataldo of Archer Industries, who came up with some money, but Garnache wasn't comfortable with the arrangement and returned the money to Cataldo. Joe's job was to buy 43 lots for $205,000 and arrange financing with U.S. Financial, a large mortgage company out of San Diego and Washington D.C., but that company found itself in trouble with the Securities & Exchange Commission. After only one home was built, the project fell apart. There was also a second failed real estate venture in Cape Elizabeth, Maine, connected to Cataldo. However, Stu Lamont was not involved in that deal.

Garnache said that Stu and Joe were a couple of "real smoothies and real fast talkers." He believed that the Phillips Maine folded on purpose, and he didn't trust Stu or Joe.

Then Castellucci went to work for Certified Laboratories, a chemical company out of New Jersey, which had contacts in the advertising business, including a man named John MacFarland. Joe was fired from that job after placing phony orders, forging sales records, and trying to blame the sales manager, Mr. Levine, because they had a bad relationship, and Joe felt he wasn't getting due credit for actual sales.

At the end of 1972, he had meetings with MacFarland to start an advertising business in Portland, Maine, that would handle local advertising similar to his previous advertising job with the *New York Daily News*. Sal Cataldo loaned him money for his startup, as Joe was always short of cash. MacFarland and Castellucci often talked about what accounts they might handle. MacFarland had been impressed with a photographer named Jon Pownall who handled political campaign photography, so he asked Pownall to attend a meeting to give advice on photography for the Miss Maine Pageant, which Pownall agreed to do.

At the end of that meeting, Jon pulled Joe Castellucci aside. Jon asked, "Instead of going into the advertising business, Joe, why don't you produce my next movie?" Jon needed someone to handle finances as he wasn't very good at it and only wanted to direct his movie.

Joe was taken aback, but his eyes lit up. "What does a producer do?"

"He arranges financing, et cetera." Jon went on to tell him about his first documentary film, *Goodbye, Fat Larry,* and then provided a synopsis of the new film he wanted to produce for the big screen with big-name actors.

As 29-year-old Joe listened to Pownall's plan to get into the movie business, he shrewdly recognized an opportunity to "make it big" and earn real money, even though he knew nothing about the business. But he could learn.

"Why don't you come by my studio—I'll show you a treatment of the movie," Jon suggested. "It's something I had in mind for a long time. I've been working on the concept for a year and a half or two years."

A few days later, Joe went to Jon's studio in Portland. Jon provided a further background on his previous endeavor, *Goodbye, Fat Larry,* how the funds were raised, and examples of the advertising that he had done.

GOODBYE, FAT LARRY

Shortly thereafter, Jon and his wife Jean went to Joe's house in Scarborough for dinner where they discussed the new film and what was needed.

Up to that point, Castellucci knew very little about the movie business except that his father-in-law's company, Globe Photo, had some connections. The next day, Joe called his father-in-law, Elliot Stern, who set up a meeting in New York City with Russ Meyer, a successful director and producer of most notably *Beyond the Valley of the Dolls* and other X-rated movies. Joe described the movie to Russ, who thought it sounded like a good concept and would make money, adding that there *might be* a need for "G" (General Audience) movies in the marketplace.

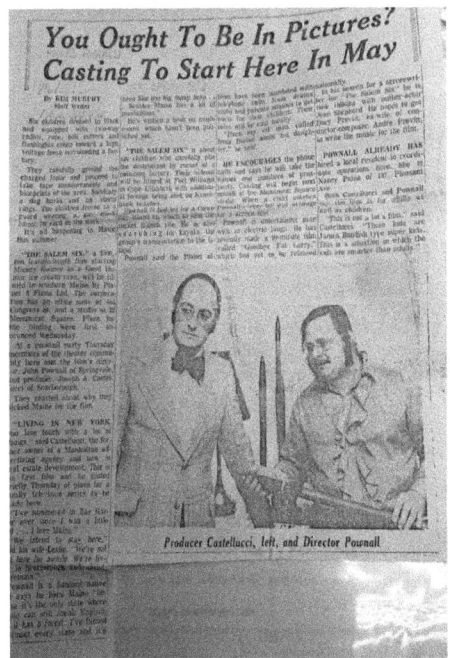

From the Portland PD Pownall case files. *Portland Press Herald,* Friday, April 6, 1973. Joe Castellucci, left; Jon Pownall, right.

In March 1973, Joe convinced Jon that he could find big investors for his new film, although he had no real connections except Sal Cataldo to whom he owed money. Jon had the talent, skills, vision, and passion for filmmaking, and Joe...well, Joe had the passion for money. To Pownall, it seemed like a partnership made in heaven.

Jon Pownall was impressed with Joe. But there was no background check done on Castellucci, no financial investigation, no business referrals. Jon liked what he heard from Joe at the MacFarland meeting. Together they formed a company called Planet 3 Films. Joe's title was Producer and Owner of Planet 3 Films, and Jon's was Director. Jon did not draw up a contract for Joe; they just agreed to work together.

PLANET₃ FILMS LTD.

Planet 3's logo.

Joe had no idea how to find people with big money and convince them to invest in the very first movie for Planet 3 Films, a risky venture, but he had to raise $450,000.

To help with fundraising, Jon arranged tentative financial co-production with Churubusco Studios in Mexico City, which would do the post-production editing. Many of Planet 3's contacts were made through their previous Chicago representative, Felipe Fabregat, who introduced Jon to the Mexican studio. Felipe was also married to Jean Pownall's sister. During the years they worked in Chicago, Jon and

GOODBYE, FAT LARRY

Jean were also officers in Video Mexico, where commercials were taped for U.S. clients.

Castellucci finally found his first new investor, a man named Maurice Parent, who committed $6,500 to the project. He also received $6,500 from Michael Doyle, an insurance agent with the Bath, Maine, firm of Chapman & Drake, who had an office above Planet 3 Films. Joe still had to raise another $437,000.

Joe knew Jon depended on him and, if they were to pay actors and crew, they had to have the money when the film was tentatively scheduled to start in September. After all, contracts were being written with big stars and they expected to be paid. There were several child actors to be hired as well. They had to get releases from parents; and even if they did not join the Screen Actors Guild, they would have to be paid the Guild's minimum wage.

Jon and Joe needed a salary, as well, and they settled on $300 a week for each.

In April 1973, Jon flew to L.A. and met with representative Gordon Wolfe from Cinemobile, which rented equipment on a per diem basis and worked with Jon on the "Son of Helicopter" car commercial. Whatever might be needed on their location—large or small movie camera trucks, sound equipment, and lighting—Cinemobile could provide it. He obtained prices but no contract could be written or signed until the movie script was finished and the set location was approved.

Things were starting to come together.

"To be a filmmaker, you have to lead. You have to be psychotic in your desire to do something. You have to push very hard to get something unusual, something different." — Danny Boyle

The Salem Six

Jon Pownall had had an unusual idea for a movie for a long time. He saw every moment in his mind. He envisioned the characters coming to life. He wanted to identify a serious evil of his time (pollution), then enlighten the world through his film, but include moments of levity and humor. And he wanted six children in the coastal New England "town of Salem" to be the activists, fighting the notorious polluting factory. Hence: *The Salem Six.*

Jon intended to open the movie with a John Denver song. It would take place in 1973. The audience would see a Good Humor Man (to be played by Jim Backus, the actor known as Thurston Howell of *Gilligan's Island* and the voice of *Mr. Magoo*) and an old lady holding a birdwatching book (to be played by Margaret Hamilton, known as the Wicked Witch of the West in *The Wizard of Oz*) riding together in the Good Humor truck. They are crossing the southern Nevada border of the United States heading for Mexico and are later seen buying tickets to Pakistan.

(The audience does not understand what is going on yet, but they recognize the actors.)

The scene changes, going back in time, with the children carrying fishing rods and walking to a nearby fishing spot on a sunny summer's day. The water had always been clear and clean, but on that day, instead of reeling in fish, they pull out a dead cat, old tires, and other debris. The children become upset and conclude that a mysterious factory upstream must be polluting their favorite fishing spot. They formulate a plan to stop the polluting factory.

Enlisting the help of their local Good Humor Man and a little old lady whose favorite pastime is birdwatching, the children (four boys, two girls, and a young "tag-along"), using charm and conniving, convince the two unwitting adults to finance their goals. With the money to fund their project, the six kids plot to bomb the factory.

What seems to be a harmless children's prank—sending homemade toy rockets toward the factory, the Good Humor Man and the Birdwatcher underestimate the children. In fact, the Good Humor Man hands out Popsicles for the event and the lady gives them little tea cakes, and the two chuckle about how adorable and spunky the children are.

Meanwhile, the kids get busy and set up their command post. The audience would then see some children with walkie-talkies in kayaks on a creek, reporting back to their teenage commander when everything was ready at each of their strategic posts.

The two adults watch as the "toy" rockets fly into the air and drop next to a truck in the factory parking lot that is unloading naphtha, and some sparks fly. Suddenly there's an explosion!

The kids cheer at their success!

The bewildered Good Humor Man and Birdwatcher suddenly realize that this "harmless prank" was no joke and that the children did exactly what they said they were going to do—blow up the factory. The two look at each other in disbelief and fear. What had they done?? They become nervous about their participation in the event and decide that it's time to skip town. They take off running for the Good Humor truck, ending the movie.

* * * * *

The Salem Six had to be a low-budget film for props, but Jon Pownall hoped that the big-name stars would draw a large audience throughout the country.

Planet 3 started looking for children to act in their film. An ad was placed in the *Portland Press Herald* for the parts of the six local children, and 425 youngsters showed up to audition. Each child was interviewed while parents filled out applications.

The children were then sent across Monument Square to Jon's studio where they were given screen tests by Jon and Jean, a lengthy procedure. It was difficult to narrow down the young actors, but they finally did so and set up training.

Charles Hall, 10, heard about the "cold read audition" and took a bus by himself to Portland and got a part in the film. His mother couldn't accompany him because she was expecting a baby.

Another applicant was Sam Patton, 11, whose dad worked at *The Maine Times* and encouraged him to try out. He recalled that Jon cheerfully pointed out to him that there was a character in the film named Sam, and he got the part.

The soon-to-be-made motion picture by the independent film company generated support and enthusiasm throughout Maine. Old Towne Canoe delivered six kayaks that would be used by the children in the movie, and StarCraft loaned them a speedboat. The film would "put Maine on the map" and generate new tourism.

Jon Pownall enjoying a casual moment with Melanie McGorrill (front) on August 30, 1973, at the Good Humor truck to be used in his new movie, *The Salem Six*. The children's athletic director, Sandy, in rear.

Photo ©Tom Jones Photography, Brunswick, Maine, courtesy of Melanie McGorrill.

Jon only wanted to direct the movie; anything else would be a distraction. It was his intention that Castellucci be the sole owner of Planet 3 Films, at least initially, and the film's producer, handling all the fundraising and business details.

After listening to Jon's needs, Castellucci went to an attorney in Portland—Bernstein, Shur, Sawyer, and Nelson—to incorporate Planet 3 Films, which took two to three months.

They estimated that they needed $10,000-15,000 in pre-production money. Possibly more. Once Joe was sure that Pownall was ready to proceed with the movie, he went to Casco Bank in Scarborough, set up an account under his own name as owner of Planet 3 Films, and got a loan for $10,000, which was deposited into the account. They had advertised for a secretary and hired Nancy Payne through an agency. Nancy was the daughter of respected Portland insurance man William Payne of Desmond and Payne. She had recently returned to Maine from Washington, D.C., where she had worked on the re-election of President Richard Nixon before the Watergate scandal.

Jon and Joe found office space on the mezzanine of 465 Congress Street, with the windows looking down on Preble Street, which ran perpendicular to Congress Street on Monument Square. Jon continued to retain his small photography studio at 22 Monument Square.

With that money they also had to pay for incorporation costs, rent, furniture, salaries, and some office equipment. It was a very tight budget. Jon had his own office equipment stored in Chicago and arranged for it to be trucked to the new location.

When the office opened, Joe and Jon set up a press party for the media and theater community in Portland, so that they would be aware of their presence and what they hoped to accomplish. It also gave them a chance to meet the press and mingle with theater directors, producers, and actors.

GOODBYE, FAT LARRY

Then Castellucci drove to New York City to buy what was known as the *Players Guide*, a list of actors and actresses who might be suitable for their movie. In March, Jon and Joe drove back to New York, where Jon telephoned Jean Shepherd, Jr., a radio personality, who was also an author, TV producer, director, screenplay writer, and humorist. Shepherd had his own TV show, *Jean Shepherd's America*, which was broadcast on public television and some private TV networks. (A few years later, Shepherd wrote the highly acclaimed and popular film, *A Christmas Story*.) Jon most likely knew "Shep" from a series of humorous short stories about growing up in Indiana and steel towns that he had written for *Playboy*. Jon was convinced that Shepherd was the right person to write the screenplay for *The Salem Six*.

While they were in New York, they also met with Nick Scott, who was given a screening of Jon's documentary *Goodbye, Fat Larry*. They discussed distribution of the film with him. Neither one of them ever heard from Scott again. Sadly, *Goodbye, Fat Larry* was never released.

* * * * *

On Jon's desk at Planet 3 Films were his August 31 round-trip plane tickets to Los Angeles inside a white envelope, which had been delivered on August 30 by Bruce Littlejohn who worked on the Conrak boards (production boards containing information on certain scenes, i.e., actors, equipment needed, etc.). After Jon met with Joe Castellucci that evening, he planned to get a few hours of sleep then be picked up in a staff car, a white Volvo, at his home in Shapleigh by another staffer, David Joy, who would drive Jon to Logan Airport in Boston.

In Hollywood, Jon had an appointment to get contracts signed for the film. Joe's job was to make sure that the investors were ready to pay these stars for their work.

Instead, the envelope containing the airline tickets was found under Jon's desk, on the floor, by Sergeant Eccles at the crime scene. Eccles photographed it, then inspected it, noting that the flight was for that same day.

Perhaps it's an important clue, Eccles considered.

It *was* a very important clue.

It was critical to the murder plan that the contracts for the two stars never be signed. Timing was everything. It was now or never.

"The love of money is the root of all evil." — St. Paul, the Apostle

The investors

It was in the news—a movie was going to be filmed right in Portland by a local film company, Planet 3 Films. It got the attention of, well, everyone, including those who saw it as a means to make money for themselves.

The "concept" for the film was registered in Jon Pownall's name in April 1973 and paid for by Planet 3 Films.

In the early stages of planning, Jon went to Mexico City to meet with his brother-in-law Felipe at Churubusco Studios, a major Mexican movie company, and a potential distributor in the American market. Even though they were very interested, Churubusco needed Planet 3 Films to make a commitment before they would follow suit, and Planet 3 Films didn't have the finances to do that yet. At the time, Jon and Joe assumed that they would co-produce with Churubusco, so Planet 3 began to make their plans. They also had some music written for the proposed script by Ed Romanoff, a singer-songwriter.

Meanwhile, Joe Castellucci went to Salt Lake City to discuss distribution with Alan Peterson of American National Enterprises, which focused on General Audience films. He expressed a great interest in Jon's "treatment" (it wasn't in script form yet). Peterson's company said that they would "four-wall" the film, which was a common practice in the 1970s. That is, they would rent "X" number of theaters, do saturation advertising, then place someone from their company inside the theaters to collect the receipts, grossing an average of $8-12 million on a film that had a million-dollar budget. That fit nicely with Planet 3's film budget.

Jon then sent Joe to New York to meet with Attorney Paul Baumgarten, who brought up insurance required by the Screen Actors Guild. This raised a red flag if they used Churubusco, which insisted on using Mexican technicians and crew. That meant work visas had to be arranged to have them work in the United States. Baumgarten recommended that Planet 3 Films use a New York firm that specialized in the film business. That was something that they needed to consider.

Film locations were checked out, and they decided on Fort Williams in Cape Elizabeth, Maine, near where Jon lived. The Town of Cape Elizabeth cleared the filming with certain provisions—not going into buildings, no large numbers of people on set during the shoot, etc. Jon had no problem with those provisions.

Jon also arranged to use an antique Good Humor truck in the film. One morning, staffer David Joy arrived at the office and Jon was already there.

"David, have you had breakfast yet?" Jon asked.

"I have."

"Well, call your mother and tell her you're going to be late for dinner. You have a flight to Hartford, Connecticut, that leaves in 45 minutes. You'll be driving a Good Humor truck back to Springvale," Jon said with a twinkle in his eye.

GOODBYE, FAT LARRY

David had never had an assignment like this. He made the flight and was met in the Hartford airport by a man holding a "Good Humor" sign. The man drove him to a factory where the truck was parked and handed him the keys. David wasn't there more than 15 minutes before he was headed back to Maine.

The problem was, David was not familiar with the area or the route. He stopped to ask directions to Maine, and Rt. 91 (ahead) was pointed out to him. He kept driving, waiting to read a familiar sign, but the only sign he saw was "Welcome to Vermont!" He stopped the Good Humor truck at a tourist stop and found that, 5 miles down the road, Routes 9 and 202 would take him directly to Sanford and Springvale, Maine. When he came back to the parking lot, there was a line of 5 or 6 people wanting ice cream! He apologized, saying the truck was going to be used in a movie.

When he finally handed the keys to Jon Pownall, Jon opened the back of the truck. To David's surprise, it was packed with ice cream treats!

On June 16, the chosen children to act in the movie (Melanie McGorrill, Luke Pickett, Charles Hall, Diane Dee, Billy Foster, Sam Patton, and young "tag-along" Geoff Stump) were invited for a boat ride, along with their parents and some family members, to Square Pond, Treasure Island, in Shapleigh, Maine. Much to their disappointment, a storm came up and the boat trip had to be cancelled. Instead, they gathered at Cape Elizabeth for a day of socializing.

Then on July 23, the young actors were to officially begin their training and rehearsals on Treasure Island. However, Planet 3 sent a letter to parents saying that the date had changed to July 30; a phone call followed, informing parents that the date had changed again to August 6. The children finally arrived on Treasure Island and were greeted by Jon. They had "house mothers and fathers" to watch over them, cook, and arrange recreational activities, such as kayaking, and to tutor them in their schooling.

Jon personally took the children water skiing, to the Acton Fair, arranged bike rides on 10-speed bikes, taught them to sing the movie's theme song, played games, and told stories. He also worked with them for about three weeks on their acting and the scenes, explaining how everything would take place.

Photos ©Tom Jones Photography, Brunswick, Maine, 1973

(L to R) Luke, Diane, Sam, Charles, Billy, Melanie, Jon.

GOODBYE, FAT LARRY

(L to R) Charles, Melanie (profile), Diane, Billy, Jon, Luke.

(L to R) Luke, Sam, Billy, Melanie, Diane, Tom Pownall, and Charles.

Initially, it didn't occur to the parents to ask why Planet 3 did not have agreements for the children in writing. There was a naïveté among Mainers, and they trusted the filmmakers to do the right thing. Joe Castellucci, in his lack of knowledge as a producer, only provided verbal reassurances. Later, some of the parents began to question the absence of contracts and it left them unsettled.

The film's budget was $650,000, but with percentages not reflected in the budget for producers and directors, the break-even point was $800,000.

A new wrinkle in their plans was brought to their attention by their attorney, George Shur of Bernstein, Shur, Sawyer, & Nelson. The Banking Commission under the SEC was concerned by the way they were approaching people to invest in the film, including the press party held by Planet 3. If Churubusco Studios would not commit, Shur had a problem with Planet 3's production schedule and how people would be paid.

On May 9, Shur incorporated Planet 3 Films, Ltd. At that time, Joe had asked the attorney to prepare a prospectus, which they said they couldn't do until Planet 3 had upfront financial backing in their bank account. Shur said that Planet 3 also needed to consider the risks concerning the securities and exchange law, Maine Banking, and Blue-Sky laws. Joe was dismissive and felt that the attorneys were being negative and not acting in their best interest. He was confident that Planet 3 could work things out.

Castellucci made a call to Joe Thomas, who had attended the April press party. Joe was the Director of the Portland Players and had been recommended by a friend of Castellucci's. Thomas had a solid reputation around town and in the theater community and agreed to help him any way he could; that is, finding investors for the film.

Two local investors, Michael Doyle and Maurice Parent, put in $6,500 apiece. Joe drew up and signed two identical contracts on June 18, 1973, which read, "It is hereby understood and agreed that (Michael A. Doyle) (Maurice Parent) is to receive stock in Planet 3 Films, Limited, a duly organized Maine corporation which will consist of two percent ownership in said corporation. Said transfer to be completed within ten working days." This document purported to sell stock in the company. *A company with no assets.* According to Joe, he received $6,500 from each investor as full payment for 8/10ths of one percent in the *film*, *The Salem Six*, not the *company*. But that's not what the contracts said.

Castellucci realized that he needed a few heavy investors with perhaps $40,000 or $50,000, rather than 50 or 100 small investors, which would be a problem when producing a prospectus to be registered with and approved by the Securities and Exchange Commission. Churubusco Studios would cover about two-thirds of the capital they needed for the film, but the investment was still on the table and no commitment had been made.

After Castellucci's phone call, Thomas came to the office and met with Castellucci to find out what was needed. A few days later, Planet 3's secretary and talent coordinator, Nancy Payne, added a meeting to Joe's calendar regarding a potential investor through Joe Thomas. It was to take place at DiMillo's

Restaurant on Long Wharf in Portland with 43-year-old Herbert Schwartz of Herbert R. Schwartz Associates, an interior design company. Schwartz was a fundraiser for the Maine Democratic Party and was called upon to curate in the first Temple Beth El Arts Festival.

The meeting at DiMillo's was attended by Castellucci, Joe Thomas, Herb Schwartz, Ken Block of the South Portland Bank, and Stanley Howard, a craftsman who had a successful contracting business working for Mr. Schwartz and who was known to patronize casinos. Jon Pownall did not attend, as securing investors was Castellucci's job. In the meeting, Castellucci outlined Planet 3's finances, distribution plans, and any commitments they had already made. He also had to answer some tough questions.

Herb Schwartz was interested. Afterwards, he went to Planet 3's offices to listen to the music score and, while there, he met Jon Pownall.

Herb, a tall, savvy, 43-year-old successful businessman, who always dressed in plaid suits, told Castellucci to forget Churubusco; that there should be no problem raising money locally. He also said to fire the attorneys of Bernstein, Shur, Sawyer, & Nelson. He suggested that they be replaced by the firm of Reef & Mooers, which Joe did on June 28, 1973. As a result, Shur resigned as Clerk of the Corporation for Planet 3.

Soon, Herb and Joe met with Reef, who offered a way around the SEC problem—to use "investor groups," selling parts of the corporation to a large group. To Joe, it sounded like an agreeable solution for Planet 3, although he didn't really understand that this would affect his own standing in Planet 3.

After that, Joe allowed Herb to handle the fundraising.

Churubusco Studios sent Nevis Morales, a liaison from Mexico City, to voice their continued interest, but by that point, Planet 3 was looking at local financing, which would lower their total film budget. Nevertheless, Castellucci didn't quite close the door on the Mexican studio and still referred to them as "an out-of-state investor" for insurance purposes.

At this point, Joe Castellucci invested $15,000 into the film (Casco Bank loans in his name). Two other investors, Michael Doyle and Maurice Parent put in $6,500 apiece. Reef told him that he couldn't "sell" anything without having something to sell. There was no script, no acting contracts, nothing. Reef warned, "It's a shell corporation with liabilities but no assets!"

Herbert Schwartz, not Joe Castellucci, claimed to have found a major potential backer, David Dickerman. In fact, Joe, as Producer, never even talked to Dickerman. Joe didn't feel guilty about that; he just felt that he had better things to do.

Jon Pownall and Herb Schwartz met a few times, and everything was going well, everyone was amicable. In July, they met at one of their favorite drinking spots, Roma Café. The small dining area was dark, lit by crystal chandeliers, and tables were covered in white linens. It was at this meeting, Herb introduced Truman Dongo to Jon as an interested investor. Truman was a wheeler-and-dealer, a salesman for his own company which specialized in car fender covers. He always carried a lot of cash, and what better way to use it than invest in a motion picture that had big-name stars? Jon welcomed him and Dongo counted himself "in."

There was more to the connection between Schwartz and Dongo that Jon knew nothing about. They had known each other since high school and had been involved in various juvenile criminal activities. Herb managed to become successful, whereas Truman was a convicted felon. Nevertheless, they remained friends.

Roma Café, 1960s, and Bramhall Pub in the lower level. Photographer unknown. No copyright infringement intended.

"When writing the story of your life, don't let anyone else hold the pen." — Harley Davidson

Horace Mann life insurance policy

April 1973

As Jon and Joe began to put their company together, their New York attorney, Paul Baumgarten, recommended that Planet 3 Films buy insurance on Jon Pownall's life in case he passed away before distribution of the film. Jon did not raise any objection. After discussing it with his wife Jean, Jon requested that Jean be a beneficiary for a certain percentage of the policy and that Joe be a beneficiary for the rest. Joe didn't have a problem with that and started researching policies. He didn't think to consult the movie's investors on their opinion of insurance since he was the sole owner of Planet 3 Films and Baumgarten suggested it.

A $400,000 policy decision was reached, based on Planet 3's initial film budget of $450,000, assuming they went with Churubusco and a higher budget. If the proceeds of the film were at least $500,000, the proceeds would be divvied up for everyone involved. Jon was to have ownership, then Joe as Producer would receive a certain amount, then the lead actor would get "X" percent, and so on. Paul Baumgarten said a producer normally would receive 40 percent, but since Planet 3 was still being formed, Joe agreed to 20 percent.

Stuart Lamont, who was currently an insurance agent with Horace Mann, reached out to Joe when he heard that he was looking for a policy. Stuart had been involved in the Garnache project with Joe previously and both had "connections," some of them rather nefarious.

"Hey Joe, can I come over and talk to you about some insurance? I'm competing to win a trip to Bermuda, and it would increase my chances if we could do some business."

"Sure, Stu, come on over!"

Once at Planet 3, Stuart laid out a particular plan based on the budget of the film.

Knowing Stuart well, Castellucci inquired, "Stu, would the policy pay even if the person who is covered is murdered?"

Stuart replied, "Yes, that's right, even if he's murdered."

Joe applied for two policies. Jon's policy stipulated that 50 percent would go to his wife Jean and 50 percent to Castellucci. A second policy was written on Joe Castellucci where 50 percent would go to his wife and 50 percent to Jon Pownall.

Joe's plan was to pay the $2,400 a year premium using the Casco Bank loan. The problem was that the initial $10,000 loan was getting low, and Joe had to be more cost conscious.

A Retail Credit Corporation rep, who investigated and verified insurance applications, arrived at Planet 3 to have specific financial questions answered by Jon Pownall for application approval. Twice when the rep tried to meet with Jon, he was told by Castellucci that

Jon was not in the office. On the third try, the Retail Credit rep finally agreed to meet with Joe instead. Castellucci told him that they were in the process of completing financial arrangements when, in fact, they had just begun. They did not have any committed, big investors yet, but Joe mentioned that they had "various investors throughout the United States." Until Screen Actors Guild problems were resolved, they could not enter into contracts with actors, but Joe told him that Jim Backus was under contract for the film. Joe said that Jon Pownall was in "a successful financial posture," owned real estate in Chicago which earned him income, and he was the Vice President of Planet 3 Films. He also informed the insurance rep that Jon had a "major film" called *Goodbye, Fat Larry* but, in fact, it was a documentary that Jon filmed but which was never distributed.

Joe told the Retail Credit man that he did not know all of Jon's financial history or exact net worth. The Credit rep said, "In that case, to the best of your knowledge, what would you estimate he is worth?" Based on what he heard from Jon during discussions regarding rental properties in Chicago, a home in Springvale, a camp at Shapleigh, and 10 percent of the film profits, Joe made an estimation of $225,000.

Joe found out much later that Jon had faced financial difficulties in Chicago and had gone through bankruptcy. Jon had also been a defendant in a number of lawsuits involving "claimed indebtedness."

The Retail Credit rep said that Planet 3 would get a follow-up letter in the mail. Unfortunately, when Joe did get the letter, it stated that the policy was declined on the amount of $400,000. However, they would consider writing a policy for a smaller amount. Disappointed, Joe never followed through with Horace Mann and, instead, looked elsewhere for insurance.

Just about that time, Michael Doyle offered his assistance. He had an insurance office at 465 Congress Street on an upper floor and had previously invested $6,500 in Planet 3 Films.

Mike mentioned that Transamerica might write an insurance policy for them, as they took on some high-risk customers. Joe agreed that Mike could look into it and let him know.

"Our intention creates our reality." — Wayne Dyer

Car ride to New York City

July 30, 1973

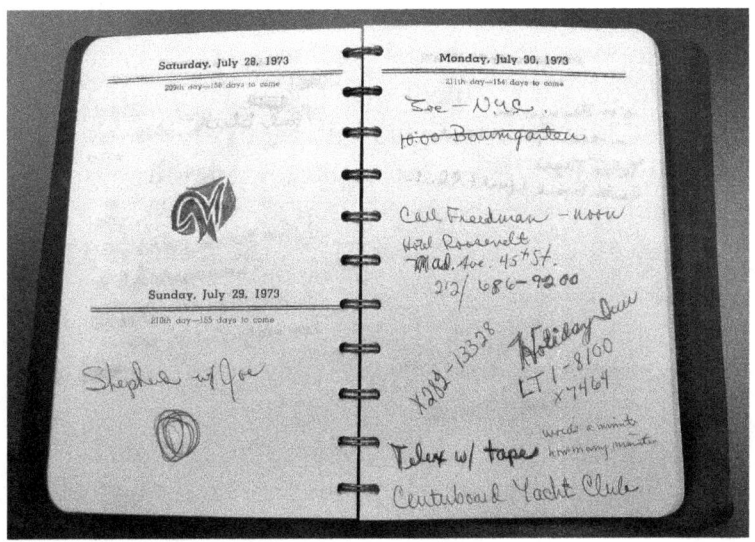

Jon's date book from evidence.

Photo ©Elly Stevens, 2022

Joe Castellucci, Herbert Schwartz, and Joe Thomas were on their way to New York City for a meeting with Jay Friedman about using John Denver or possibly Barbra Streisand for the soundtrack of *The Salem Six*.

Castellucci brought up the life insurance policies that were rejected by Horace Mann Life Insurance.

Herb perked up. "What insurance?"

Castellucci realized that he had never mentioned his insurance application to Schwartz. He explained,

"The insurance policy was written so that if I died, 50 percent would go to Jon and 50 percent to my wife. If Jon died, 50 percent would go to me, and 50 percent to Jon's wife. But that agreement was rejected."

They talked about revising the policy so that Planet 3 Films would be the beneficiary. "If Planet 3 is the beneficiary, the money stays in the business," Herb suggested.

It sounded like a good solution to Joe, and he planned to talk to Mike Doyle about it.

Joe Thomas, who was sitting in the back seat, laughingly said, "Well, we could always bump Jon off and collect the insurance! Haha!"

They all laughed. But to Herb, the thought piqued his interest.

In the hotel that night, they discussed the insurance policy on Jon again, in general terms with no mention of any crime.

But on the way back to Maine the next day, Herb brought it up again, "Well, maybe that's not a bad idea," referring to knocking off Jon for the insurance money, without saying his name or mentioning the actual crime.

They all recalled television shows, like *Alfred Hitchcock Presents,* where people committed the perfect murder and got away with it.

"Life insurance offers a man the only way where he can make his will before he makes his money."
— Anonymous

Transamerica life insurance policy

After the New York trip, Schwartz mentioned to the investors that he didn't think an insurance policy was a good idea, dismissing it as an "unnecessary expense." It didn't strike his cohorts as anything strange or unusual, just Herb's business decision and they went along with it. Castellucci also relied on Herb's business sense, as it didn't come naturally to him, and he almost always agreed with Herb.

Planet 3 Films' new attorney Norman Reef, however, told Castellucci to proceed with procuring insurance on Pownall. Joe had not spoken to Herb or asked his opinion; he just assumed that whatever Reef said also came from Schwartz. And since Joe did not understand all the rules and regulations with the SEC, he left that up to Schwartz and Reef and refused to further involve himself in raising financing.

As President of Planet 3, Joe was willing to trust the whole corporation to Mr. Schwartz' unsubstantiated word that he had investors—the entire success of the film, without question—even though he had only met Schwartz a month earlier. And Jon Pownall put his trust in Joe, even though he knew nothing about Joe's background or abilities. And Joe didn't realize that Jon operated on a shoestring and had no cash. Jon was depending on Joe to find people with money. The entire situation was a disaster in the making. The only "sure thing" was insurance money—if they could get a policy.

In a meeting with investors, Mike Doyle pointed out that if Jon were to die, there would be no film. If Castellucci were to die, someone else could step in. Jon was the key person and, therefore, the insurance policy should be a "key-man" policy.

By Tony Webster from Minneapolis, Minnesota, United States - Transamerica Pyramid, See Wikimedia.

Under the advice of Mike Doyle, Castellucci submitted an insurance application to Nancy Phillips in Los Angeles for a Transamerica Insurance policy on Jon Pownall's life. Once again, Joe lied to the credit investigator. He stated that the film could cost $700,000 to $800,000 and "sufficient financing was guaranteed," even though neither Dickerman nor any other investor he knew of had ever planned on investing that much. In fact, Joe didn't even know how much Dickerman might invest, as he had never met with him, nor discussed the books with him. Even though Joe still considered Churubusco Studios as a possibility, he had not pursued them.

Joe wrote to Nancy Phillips, "In order for our investors to physically put money into the production, they insist on insurance coverage of $400,000 for their protection, as well as my own." He based that on a meeting he had with Reef, who was now the Clerk of the Corporation. Reef claimed that "potential investors" wanted this commitment. Joe also wrote that $32,000 had already been expended on the production of the film.

In a phone call with Nancy Phillips, Joe claimed that the total budget of the picture was $650,000 and Planet 3 Films had most of the investors' money except for $200,000 that was in escrow, pending the insurance on Pownall's life.

However, the amount of financial net worth to date only came from the $13,000 invested by Mike Doyle and Maurice Parent, the $10,000 loan from Casco Bank, and a second $5,000 note from the bank. No firm commitments had been made and no other investments were in the bank. Planet 3 Films was strapped "pretty tight."

Joe felt it necessary to include a postscript on the insurance application that read, "The director (Jon Pownall) owns 10 percent of the net receipts of the film itself but does not own any percent in the production company Planet 3 Films, Limited."

When Joe inquired about the circumstances under which the insurance would or would not be paid, Nancy Phillips recalled a time when they insured a man in Texas for two or two-and-one-half million dollars, who was later murdered. They had to pay off that claim because the investigation had not been done properly and the man's worth was nowhere near that amount. That's why they began to use strict processes to be sure someone is truly worth the money they are insuring.

Even after his "go-around" with Horace Mann's Retail Credit rep, Joe still fudged Jon's net worth and the commitments of investors for the Transamerica policy.

"It's impossible to protect your kids against disappointment in life." — Nicholas Sparks

Failed promises and restless natives

The young cast members were thrilled to get key roles in *The Salem Six*. It didn't matter very much to them that the schedule was pushed back a few times. After all, it was summer, and Jon's activities kept them busy on Treasure Island in Square Lake, and his enthusiasm kept the children smiling. In addition, the children were to be paid for their roles in the film.

After the first week of training, the staff began to ask when they would receive their first paycheck. There were rumors of financial problems at the production company, but they didn't want to concern or alarm the children with those rumors. Nevertheless, it didn't leave the staff with a comfortable feeling.

Then the parents began to question why the paychecks for the children had not been received in a timely manner. Everyone hoped for the best—just a short delay, perhaps. They wanted to trust Jon Pownall, who had strong family ties to Maine, but could they trust a company which had not required signed contracts to ensure the children's pay?

In late August, Planet 3 announced that the start date of the filming was postponed until September 10, which meant the outdoor filming, including the children's swimming footage, would not happen until the *end of October!*

School in that area was due to open the week of September 3. Parents began to exchange phone calls, getting more and more irate. There was also talk about Planet 3 moving the entire production from Cape Elizabeth, Maine, to Mexico if Churubusco Studios became involved. The parents certainly did not want their children to be transported to another country and missing school!

One of the young actors, Geoff Stump, 8, whose father was a theater professor, attended the rehearsals and kept expecting to receive lines, but there were none for the part of the tag-along. His father confronted Castellucci, feeling disgruntled. Joe responded, "*We* are going to take care of Jon Pownall."

Unfortunately, Geoff ended up being cut from the film.

One day young Geoff was on Treasure Island with the rest of the cast; and the next day he was not. It was hard for a child to process.

The children and workers eventually received back pay for the time they had worked on the movie.

"If one of the partners in a partnership is losing his shirt while the other is counting his money, it is no longer a partnership." — Giovanni Bisignani

Letter to Attorney Reef

Monday, August 6

Joe Castellucci wrote the following letter to Norman Reef at Reef & Mooers law firm:
"Enclosed are four pages of conditions that Jon Pownall has set down. Please provide your feedback.

"It is my feeling that for the most part these conditions are in order, provided there are qualifications on my part. Also, the total amount that Mr. Pownall is asking (10 percent) seems to me to be a bit high and therefore would be difficult to justify in the eye of any investor. I feel that 5 percent equity in the production or even less would be both reasonable and fair. As a matter of fact, if we were to pay all of the monies requested without equity, Jon Pownall would be receiving a fair amount.

"In all areas where it is stated that the Director will have final approval, such approval must be within the confines of the production and budget and must be justified to me. There are two areas which are definitely open for argument. This is the last demand for $8,000 for supervision of editing and music, and any monies for living expenses for the entire Pownall family should editing-and-music supervision be more than one hundred and fifty miles from Planet 3 Films' Portland office."

"Joseph A. Castellucci
Enc."

* * * * *

Before August 6, Jon was to receive $30,000 for directing the movie plus 10 percent of the film.

The contract was revised to "$30,000" (and not the 10 percent); "details concerning the rights and responsibilities of the director will be defined by the firm of Reef & Mooers, Attorneys at Law, in contract form." This revision was not discussed with Jon until August 15.

"Easy come. Easy go." — English proverb

Corporation vs. film ownership

Friday, August 10

Castellucci spoke privately to Joe Thomas in his office at 465 Congress Street. "Joe, since you've been working on this film, spending time away from your own livelihood, I feel you should have some ownership in the company once things get rolling."

Thomas had signed a note for a bank loan with Herb Schwartz and felt, on the basis of that note, that he should be part owner of the film company and a beneficiary of the insurance.

Joe suggested 3 to 5 percent with the possibility that if Thomas became an integral part of the movie team, he should be given the opportunity to own a larger part of Planet 3 Films. Thomas thought it was reasonable and agreed.

But later that same day, when Joe approached Herb Schwartz, Herb thought that *he* (Herb) should have the option of owning 50 percent of Planet 3 Films if he successfully raised financing for the film. The option, prepared by Reef, was agreed to and signed by Joe that same day. As a result, Herb changed his mind about the insurance policy and wanted a commitment so that Transamerica could write the policy immediately. So, after applying for the insurance through Mike Doyle, Joe placed another call to Nancy Phillips at Transamerica in Los Angeles, and she stated that, if they had to provide an answer that same day, the answer was "no" because they didn't have enough information, and the application could go either way.

Herb said that he would try to proceed without it. He also said that David Dickerman, the wealthy Boston businessman who talked of putting $140,000 into the film, offered to cover any budget overages.

Upon hearing of Herb's option, Joe Thomas became upset. He went in to see Herb and they struck a deal, where, after the movie was released, the corporation would be divided into thirds, with one-third going each to Schwartz, Castellucci, and Thomas. Joe Thomas was satisfied with that arrangement.

Saturday, August 11

It became evident that Dickerman also wanted 50 percent of Planet 3 Films since he was going to invest so much of his money. If that happened, Castellucci would be out as owner of the company. Did Joe put 2 and 2 together? It was a possibility. Did they threaten to "eliminate" him if he didn't go along with their plan? A strong possibility.

They also discussed profits at the investor meeting that day. Castellucci explained to everyone that Jon did not want ownership in the company, but he wanted *ownership in the film*. In Joe's initial company meetings with Jon, it was agreed that Jon would receive a salary plus 10 percent ownership in the movie and whatever receipts were derived from that 10 percent.

GOODBYE, FAT LARRY

At that point, Mike Doyle proposed that Jon receive only 10 percent profits on the film, Joe 20 percent, the lead actor, Jim Backus, "X" percent, and the investors would have "percentage points" so they could recoup some of their investments. If, for some reason, Jon died *before* production, *none of the money would be spent yet*. If the film was scratched due to death *during* film production, the budgeted money would have been spent and investors would not get all their cash back. However, if he were to die *after* production, the film could still be distributed, profits made, and the investors wouldn't lose money.

In an evening meeting, Jon expressed to Herb that he was still unhappy with the Director's Contract since it wasn't in his favor. The contract's principal provision, as written, would allow Reef to determine what was "good or bad conduct" on Jon's part; bad conduct would make Jon in breach of the contract. And yet, Jon would have to finish the contract, and it would also make him financially responsible for the film. Jon also wanted a provision to keep Schwartz off the set. They verbally agreed to that point, but it wasn't in writing. About the key-man insurance, Jon made the comment, "It's weird that I'm worth more dead than alive." They never reached an agreement.

Moving on, they went over loose ends—Jean Shepherd's script was late, there were equipment needs and promotional equipment to be collected, a crew to be assembled, agents to be contacted, contracts to be signed, and so forth. No information had been posted on the Conrak board yet—the shooting schedule, day-to-day requirements—how many actors, equipment used, location, time, et al.

ELLY STEVENS

The tentative shooting start date was set for the first part of September. A lot of work needed to be done.

> Amendment to Contract dated ~~Aug~~
> Between PLANET 3 FILMS, LTD. and JON POWNALL
>
> THIS AMENDMENT TO A CONTRACT, made this ____ day of August, 1973, by and between JON POWNALL and PLANET 3 FILMS, LTD.:
>
> WHEREAS, on the 14th day of August, 1973, the parties hereto entered into an agreement by which Pownall (the Author) granted and assigned to Planet 3 Films, Ltd. (the Producer) all rights to his original concept entitled "The Salem Six"; and
>
> WHEREAS, the parties are mutually desirous of amending certain portions of that Contract;
>
> NOW THEREFORE, in consideration of $1.00, receipt whereof is hereby respectively acknowledged by the parties, and the mutual covenants contained herein, the parties agree as follows:
>
> 1. To amend sections 1(a) (line 3), 4 (line 3), 7 (line 2), and 8 (line 7) by inserting the word "original" before the word "story";
>
> 2. To add a new section "3-A" immediately following section 3, which shall read as follows:
>
> "3-A. SEQUELS AND TELEPLAY CONCEPTUAL FEES: Notwithstanding anything contrary in the contract, in the event that the concept of the original story is used for additional original motion pictures or sequels to a motion picture based on the original story, or in the event that the concept of the original story is used for an original teleplay or series of original teleplays appearing on network television, either directly by the Producer or by third persons under a grant, assignment or license from or by the Producer, the Author shall receive a conceptual fee of three hundred fifty dollars ($350.00) for each such additional original motion picture or sequel actually distributed and/or for each such original teleplay or each segment of a series of original teleplays actually appearing on network television."
>
> 3. ENTIRE UNDERSTANDING: This amendment to the contract and the contract constitutes the entire understanding of the parties and together supersede any and all prior representations and agreements.
>
> IN WITNESS WHEREOF, the parties have hereunto set their hands and seals the day and year first above written.
>
> _____   JON POWNALL
>
>   PLANET 3 FILMS, LTD.
> _____   By: _____
>   Its President

Unsigned signature page in Director's Contract.

GOODBYE, FAT LARRY

Monday, August 13

Schwartz and Castellucci asked Jon to sign the life insurance policy from Transamerica for $400,000, with Planet 3 Films as the sole beneficiary. It would cover Planet 3's "owners" in case of a catastrophe or if the film went over budget. It was a typical amount for a film of the time, but an unusually high amount for any business in the state of Maine. Yet, the policy itself stated: "Owner: Joseph A. Castellucci." "Beneficiary: Joseph A. Castellucci." Joe explained, "It was Joseph A. Castellucci doing business as Planet 3 Films." Joe assumed he was still 100 percent owner of Planet 3 Films until stock was issued to Doyle and Parent, and Schwartz exercised his stock option if he raised all the financing needed for the film. What was to happen after that was not in Joe's favor.

No one had told Jon about the option agreement that had been prepared by Reef two days before, giving Schwartz the option of owning 50 percent of the company if he secured an investor. If Jon had known, he never would have signed the policy.

However, Jon considered the insurance policy as they had written it, assuming it would protect just Joe. He really intended that his family be covered if something happened to him, but Joe told him that the policy could only have one beneficiary—Planet 3 Films.

Jon fretted over this and discussed it with Jean. He was truly worried about his financial situation, especially with three children to support. It was a difficult decision. Not signing the insurance policy could hamper progress on his film—a movie he wanted so badly to produce. It would be a threat to the entire production and that was something he could not, would not, allow. After all, what were the chances he would die?

Tuesday, August 14

In a meeting at the Reef & Mooers office, Daniel Mooers asked Jon Pownall to sign over the conceptual rights to the film. The idea behind the film was Jon's and, in April, it was registered with the Screen Writers' Guild in California. Reef said that, for Planet 3 Films to have a bona fide claim to it, Jon had to turn it over to the company.

Initially, Jon was to receive $8,000 for those rights. Jon had also been receiving a salary of $300 a week since March. In addition, he was to receive $30,000 for directing the movie. But at the meeting, he was told that the money he had already received to date would be used in lieu of the $8,000 and would instead receive only $4,000 and not until the money was placed into the bank account from the investors. Jon balked at this. There were back-and-forth "discussions," some rational, some very heated. Jon finally said, "I'm not going to argue about it. Let's go ahead and get this thing rolling and not get bogged down with this," and signed over the conceptual rights.

Jon Pownall also agreed to Castellucci's insurance terms and signed the Transamerica policy with Planet 3 Films as its sole beneficiary. It was also changed from a one-year renewable policy to a five-year renewable policy. Joe obtained a $1,200 certified

GOODBYE, FAT LARRY

check from the Casco Bank loan for the initial payment on the Transamerica policy.

Jon submitted to two physicals, which he complained about, but passed.

"Trust your instincts. Intuition doesn't lie." — Oprah Winfrey

The countdown: The altered drinks

Tuesday, August 14, evening

After the Transamerica Insurance policy was signed, several of the people who had been at the meeting went to the Old Port Tavern on Moulton Street, which had been renovated and opened earlier that year as a restaurant and bar. It was *the* place to go. When humorist Jean Shepherd came to Portland to discuss the script in early June, the Pownalls and Castelluccis treated him to dinner there.

Old Port Tavern. Photo courtesy of Old Port Tavern, Portland Maine. https://www.oldporttavern.com/

GOODBYE, FAT LARRY

In attendance were Jon and Jean Pownall, Joe Castellucci, Herb Schwartz, Nancy Payne, and some people who had come in from Chicago—Irby Smith, First Assistant Director to Jon Pownall; Bill Birch, Director of Photography; and Bill Wilson, Unit Manager in charge of budgets.

They were seated at a large table and ordered cocktails. The atmosphere was comfortable, and the conversation was amicable.

Jean Pownall stayed for a while, but then decided to leave. Jon got up and walked to the cash register to pay her bill. As Castellucci's eyes turned to follow Jon, he noticed Herb Schwartz pouring some liquid into Jon's drink.

Joe looked at Herb suspiciously. "What is that?" he asked.

"What are you talking about?" Herb replied with a grin.

Joe thought it was a bit peculiar and it made him uncomfortable.

When Jon Pownall returned to the table, Joe, who was sipping on a Coke, poured the soda into Jon's drink.

Jon cried, "What did you do that for? You spoiled a perfectly good drink!" He called the waitress over and ordered a new drink, then laughed about Joe's clumsiness.

Wednesday, August 15

Again, there was a meeting at Reef & Mooers, this time about the 10 percent of the movie *ownership* that Jon was to receive. Jon and Jean Pownall were present,

Joe, and Messrs. Reef and Mooers. Jon was told at this meeting that his 10 percent ownership of the film no longer existed.

Jon felt shock, anger, and fear. First, he signed over the conceptual rights, and now he lost his 10 percent ownership in his own movie!! Since screenwriter Jean Shepherd, actor Jim Backus, Joe Castellucci, and others were offered percentages in the film, there was nothing left for Jon.

Reef, at one point, threatened Jon that he could be let go and replaced!

Jon's face became as red-hot as his temper, and words were exchanged with Reef.

Reef admitted to Castellucci in a later side conversation, that it was a negotiation tool, trying to deal "from strength."

The situation changed dramatically that day.

Thursday, August 16

The Transamerica Insurance policy was approved, to be effective August 20.

Monday, August 20

With his money on the table, Mr. Dickerman told Schwartz that he didn't want any 2 or 3 percenters in the company. Reef & Mooers worked up an agreement with Herb Schwartz that Maurice Parent and Michael Doyle would be bought out for $3,000 each within 90 days. Up to this point they each had 2-1/2 percent in the company.

GOODBYE, FAT LARRY

After the meeting, Joe Castellucci, Jon and Jean Pownall, Nancy Payne, and members of the Chicago crew went to the Old Port Tavern for dinner and drinks.

Later, Castellucci went back to Planet 3 Films to meet with Joe Thomas and Herb Schwartz. They discussed Jon's Director's Contract until it was quite late. Herb was adamant that Jon needed to sign the contract as soon as possible, which would give Reef and Schwartz more control of the director's role.

Schwartz made a phone call to Bill Wilson, Unit Manager, who had already arrived back in Chicago. In the conversation, Wilson told Schwartz that he was furious that his paycheck had not arrived. (A check for $1,704 arrived but the bank stamped it "insufficient funds." Wilson blamed Pownall, who he claimed lied to Castellucci about his financial status. It was true, Jon had, in fact, been through bankruptcy in Chicago. However, it was Castellucci who stopped payment on the check but didn't notify Wilson until August 31.) Wilson was heard telling his wife, "If I don't get my check, you can look for me in jail!" Castellucci described Wilson as in "a killing mood."

Even though Joe had not known about Jon's bankruptcy, it was his responsibility to handle the financial matters of Planet 3, including the bank balance and paychecks. Later, it was discovered that Joe never had taxes or Social Security deducted from paychecks either.

Joe got upset and called Jon at home to confront him about the bankruptcy. Jean answered the phone and said that Jon had gone to sleep, and she refused to wake him up.

Pissed, Herb said, "Let's go right down there in the morning!"

Joe left the office and went to Nancy Payne's apartment at 3 a.m. to spend the night.

Tuesday, August 21

At 7 a.m., Joe and Nancy were picked up by Herb and, together with Joe Thomas, they headed to the camp at Shapleigh to confront Jon. They stopped at Dunkin' Donuts in South Portland for coffee. Meanwhile, Herb walked across the street to the Gateway Motel to call Dickerman. He came back 15 minutes later very angry. He had informed Dickerman that Jon had not signed the contract, and Dickerman replied that his deal was off.

"I have better places to put my money!" he yelled at Herb. Herb became even more furious with Jon.

They arrived at the camp, but Jon wasn't up yet. Joe saw that one of the boats on loan from StarCraft was on the water, so he took Herb and Joe Thomas for a ride to Treasure Island where the children were staying and showed them around. Then they headed back to Jon's where Jon was having breakfast. Schwartz began arguing with Jon about the figures and equipment. Jon calmly explained everything and straightened out the situation, cooling them down.

Nancy stayed at Jon's home to do some secretarial work. Castellucci, Thomas, and Schwartz returned to Portland.

"The mark of the coward is that he attacks the vulnerable." — Marty Rubin

Negotiations intensify

Wednesday, August 22

The following day, things became volatile again at Planet 3 Films during a meeting attended by Joe Castellucci, Norman Reef, Daniel Mooers, Herb Schwartz, and Jon Pownall and, in the evening, his wife Jean. Jon hired Attorney Richard A. Spencer to handle contract negotiations, and he attended as well.

They got into the negotiations intensively, trying to work out all the details. Jon gave in occasionally and so did Herb. Jon was adamant as to the liability of the direction in the outcome of the film, should anything happen to him.

The meeting became "explosive," in the words of Nancy Payne and Richard Spencer, with both sides screaming at each other. Attorney Spencer pointed the finger at Schwartz, calling him "very abusive" toward Jon Pownall.

At one point Jean Pownall "humphed" at what Reef was saying. Reef turned and sent an angry glare at her.

"I won't have you in here while I'm representing a client, snorting like a pig. Get out of the office!"

Jean got up from her chair and left the room in tears, and Jon followed her out to console her. The film—his dream—was turning into a nightmare.

Meanwhile, Joe and Herb also left the conference room and went into another office and shut the door. Herb snarled, "If Jon screws this thing up, I'm going to kill him myself!"

Joe didn't have time to digest that. Unbeknownst to them, Reef had followed behind. A moment later, Reef burst open the office door where Joe and Herb were having their private and dangerous discussion.

Laughing, Reef asked, "What did you think of that? Haha!" He added that insulting Mrs. Pownall was a tactic to get Jon to sign the contract. Joe and Herb exchanged glances and ceased their conversation and returned to the meeting room.

Jean Pownall composed herself and went to the airport to pick up her daughter Lynda who had been in Mexico City staying with her Aunt Molly and Uncle Felipe while attending the University of Mexico. The two returned to Planet 3, where Lynda waited in the reception area while Jean went back into the meeting.

The Pownalls, Schwartz, Castellucci, and others were in the conference room and Lynda could hear angry voices and someone pounding on the table. A man left the room and headed to the area where she was sitting. He was rather tall, with a rough complexion, and wore a plaid suit. He tried to chat with her, but all she could think about was how creepy he seemed. She eventually knew him as Herb Schwartz.

She and her mother left a short time later.

During the negotiations, Jon walked out twice, threatening to walk off the picture permanently. Finally, Castellucci calmed him down and brought him back into the conference room. However, the meeting broke up without any decisions made.

Schwartz offered Jon his Cadillac to drive to his summer home in Shapleigh. Jon took the keys and left.

Castellucci had been sitting at Nancy's desk at Planet 3, looking out the window and watching Jon go to Herb's Cadillac in the parking lot. Jon was sitting in the driver's seat for about 10 minutes without going anywhere. Joe went out to see if something was wrong. Suddenly, the headlights came on and Jon sped off.

"In the world of contract killing, there is no arbitration."
— Kenneth Eade

Contract for murder

Thursday, August 23

Joe and Herb cruised down Commercial Street[1] in Joe's car because Herb said that he was "looking for someone."

While on the road, Joe chatted as Herb silently looked out the window, "What if Jon, in fact, did not sign his contract, how would we direct the film? Would we pay someone to come in and direct? Irby Smith thinks there will be a great many problems if that's the case. Although...Joe Thomas said that he had a knowledge of cameras and could direct, if that would help."

Herb turned to Castellucci, "You need to fire Jon's ass! If you don't fire him..., so help me!"

Speechless, Joe drove by the Holiday Inn, then the Old Port Tavern, DiMillo's, and Anthony's Kitchen, then went back to Congress Street and parked the car near the construction of the Square.

Herb got out and wrote his name on the dust of the windshield.

Joe asked him, "Who were you looking for, anyway?"

---

[1] NOTE: This content is based on the testimony of Joseph Castellucci at the murder trial, State of Maine vs. Truman H. Dongo and Herbert R. Schwartz, Volume II.

Schwartz replied, "It's a good thing I didn't find who I was looking for. I hired someone to kill Jon if he didn't sign the contract. But I don't know where the guy went; I guess he's unreliable."

After lighting a cigarette, inhaling, and exhaling a puff of smoke, he continued, "I turned down Stanley Howard on a contract on Jon's life."

Joe was silent, thinking about the seriousness of it, and not knowing what to say. He decided it was best not to say anything.

* * * * *

That same day,[2] Truman Dongo met up with his old high school chum, Peter O'Donovan, at the Tavern Lounge at the Eastland Hotel.

Truman jerked his head toward the exit, "Hey, let's go for a ride." O'Donovan nodded in response. It sounded like Truman had something on his mind. They both climbed into Pete's car. Pete drove.

"There's something I don't want to talk about. It's heavy."

Pete glanced at him. He knew not to ask questions. He'd rather not know.

Dongo finally added, "You know the coast, Pete. I need to find a place where there's deep water at low tide. I need to get rid of a big guy, strap him in a van, or a Volkswagen bus, and roll the windows down, so I need at least ten feet of water at low tide."

---

[2] NOTE: This content is based on the testimony of Peter O'Donovan at the murder trial, State of Maine vs. Truman H. Dongo and Herbert R. Schwartz, Volume II.

So, Pete drove out to Cousins Island and then Little John's Island. Truman looked at water levels there.

Next, they went to Cape Elizabeth at a place called the Cunner's Club, but the water was extremely low there. Truman shook his head. "Too risky." They turned around and drove to Crescent Beach.

Pete knew that none of the sites appeared to be satisfactory.

"Let's just go to the Old Port for a drink," Truman said, finally.

After a couple of drinks, the bartender told Truman that he had a phone call. He left the table and headed for the phone. It was Herb.

Herb told Truman, "The deal is off. He won't sign." Truman knew what that meant.

Dongo went back to the table and complained to O'Donovan that "the director" wouldn't sign the policy. Pete knew he was referring to Jon Pownall, but he didn't know Jon personally.

"You want a ride back to your truck, Truman? I'm going to take off."

"No. I'm going to wait here for Herb." There was a lot the two of them had to discuss.

* * * * *

Later, in the Planet 3 Film's office,[3] Castellucci rose from his desk chair to use the restroom, leaving Herb Schwartz and Truman Dongo standing in front of Nancy's unattended desk. When Joe returned, Herb

---

[3] NOTE: The following content is based on the testimony of Joseph Castellucci at the murder trial, State of Maine vs. Truman H. Dongo and Herbert R. Schwartz, Volume II.

had a glass in his hand and shook the liquid inside, then stirred it with his finger before placing it in front of Jon, who was working and not paying attention. Joe walked over to the drink and poured Coke into it, giving Herb a questioning stare. Jon yelled at Joe for ruining his drink again, especially since he did the same thing a few days back at the Old Port. Joe poured Jon's drink down the water-cooler drain and made another drink for him.

When Jon left the office, he had trouble starting his car. He looked out the driver's-side window and saw Dongo sitting in his truck two cars away. Jon mentioned it to Castellucci the next day, saying it made him feel uncomfortable.

That same evening, after Herb and Truman left, Joe noticed a bluish capsule that had rolled out from under Nancy's typewriter. When Joe tested it on his tongue, it was very bitter tasting.

The next time he saw Herb, he asked, "What the hell is going on? What did you put in Jon's drink?"

"It was just a joke. Get over it," Herb responded.

Friday, August 24

Bill Wilson returned to Maine from Chicago. Wilson, Irby Smith, Bill Birch, Joe Castellucci, and Nancy Payne were in the main reception area of Planet 3.

Herb Schwartz was having a meeting with acquaintance Bradley Mack in the conference room off the back hallway. Castellucci didn't know anyone was using the room and started to push open the door which was slightly ajar. He witnessed Bradley handing

Herb a small, thick manila envelope and said, "This ought to do the trick."

Joe quietly walked away, considering what that might have been about.

That afternoon, Jon arrived at Planet 3 Films to meet with Herb, and they headed for Castellucci's unoccupied office. Joe was lounging on a bench seat in the reception area. As he looked out the window onto Preble Street, he saw Truman Dongo leave the building and then come back in a few minutes later. When Truman entered the office, Joe asked curiously, "Where did you go?"

"I let the air out of a tire on the [VW] bus," he laughed.

Just who is this guy? Joe wondered. When Dongo sat down, Joe asked about his past and if he had ever actually roughed up anyone.

He said that, yes, he had, in fact, roughed up some people.

"What exactly did you do?" Joe inquired.

"Oh, beat them over the head, punched them in the face a little bit." Dongo grinned. Then he added in a low voice, "You know...you could even kill him. I've got a gun." Dongo paused. "But that would be a little risky. If Jon were to be killed, another way would have to be worked out."

"How much would someone get for a killing?" Joe asked nervously.

"Herb said it would be about $35,000."

A little later, Herb asked if Joe would write a $225 check to Lane's Variety Store, to give this "fellow" Daryl some money. Herb had no cash with him or a checkbook.

GOODBYE, FAT LARRY

"Oh, fine," Joe said as he pulled out his Planet 3 Films' checkbook. He handed the check to Schwartz and the money was delivered to "Daryl." Later, Joe asked Herb what he bought for $225. Herb said a little heroin.

Herb smiled and said, "You know, enough heroin can kill you."

Joe "hit the ceiling" and grabbed hold of Herb's arm and led him out to the hallway. "What do you think you're doing? That check can be traced back to Planet 3 and me!"

"Relax, Joe. You have nothing to worry about," he said smugly.

Early in the evening, while Jon was busy, Herb brought up Jon's Director's Contract again to Castellucci, while Truman Dongo was present. "Do you think that if Jon were roughed up, he would sign his contract?" Herb questioned.

Joe replied, "It would be the coup de grâce, as far as Jon's concerned. He would walk away from the film."

Herb considered that.

Castellucci called Joe Thomas and repeated his conversation with Herb. Thomas was shocked. "That's absolutely out of the question!" he exclaimed. "He can't be serious!" Castellucci shrugged without replying.

Everyone was hungry by then, so Castellucci, Dongo, Schwartz, and Jon left Planet 3 to get something to eat at Sing's Chinese Restaurant. Truman got in Joe's car. Herb was going to ride with Jon and together they walked to Benoit's parking lot next to the building. Herb and Jon climbed into the

VW bus, then Jon started the engine and proceeded to drive out of the lot. He heard a "thump, thump" coming from one of the tires. He got out of the bus and realized that he had a flat tire.

Joe witnessed their predicament from his own car, knowing Truman had let the air out. "Why don't you all come with me?" he offered to Jon and Herb.

"Fine," Jon grumbled.

On the way to Sing's, Jon's conversation was described as "disjointed," as he talked about buying underwear and shirts, and how they all needed to take a ride on his dune buggy. It seemed very odd to Castellucci, and he wondered if Jon was high.

Herb said he'd call a place to fix the tire, but after their meal at Sing's, the tire store was closed for the night. Joe drove everyone back to the VW bus where they all got out and stared at Jon's predicament. Truman gripped the tire iron in his hand. With all eyes on him, he decided to put the spare tire on Jon's bus.

Jon said he'd be fine driving on the spare, and he left for home. He wasn't feeling quite right, so he changed his mind about driving all the way home and, instead, headed for the Stagecoach Inn for the night.

Castellucci turned to Truman and Herb, "What in the devil is going on with this flat-tire business?"

There was no answer, but Joe worried that Jon might have an "accident" on his way home.

Joe tried to catch up with Jon on the turnpike to make sure he was alright. He got off at the Biddeford exit but didn't see Jon or his vehicle. Joe then drove along Route 1. There was still no sign of him, so Joe drove home and went to bed.

GOODBYE, FAT LARRY

Saturday, August 25

After another late-night meeting attended by Schwartz, Dongo, Castellucci, Pownall, Thomas, Smith, Wilson, and Birch, Truman was sent out to buy some hamburgers and sandwiches. He drove to a Denny's by the expressway. He returned about an hour later and passed out the food. Truman handed Joe a cheeseburger, which he opened to add some ketchup. There was a strange powder on the bottom of the burger. Joe was suspicious of it, not knowing if it was just spice or perhaps something Truman had added.

Truman grabbed the burger from Joe, saying, "Sorry, this one is Jon's." Then he handed Joe the burger that Jon had in his hands, and they both ate their food without further incident.

Sunday, August 26

Everyone was getting ramped up to get the movie started, and Jon was planning his Hollywood trip. It was necessary to have another meeting at Planet 3. Herb and Truman stepped out of the meeting temporarily.

Castellucci left the conference room and saw Herb and Truman by the globe lamp in the main reception area. They had their backs to Joe.

Herb said to Truman, "We've got to do the fat bastard in!"

Dongo considered it and said, "It shouldn't be any problem."

Monday, August 27

Joe once again saw Dongo and Schwartz meet in the corner by the globe lamp. Dongo was saying to Herb, "The road to the camp is too long. You couldn't do anything down there and possibly get out in time," not mentioning what camp, but the "*road* to the camp." Joe didn't know what they were referring to, but it sounded suspicious.

Herb, Joe, and Jon entered the conference room to continue negotiations on Jon's contract. Schwartz accused Jon of lying. Jon went to the phone to call Irby Smith, who was staying at the Holiday Inn in Portland. Herb went over to Jon, yanked the phone out of his hand, cutting Jon's finger, and slammed down the receiver.

Angry and disturbed by Herb's rudeness, Jon said, "I've had enough of this," and walked out of the office.

Castellucci called Joe Thomas. "We're working against ourselves here. Jon has walked out, and I don't know if he's coming back!"

Joe Thomas told Castellucci, "One of the roles of a producer is an arbitrator. You've got to keep all sides happy."

Joe hung up and went in to see Herb. "We've got to come to some understanding. I think you need to stay out of the office for the rest of this week and let me and Jon meet. I can report everything to you." He then called Jean Pownall and explained that he had worked things out with Herb. She said that she would let Jon know when he got home.

Castellucci went home for the night.

GOODBYE, FAT LARRY

About 2 a.m., Jon called Joe, saying he was happy that Joe was keeping Herb out of the office and away from him.

Later, Castellucci claimed that Jon had said, "If Schwartz kills me, use the insurance money for the movie."

But the Director's Contract had still not been signed.

Tuesday, August 28

Jon and Jean Pownall went to see Castellucci at his home and they brought along Bruce Littlejohn who worked on the Conrak board. Jon and Joe were in agreement and discussed Jon's trip to the west coast. Churubusco was brought up again and possibly finding investors other than the ones they already had on the east coast.

Jon then called Irby Smith, who agreed to help him line up the crew in the Los Angeles area. It was decided that Jon would leave on Friday, August 31. They listened to some John Denver music and discussed how it might relate to their film. They still had Mr. Romanoff's music as well.

Before Jon left to go out on location, he asked Joe to call Herb to get the white Volvo back, which he claims he did. The car was to be used in the film. Herb told Castellucci that the car had some mechanical trouble, and Joe relayed that to Jon. Joe could tell Jon wasn't pleased. It was just one more unexpected expense he had to deal with.

ELLY STEVENS

Wednesday, August 29

On Wednesday morning, Mr. Douglas Thornsjo from Union Mutual Life Insurance asked to meet with Herb and Joe at the Stagecoach Restaurant in South Portland, since Union Mutual had an interest in putting about $30,000 into the film for promotional money. The company wanted to have a scene in the film where the children say that Union Mutual does not pollute but are "good guys." Union Mutual also offered their security services on set.

Following the meeting, Joe and Herb went to Union Mutual and had a tour and promised to consider everything and get back to them.

According to Joe, on their return trip to the Stagecoach Inn, Herb told him that Dickerman's deal had been revived and that he would be going to Boston to meet with him Friday.

Joe returned to the Planet 3, where he was interviewed by John N. Cole from *The Maine Times* about *The Salem Six* production. He also met with Bill Wilson, the film crew's unit manager from Chicago. Afterwards, Joe stopped at Nancy Payne's desk.

"Nancy, do you think I could get a set of keys to the building and office?"

"I only have one set of keys," Nancy said, "and Jon has the other. But the other day, Jon left his set at home in Shapleigh."

"I think we need to get some keys made up," Joe advised.

Nancy sent David Joy, a student who assisted Jon, to a locksmith to have some keys made up. She said she'd put together two new sets.

GOODBYE, FAT LARRY

At approximately 6 p.m., Herb called Castellucci at home.

"Joe, I'd like you to meet me back at the Stagecoach Restaurant."

"When?"

"Right away."

The urgency was noted. "Well, okay."

Joe was waiting in the parking lot for ten minutes when Herb pulled up. Herb motioned Joe to get into his car, but they didn't go anywhere.

Herb said, "The problems we've been having with Jon are done."

"What do you mean?" Joe asked nervously.

"If Jon does not sign the Director's Contract, I made arrangements to have him killed."

Joe didn't reply, but he noticed the white Volvo that was to be used in the film as it went by their parked car. "Hey, who's driving the Volvo?"

"I don't know."

Joe was angry about it. "Well, it sure as hell is our Volvo; it's got the dealer's plates on it!"

By the time Herb drove his car to the back of the restaurant where the Volvo had headed, it had disappeared.

"Well, that's certainly strange," Herb said, leaving Joe puzzled.

They went back to the subject of Herb's plan to murder Jon. Joe asked, "How much is this one going to cost?"

"Well, it would be $25,000 if paid out in a lump sum; $35,000 if paid over a period of time."

"You know, Jon complained that you haven't put a single damn nickel into this company, other than buying a few meals and taking one trip to New York City."

Herb responded, "Well, if he signs the contract tomorrow, I'll put up $1,200 for him to take to California. And if you can keep him here till Monday, I'll also take out a second mortgage on my Danforth Street property for $9,000 and put it in the bank."

"No, I won't do that. If Jon..." Joe didn't finish his thought. "I don't want to give Jon the impression that I'm not sticking up for his side of this. I think Jon will walk off the picture."

Disgruntled, Herb said, "Fine."

Joe eyed Herb. "Jon is working on the Conrak board, with the completed budget, photos of the kids, and the script before his trip to the Coast. I have an 8 p.m. meeting with him tomorrow night."

"Oh yeah? Make sure he brings in those books. I'd like to send someone to pick them up. I'm planning to drive to Boston on Thursday night and meet with Dickerman on Friday morning and we can review the books together. Then I need to get back to Portland to deposit the $9,000 in the bank before it closes."

Joe turned in the car seat looking suspiciously at Schwartz. "Herb, you wouldn't be planning on going up there yourself?"

"Joey! Would I do a thing like that?" He snickered.

Joe sat back in his seat.

Joe and Herb went inside the restaurant and continued their conversation.

"Why not bring your father-in-law to the meeting as a possible investor or a contact to find other investors?" Herb suggested.

"I could..."

"Listen, Joe. If everything goes well, if the books are there, and Jon is in reasonably good humor, come out wearing your white fedora. It'll signal my person that they can go in and pick up the books. Just leave the glass door open."

"Which glass door? The one on the mezzanine going into Planet 3?"

"No, the glass door downstairs."

"All I'd have to do is leave it ajar."

"No, the wind might blow it shut. Put something in it to keep it open."

"Why don't you just call Jon yourself?"

"No, if I call Jon, he may think I'm coming there, and I promised to stay away from him this week. But I want him to stay up there until the books are picked up."

Joe Thomas came into the restaurant and walked straight to their table, visibly upset.

"Why didn't you notify me about the meeting at Union Mutual this morning?"

Herb assured, "Don't worry, Joe, we won't make any decisions without your input. Have a drink."

Thomas ordered a drink, still feeling irritated. He left soon after his drink was gone. Schwartz and Castellucci left a bit later.

"Fiction is a web of lies that attempts to entangle the truth." — Nicholas Delbanco

The white fedora and matchbook

Thursday, August 30

Castellucci went into the office,[4] prepared to have his photo taken by photographer Tom Jones from *The Maine Times*. Reporters from a weekly newspaper had been there earlier in the day for a photo shoot with Jon and the local teens in his new film. It was quite an opportunity for those kids to be cast in a movie with big-name stars. They had visions of stardom and acting in more movies in the future.

That day, Nancy Payne provided Joe with a set of building and office keys, which he put in his pocket.

He mentioned to Jon that he'd like to bring along his father-in-law that evening for a short meeting to discuss co-financing the movie with Churubusco. If it weren't for that, Jon would not have agreed to drive from Shapleigh to Portland the night before his California trip.

Joe left early to await the arrival of his in-laws, who called and asked if he could meet them at Exit 7 of the Maine Turnpike and direct them to Cape Elizabeth, which he did. Joe took them for a boat ride and checked them into the Holiday Inn. Then they all returned to the Castellucci home and had dinner.

---

[4] NOTE: This content is based on the testimony of Joseph Castellucci at the murder trial, State of Maine vs. Truman H. Dongo and Herbert R. Schwartz, Volume II.

GOODBYE, FAT LARRY

AP Photo/*Portland Press Herald*

PORTLAND, Maine, Aug 31—ACTORS AND DIRECTOR—Movie director Jon R. Pownall, third from right, is surrounded by members of his cast. The movie, "The Salem Six," was to begin filming next month. Pownall was killed around midnight Thursday when he was shot twice in the back and head. This picture was taken Thursday by a weekly newspaper photographer.

The meeting with Jon was scheduled for 8 p.m., but Jon called and asked if 9 p.m. would be easier for him, and Joe said it would be, since his family was in town. So, they rescheduled for 9 p.m. Joe made two stops before he arrived at 8:50 p.m., buying cigarettes at the Night Owl and a magazine at Russell's on Monument Square.

It was an exciting time, but also a stressful time. *The Maine Times* had already interviewed Jon at his home recalling that "he was in good spirits but spoke of involved financial transactions connected with making a movie," which obviously concerned him. Jon would be on his way to Hollywood the next day to work out contracts. He wanted to make sure everything was taken care of before he left. There were plenty of details to handle before Joe showed up.

Joe let himself in the building using his new set of keys. However, Jon wasn't there when Joe arrived wearing the white fedora which Herb asked him to wear. Jean Pownall called to let Joe know that Jon would be a little late.

Joe stretched out on the couch, looked through the *Newsweek* magazine he had just purchased, and started a crossword puzzle. He was slightly startled when Jon entered the Planet 3 Films office.

"How did you get in? I know I locked the door behind me. I thought you misplaced your keys!" Joe remarked.

Jon chuckled, "I'm pretty good at jiggling locks."

Much to Joe's surprise, Jon handed him a belated 30th birthday present. Joe opened his gift, finding a leather hat that Jon had made at the Acton Fair.

"Thank you, Jon! How nice of you," Joe said.

Joe explained that his father-in-law was too tired to meet with them. However, he mentioned that someone would be picking up the books so that Herb could take them to Dickerman in Boston. Jon was fine with that. Jon updated Joe with what he had done on the Conrak board, and they discussed the script and the budget. Jon called Jean to get the home number of his attorney, Richard Spencer. He also made a call to his secretary, Nancy Payne, because he was having difficulty locating some papers she had worked on that day. He had expected her to be working late at the office, not knowing that Joe had sent her home early.

The partners discussed an alternate Planet 3 Director's Contract that Jon's attorney Richard Spencer had drawn up, with a "Herbert Schwartz clause," to assure that Schwartz would not go out on location while Mr. Pownall was directing. Jon did not want Schwartz trying to override his direction of the movie. Joe told Jon that he couldn't sign this major change to the new agreement without showing it first to the attorneys of Reef & Mooers.

There were additional edits that Jon made to the contract—that the $3,500 he already received for pre-production work was a *partial* payment and an additional $4,000 was still due; and clarifying that he owned "*ALL* rights" to the original concept.

Jon had also drawn up his own release of liability on location, giving him a free hand to direct how he pleased. Joe couldn't understand why he needed this, as he had already given him free hand verbally; therefore, he would not sign this paper either. They could not come to an agreement.

Looking at the office wall clock, Joe noticed that it was getting close to 11 p.m. and told Jon that he needed to head home. Joe glanced out the window and noted that the Time and Temperature clock displayed a slightly different time. According to Joe's statement, Jon was going to perhaps get a cigar and something to eat from Russell's then continue working. Joe gave Jon his set of keys so he could get back in the building without having to fiddle with the locks. They shared some humorous remarks, and Joe remembers laughing as he left the office.

In the hallway by the elevator, Joe put the white fedora on his head, went down to the main floor, and, with some trepidation and shuffling feet, wedged a matchbook in the door of the building so that "whoever was to pick up the books could get in." He matched his watch to the digital time of 10:58 flashing above the building on the corner of Preble and Congress. Jon had asked him to call him "in about forty-five minutes" if he decided "not to return to the office."

Once outside, Castellucci claimed to have seen "a black man near the Monument" and wondered if "he might be the person picking up the books."

When Joe arrived at his apartment at 11:15 p.m., he said hello to Linda Jordan, a neighbor who looked out of her window, then he went inside. After he undressed and got ready for bed, he tried calling Jon but there was no answer. He assumed Jon had stepped out for something to eat. After trying a few more times with no success, he called Jean Pownall, who said she hadn't heard from him. Joe made a few calls to nearby businesses that Jon might patronize, but no one had seen him, or the businesses were closed for the night. Then he tried calling Schwartz, but his line was busy.

Joe became agitated and decided to drive back to the office, a short drive. It was a warm, humid night with the usual fog by the water. Joe observed that Jon's Volkswagen bus was still parked across Congress Street, in the same spot as it had been earlier in the evening. All the lights were on in the second-floor offices. He had given his set of keys to Jon so he couldn't get inside the building to check on him. Concerned that something was very wrong, he drove to Nancy Payne's apartment on nearby State Street. Nancy said that Jean had called there as well, but Nancy had not seen Jon all night nor heard from him after his 9:30 call.

"Nancy, I think we need to call the police," he insisted. "I have an ominous feeling." He also reiterated that the last time he saw Jon, it was 10:58 p.m.

"No, I don't think that's a good idea—yet. What if Jon is just sleeping on the couch? We'd look silly!" she responded.

Joe thought about it and agreed that it would be embarrassing to show up with the police if Jon was just taking a catnap.

It was then Joe asked Nancy to go with him to the office and explained that he had given his set of keys to Jon earlier. Joe drove his car and parked near Jon's Volkswagen bus, which they checked out, but Jon was not inside. Cupping her hands around her mouth Nancy called up to the office windows from the street, but no one looked out at them. She unlocked the door to the building and she and Joe headed for the elevator.

Nancy pushed the "Up" button but soon noticed that the elevator was stuck on an upper floor, so they took the stairs to the mezzanine level. As they approached the office door, Joe pushed Nancy ahead. She walked in the Planet 3's office, then continued down the hall to Jon's office, discovering the grisly scene, with Joe standing behind her.

There was a body on the floor, slumped on the green-and-yellow striped couch, with one foot extending out. Nancy's hand muffled a scream. Joe spotted blood on the back of Jon's shirt. It was obvious that Jon Pownall was dead.

Nancy headed for her desk phone to make a call to the police. Joe grabbed the receiver from her hand and called the police himself, telling them that he thought there had been a murder.

After he hung up, he asked Nancy, "Do you think he's still alive?"

"No," she fretted.

"We'd better go down to the lobby in case there is still someone in here," he advised, glancing around and listening for any unusual sounds.

They took the stairs to the lobby, then Joe went outside to wait for the police. After looking up and down the street, Joe returned and told Nancy that he had seen "a man turn the corner from Preble Street to Congress."

"He might be the murderer!" Joe warned in an alarming whisper that made Nancy fearful. Joe took Nancy by the shoulders.

"Put your back to the wall so he can't see us!" he ordered. Terrified, she did as she was told. Joe also hid in the shadows.

After a time, Joe felt it was safe to go back outside to wait for the police, but no sirens could be heard. He headed to a pay phone and was about to make another call to the police when Nancy shouted out to him, "Here they are!"

A sergeant from the Portland Police Department quickly exited his police car and headed towards Joe

GOODBYE, FAT LARRY

and Nancy, who led the way back inside the building. The three of them walked up the stairs to the mezzanine level and into the Planet 3 offices. Joe and Nancy stayed in the reception area while the sergeant began to clear the offices and came upon the victim.

Joe asked Peterson, "Is he still breathing?"

"No," was the officer's blunt reply. Even though the sergeant knew the answer, he had to ask to see Joe's reaction, "Was he the type of guy who would commit suicide?"

"Suicide?" Joe was caught off-guard. "No-o," he stammered.

Other police officers started to arrive, turning the office into chaos.

Then Jon's office phone rang, surprising everyone. They stared at the phone, hesitant to answer it. Eventually, Joe asked the sergeant, "What should I do?"

"Hang it up," was his instruction, so Joe lifted the receiver, then put it back down. It rang again a few minutes later.

"Sergeant, it's probably Jon's wife. Please tell her what's going on!" Joe pleaded.

He handed the receiver to Joe.

Joe took the phone. As soon as he confirmed that it was Jean, he said, "Jeannie, he's been shot!"

* * * * *

Joe would soon become the number one suspect in the death of Jon Pownall.

"There is a point when facing the unknown stops being a longed-for adventure and becomes a terrifying reality." — Storm Constantine

The last goodbye

Earlier, August 30

Jean Pownall and her family were staying at the "camp," a lakeside cottage in Shapleigh off a dirt road. It was a family getaway where they were enjoying the last warm days of summer.

Their daughter Lynda, 16, was going to stay overnight with a friend in town. Their son, Jon ("Ricky"), 15, had an overnight guest, and Thomas ("TG"), 8, was getting ready for bed. Jon's mother Germaine and her friend Yvette stopped by to wish Jon well on his trip but left when it became late, and Jon had still not arrived.

"I will probably catch him on the road," his mom said.

At first, Jean tried to settle down with a book, but her mind went elsewhere. Looking out across the lake, her eyes rested on the island where the children were training for the movie, studying the art of the Eskimo roll, learning how to assemble toy rockets, memorizing lines, and rehearsing scenes. As she watched the full summer moon slide across the sky and hang beautifully above the lake, she heard a loon's soulful cry. She felt grateful to be spending time in such a beautiful place.

GOODBYE, FAT LARRY

But then her thoughts took her back to the heated moments when Joe Castellucci, Herb Schwartz, and Joe Thomas had confronted her husband, barging in on his breakfast at the cottage, and demanding answers to their accusations. When Castellucci had initially called, Jon had been sleeping and Jean refused to wake him up. But the next morning, they all showed up at the camp. Pounding on the door. Angry. Shouting. Pointing fingers. They showed no respect for Jon and his family.

And two days after that, there were the tense and explosive meetings at the lawyers, with Norman Reef throwing her out of the conference room and calling her a "snorting pig!"

Jean didn't trust any of them.

Jon just wanted to direct this movie and couldn't see the danger developing or the level of evil in the hearts of his associates. But the wolves were at his door, eating away the movie rights, Jon's pay, and even the company that he had just established a few months back. Now, they wanted everything, even threatening to fire him from directing his own movie and to hire someone else.

Jean couldn't imagine what Jon was going through. He seemed to take certain things in stride, as if business partners and investors were always nervous and confrontational about the finances. She could see the stress in his face, though.

Earlier tonight, after they finished dinner, Jon prepared to return to Planet 3 to meet with Joe Castellucci one more time. He explained that there were some details that had to be ironed out, and Jon was anxious to meet with Elliot Stern, Joe's father-in-law. Plus, someone was coming to pick up the books for Dickerman. Jon never questioned it; it was something that made business sense. After all, Dickerman was considering a huge investment in the film.

"Jon, do you really need to go into the office tonight?" Jean asked.

"I'm just meeting with Joe. I have to get everything ready for tomorrow's meeting in L.A."

"I'm worried. I wouldn't put it past Herb to make trouble."

"He's supposed to stay away this week. Everything will be fine," Jon assured her with a smile and a kiss.

Jean wondered if Jon really knew any of these people. They seemed to come out of the woodwork at the mention of a major movie, looking for fame and fortune. Mostly fortune.

The movie was a hardship on their finances. They had their share of financial issues when they lived in Chicago, but this was supposed to be their big breakthrough; instead, it was breaking them. First, his pay was cut; then he was forced to sign off on the movie rights; now they wanted him to sign a Director's Contract based on the "original" story only and be paid a conceptual fee ($350) on any motion picture sequels or television shows. Jon refused to sign it. That infuriated Herb Schwartz to the point he was asked to stay away from Jon for a week. Was Jon afraid of Herb? Jean thought so. Tonight, Jon was going to propose a "Herbert Schwartz clause" to Castellucci. She hoped he'd convince his partner that it would be beneficial to both of them.

GOODBYE, FAT LARRY

"What right does that cocky Herb Schwartz have to make his demands?" she'd comment. "He hasn't invested one red cent in the film or the company!" She wondered, *Why is he even at Planet 3, making major decisions? He supposedly is bringing in Dickerman, but where is the money?*

The other thing gnawing at her was that Joe Castellucci was turning on Jon, taking sides with Schwartz instead of backing his partner. She couldn't think of a single thing Joe had done as the executive producer of *The Salem Six*. It wasn't lost on Jon; he was aware of Joe's shortcomings. In the first month or two, Jon patiently coached Joe on the job he was expected to do and suggested ways to locate investors. Jean Pownall told a staff writer at the *Portland Press Herald,* "Jon found a lot of responsibility falling on his shoulders, placed there by Joe."

After that, Joe seemed to give up—leaving the producer's job in Herb's hands, and that's when everything started to deteriorate. Herb started interfering on set, complaining to Reef, demanding a Director's Contract, taking over the film company, and edging out Jon—and perhaps even Joe.

Still, Jon's goal was steadfast; his dream was about to come true. He was to fly to Los Angeles in the morning and get the contracts signed. Once there were commitments, Jon was sure Dickerman would come through with his backing. Jean was hopeful about that, too.

Around 9 p.m., Jon went to his VW bus carrying a birthday gift for Joe. Jon had a kind heart, and the hat he made at the Acton Fair was somewhat of a peace offering for some of the stressful business meetings that he and Joe attended.

Jean went out to the bus window and kissed Jon goodbye a few times. "Don't be late."

He consoled her, "Don't worry; I won't stay too long." Jon knew he had an early flight in the morning. "See you in a few hours."

"Okay. Love you."

Jon's daughter looked out the cottage door and watched her dad drive down the dusty dirt road.

Jean sighed, hoping nothing would stress Jon out any further before his trip. She called Castellucci, who was already at the office, and told him that Jon was running a little late, but he was on his way.

"Every man has but one destiny." — Veto Corleone, The Godfather (Mario Puzo)

Jon's last few hours

August 30

As the van disappeared down the winding dirt road that led from the camp in Shapleigh and headed for a date with destiny, Jon was most likely thinking about his trip to L.A. the next morning. He'd be meeting John Denver about the music for the movie and signing contracts with Jim Backus and Margaret Hamilton.

His mind wasn't capable of comprehending what was to come further down that winding road that led to Portland. He drove by the little towns and shops he had known his entire youth, driving past cemeteries, gas stations, and familiar stores in each village. He went past the streams where he had fished as a kid and went through Sanford with its factories and shoe and clothing outlets where he surely would have ended up working had it not been for this dream—the dream he was living, but soon-to-be nightmare that would never let him rest.

Jon parked his car on the street and walked to the side entrance of the Maine Bank. He was casually dressed in 1970's attire and had his long hair tied back in a ribbon. The night air was humid. There would no doubt be some fog closer to the ocean. He fiddled with the lock until it opened. The interior of the bank was dead quiet, and he could hear his own footfalls on the marble floor. He went upstairs to the mezzanine level and opened the unlocked door to the Planet 3 Films offices. Inside, Joe Castellucci, who had been lounging on the couch, sat up, somewhat startled.

After some small talk, they got to work. At the end of the night, Jon rejected Reef's Director's Contract. Afterall, the movie was his idea, the plot was his, the characters, the scenes... He refused to allow outsiders to take control of the director's role. They already cut his salary and made him sign over the rights to the movie. He would never let them take what was rightfully his. Jon offered the alternative contract from his attorney, Richard Spencer, but Joe said he couldn't sign it without Reef agreeing to it. He and Joe could not come to terms, so the original Director's Contract was left unsigned.

Jon's fate was sealed.

According to Joe, Jon told him to call at 11:45 to let him know if he was coming back to the office or not. *But those were Joe's words. Not Jon's.*

Once Joe left, Jon put a John Denver cassette in the tape deck, then went to his office off the back hallway to finish preparations for his L.A. trip. He put paper into the typewriter and started to hit the keys.

"Till my last day I'll be loving you." — Unknown

A sinking heart

Ring. Ring. Ring.

Jean's uncertainty became panic when Joe Castellucci called asking if she had heard from Jon as he had tried and couldn't reach him. Joe said that, after their meeting, Jon mentioned going out for a "candy bar" at Russell's, across Monument Square. That didn't make any sense to Jean as she knew Jon didn't eat candy bars.

That bastard's lying again, Jean thought to herself. *I need to write everything down.*

"You want to know if he called saying he's on his way home?" Jean questioned. "No, I haven't heard from him since earlier this evening," she told him. *I need to check the time...It's almost midnight.* "You called the office and there was no answer? Well, you know he didn't have any keys. That's why I called to tell you when he left, so you could go and let him in when he arrived." *Joe sounds so strange; not like himself. What is it? I'm beginning to feel so cold."*

Joe said he already met with Jon and gave him his set of keys.

"Oh, so you went back to the office and couldn't get in?"

Joe suggested that maybe Jon went to see Nancy Payne for a drink.

That's ludicrous! He has never gone to Nancy's, not even with Joe! And he would never stop there to have a drink when he had a flight to catch in the morning.

"You say you're worried, Joe? You're going to call Nancy?"

He said yes—that she was on stand-by in case Jon needed some last-minute things typed.

"That's a good idea," she replied, still not trusting him. "Call me right back and let me know, okay? Bye."

I have to focus; I can't panic. The kids are asleep... Christ! Lynda's at her girlfriend's tonight!

Time seemed to stop moving. Everything that followed seemed to happen in the same moment.

Jean dialed the Sanford Police to see if there were reports of a traffic accident. None.

She tried calling the office. No response. *Where is Jon? Why isn't he answering his phone? Something is VERY wrong!* She felt intense fear in the pit of her stomach. She kept calling.

Finally, someone answered at 12:45 a.m.

"Who is this?" she demanded to know. He refused to talk and hung up.

This time when Jean picked up the phone, she called the Portland Police. She identified herself and asked if there was a problem at 465 Congress Street.

The officer responded, "There was a squad car dispatched, but I don't know the nature of the call."

A few minutes later, Jean called the office again. The person who picked up the phone identified himself as a police officer. Jean was beside herself. Then Joe got on the phone.

"Joe, what happened?" she demanded to know.

"He's been shot!" he blurted out, then handed the phone receiver over to Nancy Payne.

"Shot?" Jean cried out. "Is he dead?"

This time Nancy responded. "Yes. Oh my God! Jeannie, he's dead!"

Her head was spinning with anguish, shock, and fear.

I need to keep my wits about me. What do I need to do?

Jean began making phone calls and continued to write notes on everything people told her.

She also needed to inform Jon's mother.

How am I going to tell Germaine? She will be devastated!

Then there were the three kids she'd have to tell in the morning. The news was not going to be easy to explain. Jean no longer had a husband; they no longer had a father.

In the following days, Jean told *Casco Bay Weekly* reporter John Lovell, "I feel like I was cut in half."

But, tonight, she could hardly speak. She managed to call back the Portland PD. All she could think about was that $400,000 life insurance policy on Jon—and the sole beneficiary, Joe Castellucci.

"I made a promise to a dead man." — Larry Cieslinski

Larry's promise

By Larry Cieslinski

The last time Lynda saw her father alive was before he left the camp in Shapleigh to go to the office in Portland. Jon was backing out of the driveway in the VW bus, and he had stopped to kiss her mother goodbye. Then the bus disappeared down the old dirt road that led from the camp.

I couldn't sleep. I wrote. I read the court transcripts over and over and the headlines in the local newspapers, all the time wondering how a man could be murdered for not signing a contract. I guess for $400,000, you might get away with murder.

It had become a fixation. I had to go to Portland.

I made a promise to a dead man. As I look back, I didn't consider just how many dangerous people I would have to deal with. The list went on and on and on—from the people who killed Jon to crooked lawyers and tight-lipped cops. And I was more of a visible target than poor Jon. I was a know-nothing kid from New York State, stirring up 10-year-old dust from the grave of a man I had never met. And every action has an equal and, well, you know... I just wasn't thinking! I needed to know more about Lynda and more about Jon.

While I was in Maine, I went through the garbage of Herb Schwartz the day after he had a party, looking for evidence. Found a signature among the empty wine bottles and paper plates coated with ice cream and cake.

Lynda, and her cousin Todd, and I went to see Ralph Lancaster, a man in his late 50s and the attorney for Transamerica. Linda recorded the conversation. He asked if I was a lawyer. I asked him what happened to the gun that killed Jon, which had disappeared from evidence while in their possession.

He scowled and said, "Don't come in here with your questions and platitudes and expect me to cooperate. What do you really want? You're not going to get it from me!"

And when I met with Lieutenant Dodd, he said in his Mainer accent, "The squeaky wheel gets the oil." It gave me chills and visions of things to come.

Statements, Arrests, and Indictments

(August 31, 1973 – February 14, 1975)

"There is no greater agony than bearing an untold story inside you." — Maya Angelou

Police interview Nancy Payne

August 31, 1973, early a.m.

When the patrol officer brought Joe Castellucci to Police Headquarters, he was directed to an Interview Room where he sat alone until Detectives Conley and Dodd were available to question him. Nancy Payne sat in another room.

Twenty-six-year-old Nancy was questioned first. The detectives knew to interview the weakest link first and then see if everyone else agreed with her story.

Conley started out with easy-to-answer questions about getting the job at Planet 3 Films. Nancy said that she was hired as a secretary in March when Jon Pownall and Joe Castellucci were setting up their business at 465 Congress Street. It was the first time she had met either of them.

Going back over the last six months, Nancy filled them in on her interpretation of events, including the press party, drinks at the Old Port Tavern with Jean Pownall and Herb Schwartz, and meetings with Reef.

Detectives asked her to go over what happened on August 30 and early hours of August 31.

She recalled that Joe Castellucci told her to leave the office at 4:30 p.m. Nancy was surprised because she normally worked until 8, 9, or even 10 p.m. Her mother picked her up from Monument Square and she had dinner with her parents at their home, then left to go to her own place.

Pownall did call her around 9:30, sounding tense and irritated. He had expected her to return that night to do some typing for his trip to Los Angeles. She told him that Joe specifically told her not to return unless she was called back in. Jon asked her where to locate some needed files. She gave him the information and hung up.

Later, she called to check in with Jon, but no one answered. She assumed that he had the papers he needed, and everyone had gone home, and she did not have to return to the office.

At midnight, Joe called and told her that he couldn't reach Jon at the office. He mentioned that he had offered to get Jon a sandwich and a drink earlier that night, but Jon turned down his offer, saying, "No, I will go to Russell's for a candy bar."

Right after Joe's call, Jean Pownall called Nancy, asking if she had heard from Jon.

"Jeannie was very upset and afraid that something had happened to Jon." Nancy repeated what Joe said about the candy bar, but Jean said, "He never eats candy bars!"

About 15 minutes later, Joe showed up at Nancy's house on State Street, acting agitated and saying that he tried calling Jon at the office but there was no response. Joe said to her, "I hope nothing has happened to him!"

Joe called Anthony's Italian Kitchen from her phone in case Jon had gone there to get something. The restaurant manager said that Jon had not been in that evening. Joe called the Planet 3 office again. No response.

He felt that they both should go to the office on Congress Street. "I have an ominous feeling," Joe had said. Nancy asked if he had the set of keys she had made for him. He didn't respond, but later told her that he left his set of keys with Jon. Nancy had her own set of keys with her.

She said that it seemed unusual for Joe to ask her to accompany him back to the office to check on Jon, especially at such a late hour, but she believed that Joe was sincerely concerned about Jon's wellbeing. While they were driving, Joe said, "I don't know whether to be angry with Jon because he is not where he's supposed to be when he is supposed to be there or be worried about him. I drove by the office on my way to your place, and all the lights were on, and Jon's VW bus was parked out front."

Joe wanted her to call police. Nancy couldn't understand why he thought that was necessary. Jon could just be napping.

When they arrived at the office, they parked beyond Jon's VW. Nancy said that they got out of the car and went around the corner to Preble Street to call Jon's name up to the open windows of the Planet 3 offices. No one appeared. They decided to head inside the bank building and, to her, Joe appeared scared.

Some other things struck her as "peculiar."

First, Castellucci offered up that, when he left Jon's office, it was exactly 10:58, and kept repeating that fact as if it mattered somehow, even though Nancy never asked. Then, the elevator was stuck on the third floor, so they used the stairs. Instead of Joe leading the way into the office and protecting her from a possible assailant, he pushed her ahead. And Joe merely looked over her shoulder when she walked into Jon's office and discovered the body. She gasped, "Joe, he's on the floor!" Instead of rushing in to help Jon or check his pulse, Joe just instructed her to call the police; but when she did, he grabbed the phone from her hand. Joe was very upset and could barely give his name, saying it was an emergency and that a man had been murdered. Then he hung up.

Joe ordered, "Let's get out of here!" Nancy followed him down the marble stairs, where she assumed they'd wait in the vestibule by the elevators. Joe said, "No. Someone could still be in the building!" Then he thought he heard a sound. "Did you just hear something?" he whispered, then dashed outside. Nancy got halfway out, keeping her foot in the door so that it wouldn't close and lock.

Joe came back inside and told her that he saw "some man lurking around the corner of the building who might be the murderer." Joe told her to stay flat against the marble wall in the lobby. No one passed their doorway. They thought they heard a siren, but it wasn't for them. She said Joe began to cry.

Joe collected himself and decided to try calling the police again, but just then a police cruiser pulled into the construction area on the Square, lights flashing. After the officer got their names, they all went up to the mezzanine offices where Nancy pointed out the body.

She recalled that the phone rang, and the officer handed the phone to Joe, who told Jean Pownall that

Jon was shot. "I also talked to Jeannie," she told Homicide detectives.

To Nancy, Mrs. Pownall's voice seemed very controlled and soft-spoken, as if she expected this. Jean asked Nancy, "Was it a shotgun blast to the face?" Nancy said no. Then Jean asked, "A bullet to the heart?" Nancy really didn't know but said it could have been. Jean asked if Jon had any keys, and Nancy informed her that both she and Joe had given him keys.

When asked by detectives if she saw any blood on the floor, she said, "There was no blood on the floor, no blood in the corridor—nothing—except by Jon's body."

In this interview, Nancy also told detectives about the "personality difficulties," the need for additional funding (about ten or twenty thousand dollars), the insurance policy, and the director's contract that Jon would not sign as it was written.

The Homicide detectives started asking some personal questions about her relationship with Joe, and she admitted that they were having an affair. She was single, but Joe was not.

The detectives thanked her and asked her to wait there. After a brief discussion of what they learned from Nancy, they proceeded to the next interview room.

"If you tell the truth, you don't have to remember anything." — Mark Twain

Detectives interrogate Castellucci

August 31, early a.m.

The police felt Castellucci was looking good for this crime. He was the last person to see Pownall alive and one of the first on scene after the crime, supposedly discovering the body.

Detectives Conley, Greeley, and Dodd noted that Joe was extremely nervous.

According to Castellucci, he and Jon met from 9 to 11 p.m. Jon had asked him to call back at 11:45 because he was going out for a candy bar across the street. Joe paired the time on the digital readout of the Time and Temperature sign with his watch. He said the sign flashed 10:58 p.m. (The detectives knew that Nancy had been told that exact time over and over.)

Joe made a point of mentioning his neighbor who witnessed his arrival home. Then he got ready for bed and made the promised call to the office. Jon did not pick up. He tried again a little later. When he did not get a response, he called Jean Pownall. She said that Jon had not gotten home yet. He also called Herb, but there was a busy signal. It was at that point, Joe "got concerned." It was a "gut feeling" that something was wrong. He decided to put on (fresh) clothes and head for Nancy Payne's house.

"Why did you go to Nancy's?"

"Well, Jon had called her earlier because he couldn't find some important papers. I thought perhaps he had been in touch with her."

"Couldn't you have just called?"

"Nancy had keys to the bank building and office in case we had to go there. I had given my keys to Jon because he misplaced his set."

Joe's story matched Nancy's, but there was still some question about the keys. Joe seemed to have an answer for everything. So far.

The detectives then pressured him on his timeline to firm up his alibi: Why did Jon insist that you call him at exactly 11:45? What were you wearing when you met him that night—were the clothes, hat, and shoes different than the ones you're wearing now? What happened to those clothes? Why did you call Mrs. Pownall from Nancy's? Are you having an affair with Miss Payne? We already know about the $400,000 insurance policy and that you are the sole beneficiary. Do you own a gun? Do you know if Herb and Truman were going to meet Jon in the office last night? Do you know who killed Jon? *Did you kill Jon Pownall?* Did you fabricate the story to Miss Payne? Did you know Jon was going to be harmed before you left the office that night? Did you force Miss Payne to discover the body? Did you know that the deed was already done by 11:45? Have you told us the complete truth here tonight?

When asked if he had gone into the Planet 3's conference room that night, Joe said he hadn't.

Castellucci was interrogated from 3:30 a.m. until 9 a.m. They didn't have enough to charge him and, as a result, released him.

The detectives needed the coroner's report and to interview a litany of other people—witnesses, possible enemies of Jon Pownall, business associates, and those close to him. After they followed up on their leads, they planned to bring Castellucci back in for additional questioning to tie up loose ends and hopefully make an arrest. Or, if he hadn't pulled the trigger, perhaps Castellucci would tell them everything he knew, including who killed Jon Pownall.

To the police, this was looking like a professional hit by someone from out of state. Conley knew of crimes by hired killers in other states, but nothing like this, ever, in the state of Maine.

Detective Greeley of the Maine State Police briefly talked to Joe, took his fingerprints, and had the State's Evidence Technician give him a nitrate test to see if he had recently fired a gun. The test was negative. Conley observed dark stains on his left shoe. He asked him to remove his canvas deck shoes so that they could be tested for blood evidence and to see if they matched the shoe prints in the Planet 3 hallway.

Since Castellucci was barefoot, Detective Daniel Ross gave him a ride to his car, and Joe drove home.

"My strength lies solely in my tenacity." — Louis Pasteur

Jean Pownall tells PPD to follow the money

August 31, early a.m.

Detective Conley and Lieutenant Dodd interviewed Jean Pownall, as she was holding up well and there was no need to detain her at length.

Jean Pownall stated that, although she didn't want Jon to go into the office that night, Jon had left their family's camp in a playful mood and headed for a meeting at Planet 3 with Joe Castellucci. Joe told Jon that he would be bringing his father-in-law, Elliot Stern, who had interest in backing the film. Jon asked her to call Joe at the office number at 9 p.m. because Jon's arrival would be a little late. She notified Joe by phone at the allotted time.

That evening, Mrs. Pownall was also watching for the arrival of Jon's mother Germaine at the camp.

Jon called Jean around 10 p.m. asking for Attorney Richard Spencer's home phone number. Jon was obviously busy and hung up after he jotted down the number. Those were the last words he ever spoke to her.

Castellucci called Jean at 11:45 after he could not reach Jon. Joe had mentioned that when he left Jon, he was going to get a candy bar. That alarmed her because she knew Joe had made that up. Something wasn't right, and she tried calling the office herself. No response.

Mrs. Pownall was so upset and suspicious about the phone call that she began to take copious notes with the times and events that followed regarding Castellucci, Schwartz, and Reef. There was also Joe's comment that he had given Jon his set of keys the day before. It didn't make sense to her, as Jon already had a set.

Someone finally answered the office phone at 12:05—but it was a police officer. When Joe Castellucci got on the phone, he told her that Jon had been shot.

During the interview, Jean pointed out to detectives that a recent $400,000 insurance policy had been taken out on Jon's life and the beneficiary was to be Planet 3 (Joe Castellucci). Jon was hesitant in signing the policy but finally agreed. Jon had wanted another $100,000 policy taken out with her as a beneficiary, but, supposedly, the insurance company would not cover him for an additional policy.

Jean said that she called David Joy, one of Jon's photographic students, to see if he had heard from Jon, but he hadn't. David expected to drive Jon to the airport on Friday morning. She also called Anthony's restaurant and Russell's Smoke Shop.

Lastly, she mentioned a strange incident that occurred on the previous Friday. Sometimes Joe and Herb kept him late at the office—sometimes 3 a.m. and even 5 a.m. After Jon became exhausted, they would bring up the Director's Contract, hoping Jon would sign it, but he never did. On that particular Friday night, when Jon went out to his car at 11 p.m.,

GOODBYE, FAT LARRY

there was a flat tire. Jon suspected that they wanted to detain him. Surprisingly, they all became "friendly" and convinced him to go to the Old Port Tavern for dinner and drinks. They kept ordering drinks for Jon. Jon thought that Herb put something in one of his drinks, as he couldn't think straight. After the spare tire was put on his car, Jon found that he had double vision and couldn't drive home. Instead, he went to the Stagecoach Inn and stayed the night.

When Detective Conley asked her about a possible suicide, she said there was no way Jon would ever commit suicide.

She asked Conley if she could notify her children as soon as possible before they found out on the TV news or the radio. After the notes were typed up, she agreed to come back in to sign them as her official statement. They said that would be alright.

The police secretary Virginia Thurlow typed up Jean's notes and said they were very detailed.

Later, Mrs. Pownall viewed the body at the morgue and noted that Jon's left hand appeared to be swollen, as if he had been in a physical altercation.

"He was pale as his undershirt, and his knees were knocking together." — Ophelia, *Hamlet,* William Shakespeare

The knock on Schwartz' door

August 31, 5 a.m.

BANG, BANG, BANG.

The unmistakable pounding signaled that the police were at the door. Herb's wife woke him up. He went downstairs.

"Mr. Schwartz, we are here to inform you that there's been a homicide at your office," the police officer said. They noticed Schwartz had a black eye.

"My office is at 23 Danforth Street. My daughter lives above it."

"The homicide occurred at the Planet 3 Films offices, sir. Mr. Jon Pownall was murdered. We have a few questions for you."

"What?" To detectives, he seemed to feign surprise.

Officers needed a verbal statement and began to take notes. "We need to know your whereabouts yesterday."

The officer told him that he would need to make a formal statement at headquarters. At that point, Herb excused himself, went into the bathroom and vomited.

As soon as he was cleaned up and ready, he went with the officer to the station.

Asked where he was the previous night, Herb told detectives, "I was in South Portland on an [interior decorating] installation at M. Reuven's apartment.

GOODBYE, FAT LARRY

Then I went to another job at my office; I called my wife and told her I would be home around 8:30 p.m. I arrived between 8:30 and 9 p.m. My wife was talking to my daughter. I told her to make me dinner—I was starving. She made me dinner and gave me a list of calls and things to do. I went to my bedroom, got undressed, and spoke to Leslie Castellucci on the phone. My call was for Joe. She told me that he was in the office. I asked her to have him call me at home if he wanted me.

"About five minutes later, Joe called and told me he was waiting for Jon to come up to wind up loose ends before his L.A. trip, and Nancy was going to be on hand for typing (budget, report, crew intention, etc.).

"I then went to bed. Watched TV, dozed, and was awakened by the TV. My wife came upstairs about 10:30, watched the news, and fell asleep during the movie *War and Peace*."

"You're either with me or against me! You have no other choice." — Lines from *Ben-Hur*

Warnings and threats

August 31, afternoon

After the intense interview by the PPD, Castellucci's wife had given him a Valium and he slept until 4 p.m. that day.[5]

When he awoke, he found that Messrs. Schwartz, Thomas, Doyle, as well as Mrs. Thomas and Mrs. Schwartz had come by his apartment at 901 Shore Road in Cape Elizabeth, Maine.

"Joe, let's step outside," Herb ordered as his head motioned toward the door.

In the parking area, Joe started questioning Herb. "What the hell went on there last night? Were you there? Do you know who did it?"

Herb just gave him an icy stare as they continued to put distance between themselves and the two-story apartment house.

"Herb, I know you threatened to kill Jon."

"Jesus, Joe, you didn't say anything to the police about that, did you?"

"No, I didn't."

"Thank God!" Herb paused. "There's talk that this was a pro hit. Whatever you do, don't say *anything* to

---

[5] NOTE: This content is based on the testimony of Joseph Castellucci at the murder trial, State of Maine vs. Truman H. Dongo and Herbert R. Schwartz, Volume II.

the police. If you do, your head could be blown off. He's killed once and he could kill again," he warned.

Castellucci was taken aback.

Herb continued with another threat, "You wouldn't want your wife to find out about Nancy Payne, now would you?" Castellucci swallowed hard, as Herb went on. "You are as much involved in this as anyone."

"What do you mean?"

"You were the one who placed the matchbook in the door to let the killer in!" Herb went on to say, "When I talked about a killer, you didn't believe me, did you? Well, I did tell you that Jon would be killed." He paused, inhaled his cigarette then exhaled. "I want half of the insurance money."

"Herb, if the insurance money comes in tomorrow and I give you half of it, the police would arrest us in ten minutes!"

"I need to pay the killer. Let me worry about how it would be worked out—the payment—without any consequences to you. If you testify against me or anyone else, mentioning threats against Jon, you may never make it to the witness stand."

"What?"

Clenching his teeth, Herb warned, "Figure it out. If you say anything that might point the finger at me, I will deny it. I want to know where you are every second of every day. I don't want you making any comments to the newspapers or the police. Do you understand?"

Joe nodded. "Did you do it?" he asked Herb.

"Dammit, Joe! I had to use Truman! I had no other choice!"

Thereafter, Herb insisted that Joe meet him for breakfast every morning at the Pancake Kitchen and required his presence at lunch and for meetings.

But sometimes it's impossible to control the situation. The next day, on September 1, Joe was picked up and taken to Police Headquarters to be interrogated again by the Portland PD and State Police.

"Read all about it!"

Breaking news across the nation

September 1, 1973

Slain Director (excerpt, *Biddeford-Saco Journal*)

Authorities say film producer Joseph A. Castellucci and director Jon Pownall engaged in a late-night meeting shortly before Pownall was found shot to death.

Castellucci and a secretary for Planet 3 Films Ltd. later discovered the body in the company's office in downtown Portland early Friday morning.

The 39-year-old director had been shot twice...in the back of the head and in the upper back. Officials said that Pownall also appeared to have been stabbed in the throat.

Pownall's death followed by less than two weeks of a $400,000 insurance policy on his life. The policy names as beneficiary Planet 3 Films.

"Murder is a bad feature." — Herbert R. Schwartz

Shock and tears

The news of Jon's murder spread like wildfire, not only in Portland, but Boston, New York, Chicago, and Hollywood. And on Treasure Island.

Cast member Billy Foster, 12, awoke in the early morning hours of August 31 after hearing the camp's only phone ring. He answered it. An agitated person on the other end asked, "Who is this? Let me speak to someone in charge!" It left him distressed and sleepless the rest of the night.

The next day, as the cast sat around the breakfast table, Tommy, their manager, broke the news to them. Jon had been shot and killed.

One boy kept repeating, "Shot and killed. Shot and killed. I can't believe it." It stunned the young actors who never knew anyone who had been murdered.

As reported by John N. Cole of *The Maine Times* in his article "Murder at Planet Three" on September 7, 1973, Jon Pownall, their friend, instructor, and movie director for the last three weeks was dead. The children were in tears and disbelief most of the day. Their dreams of being in a motion picture were dashed in an instant. Their excitement turned to sorrow and fear. Who would do such a thing to Mr. Pownall? He was so good natured and kind!

Billy thought back to the previous day. Jon had looked into his eyes and said "Goodbye, Billy." Then he gave Billy an embrace that wove a cocoon of concern around Billy. Time stopped for both of them until the embrace concluded. *Could Jon have anticipated what was going to happen?*

One of the girls, Melanie McGorrill, said that Jon had shared something with her in a private moment before his death. He had said, "If I were to die, my family would not get any money." At the time she scoffed it off, not believing something like that would ever happen.

If they thought for a moment that someone else would complete the movie, it was just wishful thinking. All they had were their memories. *The Salem Six* movie died with Jon.

Back then, there was no counseling for the children. They were expected to go back to their normal lives. The kids didn't see each other again for decades and there was no social media to make it easy to contact each other.

It also ended the concern parents had about filming the swim scenes in late October, relocating the young actors to Mexico, and having them miss their normal schooling. But now they had to deal with children who were emotionally disturbed and frightened.

After Nancy Payne's statement to police, her father whisked her off to the family farm to shield her from phone calls and the press.

Planet 3 Films' neighbors on Monument Square and inside the Maine Bank building were shocked to hear that Pownall had been murdered in his own office late at night. How did they get inside? Was it an inside job? Or was it a professional hit, as the local police department suggested? They had heard of such things in cities like Chicago, but Portland, Maine? Never!

According to the Maine State Police, there were **12** homicides in the **entire state** in 1970, 24 in '71, and 36 in '72.

Joe Thomas of the Portland Players told journalist John Cole, "I'm 43 years old, and this is the first time I've ever known anybody who's even known anybody who was murdered!"

Cole also quoted Herb Schwartz' single-line statement, "Murder is a bad feature."

When Cole reached out to the law firm of Reef, Mooers, and Hardy, they had no comment, The insurance company and the major investors did not wish to comment either. How could they until they had all the facts?

As reported by staff writer Mike Scanlon, *Portland Press Herald,* the Bayside for Kids director David Berenson pointed out that Jon had worked for the project, first as a consultant, then as a full-time employee, for about five months, instructing kids on filmmaking techniques. "Pownall was strong-willed. He was not easily dissuaded. If things weren't done his way, he wouldn't accept it without a bitter fight. He may have aggravated a lot of people." While that may be true, it was Jon's story, Jon's vision, Jon's direction. Everyone else's job was to make it happen. Berenson added, "He had an incredible amount of energy, and was incredibly knowledgeable about filmmaking. And he had a deep and powerful feeling of love for young people."

Part-time consultant John Sutton believed that "Pownall's personality was strongly attractive. That laugh (of his) stirred up a lot of people. It attracted people to him, and they opened up to him."

GOODBYE, FAT LARRY

The viciousness of Jon's murder had a widespread effect—Maine residents began to lock their doors, keep their hunting guns nearby, and train their dogs to attack on command. They wanted Maine to stay exactly the way it had been before the murder, but they knew in their hearts that, once you invite evil in, it never leaves.

"It is better to offer no excuse than a bad one."
— George Washington

Reef accompanies Schwartz to PPD

September 1, 4 p.m.

Herb Schwartz arrived at Police Headquarters with attorneys Reef and Mooers, who remained present during questioning.

Herb complained to Detectives Conley and Greeley. "I'm very upset with the way I was notified of Pownall's death."

He complained how a policeman knocked on his door at 5 a.m. and informed him that "a homicide had occurred in his office," to which Herb countered, "My office is at 23 Danforth Street. My daughter lives above it."

Conley thought that was a peculiar thing to say, as if Herb knew it didn't occur in his interior design office.

Detective Conley asked, "Why didn't you pick up the phone last night when we called? We tried numerous times."

"You must have dialed the wrong number," Herb suggested.

"We also banged on your door earlier, but you didn't answer until 5 a.m."

"Oh, I had the air conditioner on. I must not have heard you knocking."

Conley asked him to go through his day on Thursday, August 30, again. *His story changed.*

Herb now stated that he was out of town, meeting with David Dickerman, an investor, and didn't get home until 7 p.m. At that time, his wife was on the phone with Gerry Dongo, who asked if they wanted to go to a drive-in movie with them to see *Last Tango in Paris*.

When asked about his relationship with Pownall, Herb agreed that there was friction between them because Pownall refused to sign the Director's Contract. Joe Castellucci had asked him to stay away from the Planet 3 offices for a week, and he said he did.

The detective wanted to know what happened to the white Volvo that David Joy was going to use to drive Jon to the airport. Herb replied, "I don't know anything about Jon wanting to use the Volvo on Friday morning."

Schwartz agreed to undergo a nitrate test for gunpowder residue, which was administered by Deputy Sheriff Al Daigle. Schwartz signed off on his statement voluntarily, after which it was okayed by Attorney Daniel Mooers in front of Detective Conley. The nitrate test was negative.

"No matter how careful you are, you will get caught."
— Unknown

Castellucci questioned again

September 2

Joe arrived at Police Headquarters with Attorneys Norman Reef and Daniel Mooers where he was questioned by Maine State Police Detective Ames and Portland Police Detective Peter Conley and Lieutenant Clement Dodd. Also present were Deputy Attorney General Richard Cohen and Chief McClard.

Joe went through events from Thursday, August 30, 1973, again, with no major changes to his story.

Upon questioning, he denied that he tried to set up an early meeting with Schwartz that night. Joe also denied that he was bringing his father-in-law to meet with Jon.

"Mrs. Pownall may have heard her husband say to me on the phone, 'Come alone. Don't bring anyone,'" inferring that it was *Jon's request* not to bring his father-in-law because they had too many things to cover before the trip.

Detective Conley inquired, "Did Jon have the power to sign his own checks for Planet 3 or not?"

"It was a policy that I would be the only one to write checks, although Jon did sometimes question them, especially in the beginning of the company."

Joe also told police that it was Nancy's idea to make the keys, and he was unaware that a set had been made for Jon. He also reiterated that Herb was asked to stay away from the office for a while. "Herb liked to think he was the boss."

"Is it true," Conley asked, "that you and Nancy Payne are having an affair?"

Castellucci became visibly shaken by the question, and almost broke down. "Do you have to release that information? I did have a brief affair, but it's cooling somewhat. Things are going better with my wife at home."

Attorneys Reef and Mooers were also questioned about their part in the contract negotiations.

To Reef the detective asked, "Did you make a comment to Jon Pownall telling him that he was fired?"

Reef brushed it off lightly, responding that it was just a "contract tactic" to scare him into signing.

Joe spoke up. "I reassured Jon and told him that no one was going to fire him as long as he was the boss."

Reef did admit that the contract meetings were "stormy" with Mrs. Pownall and Herb Schwartz taking an active role.

"Mr. Castellucci," Conley continued, "how do you think Pownall was killed?" asking his opinion.

"I think the killing was done by outside contacts Jon made in Chicago. He must have had trouble with them."

"Will you take a polygraph?"

Joe hesitated. "It depends on what my lawyer says."

When asked about the white Volvo, Joe stated that he had talked to Schwartz on Thursday afternoon about Jon using it to go to the Boston airport that morning. Herb had said that it was not running perfectly. Lt. Dodd felt that was strange, as David Joy knew nothing about that, and Schwartz denied knowing anything about Jon needing the car.

"Well, it slipped my mind to inform David Joy," Joe added.

Dodd wanted to know more about the key sets that were made.

Joe mentioned that he had given his set to Jon. His story was that, when he got to the office, he saw a set of keys under the blotter near the rubber plant on Nancy's desk. He assumed they were the keys he had given Jon and put them in his pocket. He said they were currently at home.

At this point in the interview, Conley was notified that Nancy Payne was at his office with her lawyer. The meeting broke up with the understanding that Castellucci would speak with his attorney and a time for the polygraph would be set up.

"Lie low to the wall until the bitter weather passes."
— John O'Donohue

Lying low

September 3

A service was held for Jon Pownall at Springvale's Heald Funeral Home the Monday following his death. Jean Pownall and her three children, as well as Jon's mother Germaine and his brother Richard, sat upfront. Among the other 125 people in attendance were Joe Castellucci and his wife Leslie, Michael Doyle, and Joe Thomas.

Pownall's death was described as "a tragedy without conscience," by a speaker at the service.

Earl Lederer of Acton, Maine, a presiding overseer at the Jehovah's Witnesses Church at Sanford of which Jon's mother was a member, noted that the shooting was a "symptom of today's society." He said society will be changed by God, who will also solve major world problems "in the near future."

Lederer went on to say that "the recognition of this tragedy by so many who recognize the difference between right and wrong clearly substantiates the existence of God."

A few days after the funeral, Detective Peter Conley requested that Jean give a second statement to the police.

Mrs. Pownall told Conley, "At the funeral, I was suddenly face-to-face with Joe (Castellucci), and until that moment, I was unaware that he was present. He put his arms around me and said, 'Jean!' I embraced him and asked, 'You know Jon loved you, don't you, Joe?' At this time, his face was on my chest. I put both hands on either side of his face and raised it to mine. I wanted to look into his eyes. He looked at me very briefly and then averted his eyes to my chest. He said, 'I loved him, too.' I kept raising his face to look into his eyes. His wife Leslie was standing next to him and offered her sympathy. They were followed by Mike Doyle and his wife. I said that I was glad they had come in spite of the ugliness in the newspapers."

Jean continued, "Then we left the funeral parlor and went to the Riverside Cemetery in Springvale. Joe stood in the narrow dirt road with Leslie beside him. They were at the foot of the coffin, and I stood to the left of Joe on elevated ground. At the completion of the services, I became aware of Joe sobbing loudly, and his wife hanging onto him. I went over to comfort him; and I felt compelled to look at him. I kept thinking I would see something in his face, but he seemed to have trouble making eye contact, and he kept looking at the ground. Leslie said to him, 'I almost expect to hear Jon's big-hearted laugh at any moment!' and that is when Joe began to sob. I told him that they were welcome to come out to the cottage after the service. My motive for inviting him was not necessarily benevolent; I was interested in observing him and his reactions.

"I had some fears that my brother and cousins were contemplating unpleasant words with Joe at the cottage. I took my brother aside and told him to tell everyone to treat Joe with courtesy. Joe stayed for several hours. My brother-in-law Richard and Joe sat in the car for quite a while having a conversation. Later, I assured Joe that everything would work out. I said, 'Life isn't like Perry Mason, but things will work out.' I got to the point where I felt I just could not continue the conversation with him, yet I knew I should listen to his conversations very carefully.

"Joe completely regained his composure, and we continued to talk. I mentioned that I heard that Bill Wilson had a registered .38 caliber pistol. Joe told me that on Wednesday before Jon's death, that he (Joe) had stopped payment on Wilson's paycheck. Bill Wilson's wife Nancy claimed that Bill was angry and had threatened to 'see that the movie was never made.' He apparently made a phone call to his wife telling her that, if he didn't come back, she could find him at the County Jail. I found it hard to believe that Bill would be capable of such a thing.

"Joe also told me that, once the insurance paid off, he would take care of Jon's funeral expenses. I didn't tell him that the bills were already paid. He said that the loan for the VW bus was in his name and Jon was just a co-signer, so the insurance would not cover that. I told him that I would like to keep the bus, as it was so much a reflection of Jon.

"During our casual conversation, *Joe asked me if I knew that Jon's throat had been cut.* I replied, 'No, but I did hear there was a stab wound in the throat.'"

Jon's brother, Richard Pownall, accompanied Jean to Police Headquarters. Richard told detectives that after the funeral, Joe would not make eye contact with him. However, Joe did mention to him that he saw Herb Schwartz with Peter O'Donovan, who Joe described as a "local hit man."

Detective Conley asked Jean about Herb Schwartz. According to Jean, Herb called Joe the night of the murder, telling him where to find the money he was leaving. "Joe had told me that Herb was going to invest some of his own money, which was a surprise. Jon was always saying that Herb had an awful lot to say for someone with no real interest in the film. I asked Joe if he had to pick it up from a hiding place. Joe responded, 'Yes; they were being careful because it was cash.' He mentioned $9,000. That was strange because Joe's wife Leslie said Jon was going to take [Herb's] $1,200 to L.A. Joe became irritated with Leslie and sent her back into the cottage against her protest.

"We also discussed the upcoming article in *The Maine Times* by John Cole. I said to Joe that it could be ugly. Joe then told me that he had been asked by the police if he had an affair with Nancy, and he admitted to them that he had."

After the discussion with Jean Pownall, Detective Conley reached out to the Chicago Police Department and requested a report on William Wilson. A year earlier, he had been arrested for Failure to Register a Firearm.

"It is during our darkest moments that we must focus to see the light." — Aristotle

The missing Volvo, the wallet, and a check for heroin

September 4

David W. Joy

David Joy was a high school senior when he attended Jon Pownall's class on 16 mm motion picture photography at Bayside for Kids in the fall of 1972, and they developed a working relationship and a bond. When the Pownalls rented studio space in Portland, David started assisting them in various jobs.

David remembered, "I helped Jon in finding a location for the movie he had in his head. There was one spot—an old mansion in Kennebunkport with its rocky shoreline [close to what was later known as the summer home of George H. W. Bush]—where we discussed how it would be viewed at what angle through the camera."

In his statement to detectives, he was working at the photo copier in the Planet 3 Films office when Herb Schwartz came storming in, sputtering and swearing. David knew he was complaining about Jon. Herb went into Joe Castellucci's office. A few minutes later, Joe came out and gave David $20 to buy a bottle of Cognac Courvoisier from the liquor store five blocks up the street. David didn't like Herb or Joe, but he did what he was asked to do.

A couple of days before Jon's trip to L.A., David stayed at Jon's camp but left (in his own car) on August 30 to return to his parents' home in Portland.

Early on August 31, the plan was to pick up the white Volvo belonging to Planet 3 Films in the dirt parking lot by George's Restaurant, drive to Shapleigh to pick up Jon, then drive him to Logan Airport in Boston for his early morning flight to L.A.

But when he looked for the car on August 30, it wasn't there. David called Jon at 7:30 that night to find out about the car. Jon wasn't sure of its location, but he would make some phone calls and confirm the details. He said he'd see David in the morning and hung up.

At 8:30, David went to bed because he had to get up at 3:30 a.m. on Friday. However, around 10:45 p.m., David kept thinking about the Volvo and what he had observed with Schwartz and Castellucci. It made him feel uncomfortable. He decided to make sure the car was where Jon said it should be.

David asked his father to go with him to the parking lot.

The white Volvo wasn't there.

David and Donald noticed that the lights were on in the Planet 3 offices. Jon's VW bus was parked on Congress Street and a box of Marlboro cigarettes was visible on the dash. He knew Jon didn't smoke, so David wondered if Joe Castellucci had driven Jon's VW and parked it there.

David went to the entrance and noticed *a matchbook wedged in the door.* He was very confused.

He thought, *Maybe somebody who works here just stepped out for a minute and doesn't have keys.*

It made him feel scared, and he didn't want to go up to the mezzanine and run into Herb or Joe. He and his father headed home.

When the phone rang in the middle of the night, it woke him up. He thought it was Jean or Jon making sure he was up since they had a 130-mile drive to the airport. But it was Nancy Payne, informing him that Jon had been murdered.

David recalled, "I went white. My knees buckled. I was in total shock. I knew I had to go to the police and tell them what I knew."

Donald G. Joy

David W. Joy asked his father, Donald G. Joy, to come along to Planet 3 that Thursday night since he was staying with him for a few days.

The elder Joy told Detective Conley, "We noticed the lights were on in the Planet 3 offices." He also saw that Jon's VW, which his son identified, was parked across Congress Street.

He said to his son, "Why don't you write a note and leave it on his car?" His son claimed that he didn't know what to say, since the Volvo might be in the parking lot by morning.

Donald said that he saw a man in the Square near Russell's, but he was unable to describe him. There was also a man on the corner of Casco and Congress, just standing there.

(The white Volvo was located that night, seized, and towed to the Portland Police Impound Lot for an evidence search.)

Bruce Littlejohn

It was Bruce Littlejohn's hope to become a member of Jon's staff at Planet 3 for the production of *The Salem Six*. Bruce was hired by Joe Castellucci on August 13, 1973, and agreed to the salary offered. He was assigned to work on the Conrak board with Jon.

Bruce said in his initial interview with detectives, "I spent time with Jon, his wife Jean, and their three children at Square Lake, Shapleigh, Maine. Jon conducted a great deal of his business from there, although he and I traveled to Portland for matters requiring use of the office."

From about 1 p.m. to 7 p.m. on Friday, August 24, Bruce told detectives that he picked up the Volvo and staff cars, repaired bicycles, and answered phones. Joe gave him $20 to buy a fifth of Cognac Courvoisier in Falmouth (similar to David Joy's statement). When he returned to the office, Jon, Joe, and Herb were there. Jon refused to drink, saying he was "not going to give in to their methods of drinking and long, circular conversations."

"On the following Tuesday, Jon, Jean, and I left Square Lake in a blue Volvo to meet with the Salem Six cast at the doctor's office where the insurance physicals were to be given. We were late, and it had to be rescheduled for the next morning. After the appointment on August 29, we proceeded to Fort Williams to plan the stylization of the hide-a-way sequence for the film. We also stopped at Joe Castellucci's house where Jon told Joe that Herb Schwartz 'would no longer be involved' with his film. Joe appeared to be in agreement. Jon made the

GOODBYE, FAT LARRY

remark, 'I was really annoyed by the incident where Herb grabbed the phone out of my hand.'"

On the morning of the 30th, Bruce met Jon at Square Lake, and they immediately began the production breakdown. Bruce prepared the location board. A couple by the name of Jean and Gale Lawrence were compiling a list of props for the day's shoot. A photographer, Tom Jones from *The Maine Times*, spent the previous night on the island with the children, but that day he planned to photograph Jon in the Good Humor truck. Jones also took several photographs of them working on the production layout.

"Jon called Joe at the office and mentioned that Gale and I were on our way to Planet 3 to prepare a master notebook which he would take to L.A. in the morning." Jon also told Joe he had revised the Director's Contract and passed it by his attorney, and that Joe needed to read it that evening.

Later that afternoon, Bruce and Randall Brown completed the notebook for Jon, then Bruce delivered a check to Jon's attorney, Richard Spencer, who also had an office in the Maine Bank building.

"Around 5:15 p.m., Jon gave me permission on the phone to go home to Wells, Maine. I left the Maine Bank [Planet 3] at approximately 6:15 p.m., and walked across the street to Benoit's parking lot, where I picked up the staff car to drive home. When I got in the car, I noticed that Jon had left his wallet in the glove compartment. I felt that he would most likely need the wallet for the next day's trip, so I decided to return to the office and place it with the notebook I had assembled.

"When I arrived at 465 Congress Street at 6:30 p.m., the doors were locked. I rang the bell several times. A businessman from another office happened to be leaving and let me in. As I entered the lobby, the elevator opened, and the janitor exited. I asked him if he would be kind enough to open the mezzanine door, but he did not have the key. He took me to the second floor and summoned the cleaning lady, who had the proper key. She led me downstairs [to the mezzanine] and opened the door. I placed the wallet in the conference room on top of the notebook that I had prepared and delivered earlier. I walked out of the Planet 3 Films office and the woman locked the door. I left for my home in Wells, Maine, at approximately 6:45 p.m."

September 7

Officer Myron Gold told detectives that a man on Commercial Street reportedly tried to cash a $250 check from Jon Pownall's company for heroin. Conley did a quick check with the banks in that area, but no one had any recollection of the incident regarding Pownall. Officer Gold's source, an attorney, also provided some background on Herb Schwartz. About 11 years ago Schwartz had a .32 caliber gun.
    Later that morning, Herb, and his personal attorney William Troubh, came to the Detective Bureau for another interview. He was asked by Lieutenant Dodd and Detective Conley about his involvement with Planet 3 Films.

Herb claimed that the film was not at the point to bring in any backers. The company's attorneys, Reef and Mooers, said they did not need any yet.

He said he was introduced to Joe Castellucci and Joe Thomas at DiMillo's Restaurant, where they discussed the proposed film.

Detective Conley asked, "How did the 50 percent option to buy into the company come about?"

"Initially, Joe Castellucci and Jon Pownall, each, were to raise half the money. Later Joe told me that he had assumed full liabilities but didn't feel he could do it alone. He asked if I would help him. I consulted my business attorneys Reef and Mooers, who felt I should have an option to buy into the corporation."

"Was this before Reef and Mooers became the Planet 3 attorneys?"

"Yes."

"Take us through your day on Wednesday, the day before the murder."

"Castellucci called and said his account was overdrawn. He wanted to meet me at the Stagecoach Inn in South Portland. He asked me how much cash I could raise. I said $1,200." Schwartz told Joe to contact him when he needed the money.

Sensing that Schwartz wasn't telling the whole truth, Lt. Dodd decided to tell him about Castellucci's side of the story. Suddenly Schwartz began to recall more of the money conversation.

"When I talked to Joe on the phone Thursday night, he may have mentioned the $1,200 or an additional $9,000," an amount that he claimed was also discussed at the Stagecoach Inn. "I told Joe the money was in my drawer at my office on Danforth Street." Joe was going to "pay Jon in checks."

"Tell us about the Director's Contract."

Herb informed the detectives that Jon was holding up the entire program by not signing the contract. "I'm unaware whether Jon was ready to sign it on Thursday night. I assume not."

"Did you ever check out Joe Castellucci's background? His past business dealings? His failures?"

"No, I don't know of any of that, and I never asked. I was more interested in the 'vehicle' [film concept itself], than I was with the producer. The producer is only a money-maker and nothing else."

Herb also mentioned that he had also signed a $15,000 note for Planet 3 earlier.

The detectives asked about the white Volvo. Herb stated that he had informed Joe that the Volvo could not be used for Jon's trip to Boston because he claimed that he loaned it to a female friend of Dickerson. Joe had responded, "No problem. I'll let the kid [David Joy] use my car."

"Have you ever touched a gun, Herb?"

"Never."

"Denial is a save-now, pay-later scheme." — Gavin de Becker

Police bring in Dongo

September 12, 4:40 p.m.

The police picked up Truman Dongo for an interrogation at Police Headquarters.

Dongo stated that he met Jon Pownall in June when he went to Planet 3 Films' office to meet his close friend Herb Schwartz for a dinner engagement, along with another friend, Pete O'Donovan.

Conley asked, "Did you introduce O'Donovan to Herb as a hitman?"

"I may have introduced Pete, but I did not introduce him to anybody as a hitman."

Truman described O'Donovan as someone he had known since his school days. "Pete is anti-Semite and does not like Herb Schwartz and would not do *anything* for him." He added that he doesn't know about any of his friends or enemies or whether he had a gun.

When asked by Conley about the last time he had been at Planet 3, Dongo recalled that it was two or three days before the murder. There was a meeting regarding Jon's director's contract. "I used to go to some of those meetings just to tag along with Herb Schwartz." He claimed that he had gone to Planet 3 about four times in the weeks prior to the murder.

"A few months before, Joe Castellucci was trying to drum up some investors. Herb invited Joseph

Angelone, Norman Reef, Daniel Mooers, Robert Zilko, and a couple of others I didn't know, to the Roma Cafe. One was a potential investor named 'Dickson' [Dickerman] who was a millionaire from Boston. The investors were supposed to put in 10 or 20 thousand apiece and then get a percentage in the film."

"Where were you on the evening of August 30?"

"I was home, watching TV."

Conley asked point blank, "Who do you think killed Jon Pownall?"

Dongo replied, "I have no idea, but Joe Castellucci might have a good motive to kill him, as well as 'Fat Larry' in Chicago." He was referring to the fictional "landlord" in Jon's documentary, *Goodbye, Fat Larry*. Truman called it "A box office failure," when it hadn't even been released.

Dongo also stated that Herb "has been very upset since the murder."

In his statement, Dongo admitted that he had been arrested previously for breaking, entering, and larceny.

When Conley asked Dongo if he was willing to take a polygraph test, *Truman said that he would not take one*. "I don't believe in them."

"You can run from your past all you want, but it will always follow you. Forever and ever and ever..."
— Orihara Izaya

Paul Turnage calls detectives

September 10

Lieutenant Dodd received a call from Paul Turnage of Saco, Maine, who believed that he had some information relevant to the case. Dodd assigned the interview to Detectives Joseph Pelletier and Peter Conley.

Turnage informed the detectives that he had been working for Phillips Maine Corp. at the time the company went through a hostile takeover by Stuart Lamont and Joe Castellucci. After the takeover, the company's name was changed to North Atlantic Industries. Although run by Stu and Joe, it was owned by a medical supply company in Massachusetts. During the five months Turnage worked for them, he was paid with six bad checks. Neither Stu nor Joe knew anything about plastics and relied on Turnage to attend product meetings. The company folded in May 1972 after Stu and Joe got their hooks into it and bled it dry.

Joe had mentioned to Turnage on several occasions that his wife's family was worth a lot of money.

Turnage stated that both Stu and Joe had guns and knew for a fact that Stu had a .38 revolver. He also recalled that a former Saco police officer, Ernest

LeClair, came to work at the plant and tried to sell them his .357 Magnum.

Turnage passed along the name and phone number of the company's secretary, Marie Smith, who had additional information on their guns.

The detectives followed up with Marie who stated that she had seen Stu Lamont with a .38 caliber pistol in his possession many times. He carried it in his suitcase or on his belt. "I know what a .38 caliber gun looks like," she asserted with confidence.

"You should also call Joseph Sparks who used to work for Joe and Stu."

The interview was concluded.

Stuart Lamont was asked to come to police headquarters for a statement.

September 14

When Lamont met with the detectives, he claimed that he was one of the top insurance agents in the country. He had written two $400,000 policies for Castellucci and Pownall, but both policies were turned down "for unknown reasons."

When asked about his associations with Joe Castellucci, he said that he met Joe when he needed car insurance in Bar Harbor, Maine, and Stu sold him a policy. Stu said that he later ran across Joe again when interviewing for a job at Bar Harbor Candles where Joe had been a stockholder. Unfortunately, they were both let go "for no given reason." Next, he and Joe went to Phillips Maine, a plastics company, where Joe was hired for his marketing ability. That firm eventually closed down. "It was never really successful, but not in trouble when Joe and I arrived," Stu claimed. Although the chief stockholder was Mr. Lundstrom, Stu and Joe were in management positions and could sign checks for the company. However, he told the police that he did not recall ever writing any bad checks.

That's when Stu got a job with Horace Mann Insurance Company in June 1972. Joe went on to real estate.

Investigators asked Lamont if he ever owned a gun or carried a gun, he stated, "I have never *carried* a gun in my life." However, he said that he currently owned a .44 Magnum rifle, a .22 caliber pistol, a 30.06 rifle, and .22 caliber Ruger rifle, and an antique .22 caliber pistol. And when he lived in Chicago, he owned a Waltham PD pistol for about six months.

"Mr. Lamont," Conley questioned, "are you carrying a gun right now?"

"No, I am not."

"Do you have a gun in your car?"

"No."

"Has Joe ever owned a gun?"

"I have never known Joe to have a gun."

"Is there any other time you owned a gun?"

"Well, once I had a gun on my desk that belonged to a Reserve police officer named Ernest LeClair, when I was working at the plastics company. LeClair wanted to sell the gun. I didn't buy it."

"Have you ever been in a police station before?"

"Once, when I had hubcaps stolen in New York."

"What were you doing on the night of August 30, 1973?" Conley asked.

Lamont said he had dinner with his mother-in-law in Queens from 5 p.m. to 6 or 7. Everyone went to bed at 12 or 12:30 a.m.

He agreed to take a polygraph test.

September 17

Phillip Dunham from Phillips Maine was asked to come in for an interview.

It was Dunham's opinion that Stu and Joe were "pulling a swindle" and using the Phillips Maine company to set up their own business. "I told Mr. Ingstrom, the owner, and shortly thereafter, Castellucci and Lamont were fired."

"Did you also leave the company?"

Dunham stated that he was let go by the Board of Directors. At that time, he started a plastics company of his own in Biddeford, Maine.

"Castellucci showed up at my new business and accused me of stealing equipment from Phillips Maine Corp. He was accompanied by a Reserve officer, Ernest LeClair, in his police uniform."

Joe had said, "I have the law with me, and I want our equipment back."

Dunham laughed, thinking about it.

(Conley was unable to locate Ernest LeClair, but the State Police said that they would contact him.)

"Is there anything else you can tell us, Mr. Dunham?" Conley asked.

"Since all that happened, I met a Mr. Duffin, the marketing man from Colonial Candle out of Stanford, Connecticut. Duffin told me that he used to work with Stu Lamont at Xerox Corporation in San Francisco and that Stu was fired for selling another man's accounts. He was a real crook."

"Do you recall ever seeing Castellucci or Lamont with a gun?"

"As big a pair of crooks that Joe and Stu are, I have never personally known them to carry or use a gun."

"Thank you for coming in."

After this interview, Conley reached out to Joseph W. Sparks of Saco, Maine. Sparks used to be employed by the Phillips Maine Corp.

"I really don't want to get involved in anything," Sparks said nervously.

"Just tell us how you know Stuart Lamont and Joe Castellucci."

"I've known Stu and Joe for two or three years," he stated. "On the day Dunham was forced to resign, I saw Stu wearing a revolver to work." He had also once witnessed Stu firing a pellet gun at work.

"Men who take advantage of one woman take advantage of them all." — Merle Shain

Jean Pownall's updates

September 14

Jean Pownall returned to Police Headquarters, along with her daughter Lynda, to meet with Detective Conley for an updated statement.

"Detective Conley always came across as having an inner conviction of balance," recalled Lynda. "He was self-confident, but not in an egotistical way. There was a sense that he was imperturbable—very composed, calm, intelligent, articulate, and cautious. He was also committed to getting justice for our family."

According to Jean, on the night of Jon's murder, one of Jon's former students, a boy named Larry, was in the Square and saw the lights on in the office while the police were present. A police officer pointed him out to Nancy, but she didn't want to go downstairs and tell him what was going on. She dismissed him, then thought about it later. She knew he was acquainted with David Joy, and he might have had information regarding the murder.

Jean had also heard a few things about Joe Castellucci and Herb Schwartz. Nancy told Jean that Herb was a gambler and involved with a weekly poker game.

Nancy was also upset with Joe Castellucci, calling him a coward and a weakling—a coward because he pushed her ahead in Planet 3 Films when they arrived that night, and a weakling when he had a glimpse of Jon's body and ran out of the office. Joe had told her that he had two nervous breakdowns in the past, one occurring two days after his marriage and one while he was in the Army.

She was also convinced that Herb was directly involved and possibly two or more other people. She called him an "overgrown bully" and told Jean that he had been involved in a domestic violence case, beating up his first wife, and had a violent nature.

Jean said Nancy had also speculated on a number of things, including why Jon's throat was cut, and that all their phones were tapped. Nancy handed in her resignation and, in fact, had already started job-hunting before Jon's murder.

She was relieved that journalist John Cole had been kind enough not to expose her affair with Joe in the newspaper, even though she was sure he knew about it.

Whenever new evidence developed, Jean Pownall and her daughter Lynda checked in with Detectives Conley and Dodd, as well as Deputy Attorney General Richard Cohen and Assistant Attorney General Vernon Arey.

"Damn it! How will I ever get out of this labyrinth?"
— Simón Bolívar

The pressure is on

A couple of weeks after Jon's burial, Joe Castellucci needed to get away from the nightmare he was living in. The police did not order him to stay in town, even though they continued to eye the insurance policy as a possible motive.

His parents had a place in Bar Harbor, so he drove up there for a few days. He knew he couldn't stay there indefinitely, though.

When he returned to Portland, he did not go back to the apartment he shared with his wife, for the obvious reason—the truth was out about his affair with Nancy. Instead, he bunked with Joe Thomas for two months.

Schwartz kept watch over Joe's movements and there were several meetings in Herb's office and the Old Port Tavern. Occasionally, they met with Reef at the attorney's office. Joe was again warned by both of them that he should "shut up" and not talk to the police or cooperate in any way. "The more you talk, the more they are going to hound you. It's a case that will never be solved!" Reef said assuredly. Reef also threatened to drop him as a client if he talked to police, making him wonder how much Reef knew about the murder. However, Schwartz and Reef didn't care that the police were eyeing Joe for the murder or even if he went to jail.

GOODBYE, FAT LARRY

In late September, Herb picked up Joe in his car and the two drove to Lewiston, Maine. There were more warnings from Herb.

"You know the police are following you, right?"

"No, I didn't!" Joe glanced around.

"Most likely your phone and car are being bugged, too, so keep your mouth shut!"

After seeing Joe's tense reaction, Herb added, "Hey, I'm just trying to protect you."

Or was he?

* * * * *

At this point, Reef thought it best that Herb and Joe be represented by separate attorneys and hired Alexander MacNichol for Castellucci and Jack Simmons for Schwartz. However, Joe was concerned that MacNichol was closely associated with the police department and perhaps would not abide by attorney-client privilege. He also knew that MacNichol wanted him to cooperate fully with the police and tell them everything, just the opposite of Reef's advice.

October 28

Toward the end of October[6], Joe took his family to New York so that they could live at his wife's parents' home until the Pownall case was over. Joe flew back to Portland alone on October 28 and Herb picked him up at the airport. They drove to the Bramhall Pub, the

---

[6] NOTE: This content is based on the testimony of Joseph Castellucci at the murder trial, State of Maine vs. Truman H. Dongo and Herbert R. Schwartz, Volume II.

rathskeller below Roma Café on Congress Street in Portland, where they had a few drinks.

"Say, Herb, did you happen to see the article in today's paper about the discovery of a .38 caliber gun? Do you suppose it could be the gun that killed Jon?"

"They haven't found any gun," Herb remarked dismissively. "They're just trying to smoke someone out."

Joe nodded in agreement.

They left the pub and went to Herb's house for dinner.

Bramhall Pub. Photographer unknown. No copyright infringement is intended.

October 30

Schwartz walked into his office where Castellucci was sitting, waiting for him.

"That's the gun!" he announced.

"How do you know?"

"Well, there were two shots fired."

"How do YOU know how many shots were fired?"

GOODBYE, FAT LARRY

Herb hmm'd. "Well, maybe you're right."

Castellucci leaned over Herb's desk and looked at him. "You're involved in this, aren't you?" Herb stared back, never admitting or denying it.

Herb did, however, tell Joe about a man he met up with on the turnpike earlier that same day. "I met the man who killed Jon. I paid him $5,000 and asked him if the gun that was found by Long Wharf was the gun he used to kill Jon. He said, 'Yes, so what? That's your problem!' He demanded the rest of the money he's owed, which is $20,000, and said that I have 30 days to come up with it."

Joe believed him. "So, what else do you know?"

"I'm the only one who knows the entire case from A to Z. If I tell you anything more, I'm afraid you'll spill it to the police."

After Joe left Herb's office, he went to see Alex MacNichol, his defense attorney. Later, he returned to Schwartz' office. This time, Truman Dongo was present, along with Joe Thomas, and a man named John Colonna.

Herb took Castellucci aside, putting his arm around his shoulder, and said, "Look, Bubby, I don't want to see you hurt by any of this. It was the gun, okay? It belongs to Truman, but it's not traceable to him because no one would admit to selling a gun to a convicted felon."

He continued, "Joey, is there any way you could help me out here? I owe guy on the turnpike $35,000. Maybe you can ask your aunt and uncle in Miami for the money. You know, Joe, they know where your wife and daughter are staying. No one is really safe." Herb smiled. "Let's go to lunch! We can talk more about this later." He patted Joe's back.

Joe tried to think of a way to ask his uncle for that amount of money. *Why should I be the one to come up with the money?* he wondered.

Before leaving Herb's office for lunch, Truman wanted to add his two cents to Joe's. "It's a sad and unfortunate thing as to the way the gun was disposed of."

Dongo sat in the passenger seat as Joe drove to the restaurant and continued his earlier conversation. "I'll admit it; it's my gun. Would you believe that a police officer sold it to me? No cop would admit to selling a gun to a convicted felon! Besides, it can't be traced to me. I'm not going to worry about it."

After they were done eating, Joe drove Truman back to the parking lot at Herb's office with a few parting words. Then he drove straight to see his attorney in South Portland.

October 31

Herb called a meeting at his home at 8:30 p.m. When Joe arrived, Herb wasn't home yet, but Bradley Mack had come by. They were both waiting for Herb.

Schwartz came in and said to Joe, "Let's go for a ride." They just went to the gas station on Forest Avenue and back.

Curious, Joe asked Herb, "Aren't you afraid to meet this guy on the turnpike and be followed?"

"Of course. That's why I need to get the money and pay him off. He's a big spender and is desperate for the funds. I need another $21,000."

GOODBYE, FAT LARRY

Joe tried to understand the math. Earlier, Herb said he needed $20,000. Now, he was saying $21,000. Herb continued, "I paid the guy $4,000, leaving me with $1,000. I owed Buddy McIntosh $700 and kept $300 for myself." Buddy was a gambler and owned a general store and the Gateway Motor Inn.

It was all confusing to Joe.

Herb turned to his passenger, "You know, Joe, I have a contact in the police department. The police have their eyes on you. They say you're waiting to get your hands on the insurance money and run away with Nancy."

Castellucci wanted to object, but he knew that Schwartz was manipulating him.

"Joe, do you really think that it was Truman's gun?"

"You told me so!"

"Because you're a fucking idiot! That's not Truman's gun! And I had nothing to do with Jon's death! The guy on the turnpike? That's just a gambling debt. I was just testing you to see if you'd bite. It's what the police are going to do when they talk to you. I've been testing you, you moron, and you FAILED!"

Joe wasn't sure where this was going. Herb continued to admonish him about talking to police and telling lies. Then he told Joe to make arrangements to fly to Florida and get $50,000 or $60,000, if possible, from his aunt and uncle.

"What I want you to do, Joe, is call them from a phone booth and tell them you're coming down to Florida. Then, if you get the money, call me and say, 'My aunt had been ill; now she's feeling better,' which will indicate to me that everything is cool, and you have the money. Then I can pay off the $21,000 debt."

He was still trying to do the math. It just didn't add up, but he didn't say anything to Herb.

The next day, Joe went to see Attorney MacNichol again and relayed what Schwartz had said to him. After their meeting, MacNichol asked Joe to repeat what Schwartz said to him to detectives.

Afterwards, Joe left Maine and went to join his family in New York City.

* * * * *

November 15

Truman Dongo was asked to come to the police station for another written statement. He showed up a short time later.

At that time, he was read his Miranda rights.

"Do you understand your rights?" asked Detective Conley.

"Yes." He had been through this before on several occasions.

Truman was asked where he was on the evening of August 30.

He replied, "I was at a drive-in movie with my wife."

Conley noted that he changed his story, and it matched the recent story of Herb Schwartz.

The next day, Attorney Reef gave him hell for talking to the police and not asking for his attorney.

"Desperate men do desperate things." — Michael Brooks

Mounting debts and insurance money

When Castellucci lived in New York in his younger days, a "shoot out" took place between the Colombo and Gallo gangs, and the Gallo gang members lived in Joe's apartment building. He often bragged to them that he was wealthy and that his money came from Maine. Of course, it wasn't true at all. In fact, Castellucci was broke and in debt.

In less than a decade, Joe had multiple jobs and was let go from most of them, if not fired. Then in 1972, Joe asked Sam Cataldo to loan him $1,500 for the Archer Industries real-estate deal, which failed. The loan was never paid back. Sal also gave Joe startup money for an advertising firm with Mr. McFarland which never materialized. Instead, Joe jumped at the chance to make it big with Jon Pownall as his movie producer, a job that he knew nothing about and one for which he had zero qualifications.

When Jon Pownall gave Joe the go-ahead to set up Planet 3 Films, rent office space, hire a secretary, etc., Castellucci went to Casco Bank and obtained a $10,000 loan on a 90-day note. His weekly income was only $300.

One of Joe's jobs was to find investors and accumulate $450,000. He brought in Maurice Parent and Michael Doyle who invested $6,500 each. Joe felt he contributed by researching his job through an X-rated film director and producer, Russ Meyer. Pownall had the Churubusco connection since his brother-in-law Felipe worked there, and Schwartz and Thomas brought up Dickerman. Joe attended meetings, went to lunch, shared a few drinks, and added the charges to his credit card.

Then, in August, Casco Bank notified Joe that he had exceeded the credit limit on his Mastercard®. He had a credit of $1,000 but the balance was $1,323 at the end of August. He had not made a payment since July 2, 1973.

Also, the $10,000 note from the bank was to be paid in full on September 2, 1973, just three days after Jon's murder.

The film project was abandoned after Pownall was slain, which ended Castellucci's source of income.

In addition, Castellucci had a second 90-day note which was due in October, and his personal line of credit had a balance of $5,029, also in arears with an August 20 payment yet to be made. As a result, his Money Manager Line of Credit was cancelled by the bank. Joe owed $9,195.45.

Joe was in desperate need of money. The pressure was real. The need was real. The Portland police saw it as circumstantial evidence. Enough to kill Jon Pownall for the $400,000 insurance money? The possibility was there and could not be denied.

Nancy, Joe's secretary and lover, had been told by Castellucci that Sal Cataldo "was a money launderer," which he later denied ever saying. But Joe did admit to telling her that Sal always "sits with his back against a wall" in his business. Detectives understood the reason for that. Castellucci also inferred that Sal had Mafia connections, but he did not know that for a fact; it was just to make an impression on Nancy. He asked Nancy not to mention his name in connection to Sal's, but when asked by police about a birthday card from Sal, Joe denied it, although Nancy told the police that he had received one.

Joe also bragged that he owned $1.4 million stock in Archer Industries, which was untrue and later denied. But he did admit to being in debt to Cataldo.

Evidently, Castellucci liked to instill fear in Nancy. A "control" thing? It may have made him feel more powerful, more important. After all, he was a braggart.

Just how many of Joe's statements were exaggerations? Lies? Joe was not a person to be trusted.

Detectives Conley and Dodd had their work cut out for them to unravel this puzzling case. Did they have enough for an arrest? Or for a conviction? Were they all in it together—Castellucci, Schwartz, Dongo, Reef, O'Donovan, Stanley, Mack, Lamont, etc.? Was the killing done by a professional hit man hired by all of them? The murder was certainly well thought out and carried out, in every step, every action, every word, every response. An art. Who was the brains behind it?

Was there more than one killer—perhaps one with a gun and one with a knife? Could the killer have used Jon's missing letter opener (and not a knife), making the stabbing a crime of opportunity? Did he know where to stab the victim in the throat?

Were there two .38 caliber guns used in the murder—Truman's proven murder weapon based on the slug found on the carpet at the crime scene, and an additional weapon that was used to shoot Jon along with Truman's gun?

They knew this case might have to be built on circumstantial evidence, and that was a long shot. It wasn't what they knew to be true, but what could be proven.

Conley and Dodd depended on Deputy District Attorney Cohen to do what he does best in court—convince a jury that the circumstantial evidence added up beyond a reasonable doubt.

"Business opportunities are like buses, there's always another one coming." — Richard Branson

Dickerman's statement

December 5

When Portland Detectives Conley and Ames traveled to Canton, Massachusetts, to meet with businessman David Dickerman, Dickerman showed up an hour late.

Dickerman stated that he first met "Herbie" Schwartz through a friend, Bob Anderson, sometime around July 1 of that year. Bob thought investing in the Planet 3 film might be a "pretty good deal" for him. Dickerman told Bob to bring his friend Schwartz to Canton to discuss the deal.

At the Canton meeting, Schwartz told Dickerman that it was his job to find investors and he had "a lot of investors" back in Portland. Harry Baker was one of the names he mentioned who had already put in some money. Herb wanted Dickerman to invest $30,000 or $35,000 in the movie. "It was about selling some points and about me buying some points," Dickerman stated. Herb provided a resume of how he was setting up the movie.

"I told him I would want further information, some solid information."

Dickerman's first impression of Schwartz was that he was a "bullshit artist," and gave no commitment. The next day, after Dickerman met with his attorney, he was advised not to get involved with Planet 3. He then told Anderson that he wanted nothing to do with investing in Planet 3 or the movie.

Herb wouldn't take no for an answer. Shortly after their initial meeting, Schwartz met with Dickerman again, this time at the Gateway Motel in South Portland, where Herb offered Dickerman 50 percent of the company for investing between $90,000 and $150,000.

"For that type of money, I would be interested in taking a majority position. I wanted to see the Director's Contract which Herbie said was pending, and his position. Everyone's position!" Schwartz didn't have the information with him.

Dickerman thought about it overnight and, once again, decided to pass on it. "That was the last contact I had with anybody regarding this issue."

He told Detective Conley, "If Schwartz has been stating that I was going to invest in the film, he's full of shit."

When asked if Schwartz met with him in Boston on the afternoon of August 30, 1973, he said he did not. That contradicted what Schwartz told police on September 1.

"The pathways of crime are clearly marked. There's a double cross on every corner." — Chester Gould

Planet 3's option agreement

Late December

Castellucci was re-reading the August 10, 1973 "option" agreement that Herb Schwartz wanted, in which he would own 50 percent of Planet 3 Films, providing certain financial requirements were tendered and could be proven. As far as Joe was concerned, those financial requirements were never met before Jon's death and the demise of Planet 3 Films. When he came to page 2 of the 3-page legal document prepared by Norman Reef, he immediately noted a new paragraph that he hadn't seen before, or perhaps didn't recall, or was perhaps added after he signed the option agreement. He didn't have a copy of the original document to compare it to.

Joe wrote to his attorney, Alex MacNichol, saying, "The first document has obviously been changed," and that "Norman obviously lied to the police and Richard Cohen when he explained the detail of the option agreement."

It was now written so that Herb Schwartz would have the option to buy 50 percent of the stock in Planet 3 for $10,000 and have ten years to pay for it, giving him virtual control of Planet 3.

Joe knew that if he was not indicted or convicted of Jon Pownall's murder, the $400,000 life insurance policy from Transamerica might be paid out to him.

His fear was that Herb might claim that he was entitled to half the insurance money as 50 percent owner of Planet 3 Films, even though Joe was listed as the sole beneficiary.

At any rate, Joe knew this information would be revealed during the trial. He could also very well get screwed by Schwartz and Reef. Just like they did to Jon.

He didn't trust either one of them.

Attorney MacNichol took both versions of the Option Agreement into the police. In his opinion, when this agreement was signed, it was Jon's death warrant. Detective Greeley agreed that it did provide a possible motive for Schwartz, since the option agreement was carefully altered before the murder.

"Train your mind to be stronger than your emotions or else you'll lose yourself every time." — Unknown

Visits to Schwartz and Doyle

Due to a change in the law in 1974, the Attorney General's office designated the Portland Police Department to be the first department in Maine (besides the State Police) to investigate its own homicides. However, the PPD continued to work with the State Police investigators in Jon's murder.

January 2, 1974, 5 p.m.

Sergeant Murdock confronted Herb Schwartz at the back door of his office on Danforth Street as Herb was locking up for the night.

"Now what?" Herb asked. "I'm on my way to an important meeting with my attorney. We're discussing fundraising for George Mitchell's gubernatorial campaign."

"Just a quick question, Mr. Schwartz. Have you ever touched or handled a gun?"

Schwartz clenched his teeth. "No! If anyone stated that I have, he's a fucking liar!"

"I just needed your statement."

"And why are the police questioning my clients and associates and leaving calling cards at their businesses? You're ruining my reputation!"

"Mr. Schwartz, if you would take a polygraph, perhaps we could eliminate you as a suspect."

"I told you once, and I'm telling you again—I don't believe in polygraphs!"

"Why is that, Mr. Schwartz?"

"I have no confidence in scientific equipment."

Sergeant Murdock made a report based on their conversation.

* * * * *

January 2, 7 p.m.

Detective Conley and Sergeant Murdock interviewed Michael Doyle at his home. The interview was conducted in Doyle's basement with his wife present. Doyle taped the interview.

Doyle stated that he had made calls to Transamerica Life Insurance Company, but never made any conference calls with Herb Schwartz or Joe Castellucci.

Conley asked, "Did you ever make the statement, 'Is that enough for you, Herb?'" regarding the value of the life insurance payout.

"I don't recall saying that," Michael responded.

"Did you ever hear Herb Schwartz threaten to kill Jon?"

"Yes, several times."

"When was that?"

"In July. Herb said to Joe Castellucci that he would kill Jon Pownall if he fucked up the deal, but then Herb always followed that up with 'I'm only joking.'"

"What do you mean by 'the deal'?" asked Conley.

Michael thought that Herb was referring to his 2% of stock he invested in Planet 3.

"Were you a stockholder at the time you wrote the policy?"

"No. Herb said that Dickerman didn't want two-percenters in the company, and I'd have my investment returned."

"When was that?"

"About a month later; around August 20th."

"As the insurance underwriter, did you try to get a double indemnity policy?"

"Never."

"When was the last time you met with Joe Castellucci?"

"I went up to the Planet 3 offices the day after Jon's funeral and talked to Joe when he was packing up."

* * * * *

January 4

Detectives Conley and Greeley interviewed John Colonna and his wife at their business (The Frame Shop). Colonna stated that he did business with Planet 3 Films, and they still owed him $1,600. He had receipts from July 5, 1973, through August 27, 1973. When he brought the bill to Herb's attention, Herb said Reef would take care of everything.

When detectives asked Colonna, "Do you play cards with Herb or Truman?", he stated that he did not.

Colonna added that Herb does not owe him money personally, nor has he approached Schwartz for any money.

"Karma has no menu. You get served what you deserve." — Unknown

Follow-up with Dongo at home

January 7, 8:57 p.m.

Detectives Greeley and Conley knocked on Truman Dongo's door. They were met at the door by Truman's wife Geraldine, who invited them inside.

"Truman's in the bedroom."

"We'd like to talk to him for a few minutes," Conley said. She went to get him.

Conley pulled out a card and read Dongo his Miranda rights. He said that he understood his rights and agreed to talk to the detectives.

"Reef gave me hell for talking to you the last time, but I'll talk to you now."

He was advised that he could call his attorney at any time during the interview and cease talking with them. Dongo nodded in agreement.

They sat down.

"Truman, the murder weapon has been found and traced to you. It's your gun."

He made no denial at that time.

Conley continued. "We can't make any promises to you for talking to us. We had this information the last time we talked to you, and we thought you would come forward to us with more information. We know you weren't the only one involved in this."

Dongo was visibly shaken and concerned.

GOODBYE, FAT LARRY

"We cannot see you gaining financially from this murder, as some of the others may."

Dongo responded, "I'm aware of Herb's agreement for 50 percent of the company and the unwritten agreement that Joe Thomas included in it. I had nothing to gain, money-wise, from Jon's death."

Greeley speculated, "Perhaps Jon wasn't meant to be killed. Maybe someone wanted him to just be roughed up" to get him to sign the contract.

"Maybe an accident at first, but that had been complicated recently by the money," Dongo said. He did not elaborate on this statement. "I know that Joe Castellucci had fingered me to be involved in this murder. I told him I had done it, but I was only joking."

"Truman, our information on the gun did not come from Joe."

"I know he has been talking to the police and took a polygraph."

"Are you not telling us what happened because you're in fear of your life or are being threatened in any way?"

"No. I would like to help you out, but I believe I need to talk to my attorney first."

"Would you like to call him now?"

"Yes." He went to the phone and called Reef at his home number. However, he was not home, so Truman called Attorney Mooers at his residence. "The detectives are here and advised me that they have the murder weapon and traced it to me." Mooers responded and Truman listened.

Truman turned to the detectives. "Will I be going to the police station with you tonight?"

"Not at this time."

Truman informed Mooers and hung up. "I've been advised to meet with my attorneys in the morning. I will contact you sometime tomorrow after the meeting."

The interview was concluded at 9:55 p.m.

"There ain't no such thing as a free lunch." — American proverb

Bramhall Pub

January 22

Castellucci couldn't escape the long arm of the law or the clutches of Herb Schwartz and Truman Dongo. He was knee-deep in this case and knew he needed help.

After conferring with his lawyer, Joe called an evening meeting with Truman at Bramhall Pub.

MacNichol assured him, "It'll be alright, as long as there are police officers present." The officers would be in plain clothes sitting at the bar, listening to both sides of the conversation.

"Forget you're a friend of Herb Schwartz and focus on the pressure being put on everyone by the police," advised MacNichol.

Detective Greeley and Sergeant Murdock entered the pub in plain clothes, sat down on barstools, and ordered drinks.

Joe came down the steps from outside, walked over to the table where Dongo was already seated, and sat down.

The server took their orders and brought drinks to the table, then went back to the bar.

Joe began. "Let's not start out bullshitting each other. I'm aware of your arrest history and your recent confrontation with police," Joe pointed out. "By the way, I'm not wired up for sound. We can talk freely.

Up to now I haven't stated anything to police that has been incriminating."

Truman took that with a grain of salt. "I appreciate that, but I'm not worried, even if you did say something to police."

"Truman, was it really your gun?"

"Of course not," Dongo replied with irritation.

"You know, I think we're in a similar situation. Schwartz is trying to screw me—and maybe you, too. If you know anything about Jon's death, you ought to say something about it—clear your name. And if you know anything about the gun, or who was up at Planet 3 that night, go to the police and tell them what you know! They may give you immunity."

"Immunity! Shit! That's not worth a damn! The judge would throw it out in court. I know how they operate."

"If you weren't the one who pulled the trigger, you need to clear your name."

"They must know it was my gun, but I'm not sure how. No cop would admit selling a gun to a convicted felon."

Joe and the two policemen heard Dongo admit to owning the murder weapon.

Truman talked about ballistics and how a gun in salt water for two months could never be operable. Joe disagreed.

"The police told me that their tests showed it was the murder weapon!"

"I don't believe them for a minute. They're just sifting sand. Besides, I could pass a lie-detector test. But I won't take one."

GOODBYE, FAT LARRY

"I may have to take another polygraph," Joe said. "This time they're going to ask me if I know who killed Jon. Were you involved, Truman?"

"I don't know anything about it. I even told Norman [Reef] that I told you I killed Jon."

"What did he say?"

"He laughed! He said it's important to tell your attorney everything and that it's my word against yours."

"Do you know any of the details? Who was there with you?"

He wouldn't answer Joe's question.

"You're too curious, Joe. You really wouldn't want to know."

"Whoever did this to Jon didn't do it alone."

Truman smiled, as if to say Joe was wrong. He admitted, "I have the perfect alibi for that night."

Truman looked at Joe. "I expect to be indicted for this, Joe, but I have a contingency plan worked out. If I am arrested, Reef told me I'd be out in no time. And I said I'd scratch his back if he scratched mine, heh heh. You know, I'd do him a favor if he does one for me."

He went on. "The only thing that bothers me about being indicted is what the legal fees would cost. There's no bail for murder and no statute of limitations."

Truman added, "We should set up a meeting with Herb to iron out our problems." He eyed Castellucci. "Your 'fate' is not to cooperate with the police, if you know what I mean."

"Fine," Joe replied nervously.

"And if you do get arrested, I have a $30,000 home I could sell to help bail you out...as long as you keep your mouth shut."

"I think Herb was behind all this. Just how well do you know him?"

"Quite well." He continued. "Herb's feelings were hurt that you tried to fight the option agreement."

"What? How could he exercise the option if he never raised the money?"

He said you were being 'unreasonable,' and you should be 'a decent guy' and let him have his share of the money. Then everyone could be friends again." He smirked.

"He tried to screw me out of the Planet 3 ownership! One time he said that the killer was a pro, then he said Stanley Howard, and other times he said it was you. The point is, if Herb would try to screw me, he'd do the same to you." He paused. "How much do you trust him?"

"Quite a lot. If Herb ever got arrested for this, he's a pathological liar and could hoodwink the cops. They'd believe anything he said. So would a jury."

They finished their drinks.

"Do you need a ride, Joe? I can drive you where you want to go."

"Thanks, but no. I need to meet with my attorney."

They shook hands and Truman left.

* * * * *

Alexander MacNichol, Joe's attorney, pushed Homicide to make Joe the State's star witness based on all the information he had provided and continued to provide. The Homicide detectives considered everything, and since Castellucci was cooperating with them, they asked Deputy District Attorney Cohen what he wanted to do. They agreed to make Joe Castellucci the State's star witness for the Prosecution. He was *not* given immunity, nor were any promises made by the state to protect him from charges.

"A half-truth masquerading as the whole truth becomes a complete untruth." — J. J. Parker

Miranda rights read to Castellucci

March 5

Sergeant Small of the Maine State Police administered several lie detector tests on Joe Castellucci. When Joe continued to show deception on his knowledge of the crime, Small confronted Joe and took him off the machine.

Joe, now shaken, said he wanted to talk to Detective Conley with his attorney present. Small contacted Alexander MacNichol and asked him to come to Police Headquarters.

On March 8, Joe was read his rights, and he said that he understood.

In the presence of Attorney MacNichol, and Detectives Conley and Greeley, Joe said he had been withholding information for three reasons: he had a fear of going to jail; he did not want to be killed; and he did not want to lose the $400,000 from the insurance policy.

He admitted that he met with Herb Schwartz before the murder at the Stagecoach Inn in South Portland. Herb told him that the "problem with Jon" was over and that he had arranged to have him killed. To kill Jon, it would cost a total of $25,000, or $35,000 in installments. The plan was for Joe to meet with Jon and make sure Jon was alone when he left. Joe said he was to leave the door ajar so someone could get in without keys.

"When I left, I placed a matchbook in the door so it wouldn't shut. I knew for certain that someone was going to Planet 3 that night and something was going to happen. I wasn't certain if he was going to be threatened, beat up, or killed."

Detective Conley knew that Joe had omitted that information in his sworn deposition after the murder.

Joe went on to say, "When I learned the next day that Jon had been murdered, I knew I had 'unwittingly' allowed in the killer."

Joe signed off on his statement.

* * * * *

Conley went back over statements made just after Pownall's death and came across the one from David Joy. He and his father had gone to the parking lot near Planet 3, looking for the white Volvo. They didn't find the car, but they discovered a matchbook wedged in the outer door to 465 Congress St. That could only mean one thing: Joe Castellucci had just placed the matchbook and that a certain "someone" had not yet gone into the bank building to kill Jon.

"Justice is like a train that is nearly always late."
— Yevgeny Yevtushenko

Arrests and indictments for murder

December 1974

Cumberland County, Maine, which encompasses Portland, called a special session of a grand jury in the Pownall murder case.

A grand jury acts as an investigative body, independent of either the prosecuting attorney or judge. It is not up to the grand jury to determine guilt or punishment.

Criminal prosecutors presented their case against Truman H. Dongo to members of the grand jury. The prosecutors attempted to establish probable cause that a criminal offense had been committed.

The grand jury determined that there was sufficient evidence to pursue prosecution of Truman Dongo for the felony crime of murdering movie director Jon Pownall. Dongo was arrested on December 20 and arraigned on December 23, 1974, at which time he pleaded not guilty.

Due to the Christmas holiday, the case was continued until Thursday, December 26, when Justice Harry P. Glassman scheduled a hearing on a defense motion that Dongo be released on bail.

The defendant, a salesman and father of four boys, was held without bail through the Christmas holidays until the hearing.

GOODBYE, FAT LARRY

When the defense motion was heard on December 27, bail was denied by the Superior Court Justice.

After bail was denied to the defendant, Dongo's lawyer, Daniel Lilley, took the case to the State Supreme Court.

On January 8, 1975, State Supreme Court Justice Sidney Wernick heard Lilley's bail appeal of Truman Dongo.

Bail was denied again.

Then, over a month later, Herbert R. Schwartz was named in a secret indictment handed down by a Cumberland County grand jury. The indictment charged Schwartz with conspiring to commit murder.

Interior decorator Schwartz was arrested in his Portland office on Friday, February 14, 1975, and held at the Cumberland County Jail in connection with the slaying of Jon Pownall.

A second indictment charged Schwartz with being an accessory before the fact in the slaying of Pownall.

Deputy Attorney General Richard Cohen said Schwartz was being held at the county jail pending his arraignment.

No other indictments or arrests were made in connection with the Pownall murder.

After a revealing article in the *Portland Sunday Telegram* on March 21, 1975, a gag order on the Jon Pownall murder case principals was issued by a Supreme Court Justice.

"The trouble with the rat race is that even if you win, you're still a rat." — Lily Tomlin

Jailhouse snitch

March 10, 1975

Detective Corporal Martin Greeley and Detective Peter Conley went to the Kennebec County Jail in Augusta to interview Roland Dube, who was incarcerated for bank robbery, a federal violation. They asked if he would talk about any conversation he might have had with Truman Dongo and Herbert Schwartz when he was held in the Cumberland County Jail in Portland.

Dube asked to contact his attorney, Peter Murray, before making any statements. Arrangements were made and the investigators returned later the same day for the interview.

Truman Dongo had been placed in the "bound-over" cell with Dube, and they became quite friendly.

Dube said that Truman looked to him for advice. "Do you know whether or not someone's statement could be used in court without the witness being present?" Truman asked him. He was specifically inquiring about Castellucci's detailed testimony to the Grand Jury.

Dube thought about it, then replied, "I think they can in certain circumstances."

Was Truman contemplating having Castellucci "permanently disposed of" to help his case?

Curious, Dube asked Truman point-blank, "Did you do it?"

GOODBYE, FAT LARRY

Lying on his back on his cell bunk, smoking a cigarette, with a blank stare on his face and showing no emotion, Truman said, "I shot him with my handgun. I always carry a 'piece.' There was a knife wound in his throat, too." He didn't admit to working alone or inflicting the knife wound himself.

"You have been working on your job for 14 years. Why did you do it?"

Truman laughed. "For the money! Schwartz was going to pay me $35,000!"

"Did he?"

"Not one red dime," he scowled. "And he was supposed to pay $2,500 for my attorney, but he didn't come across for that either. If I was arrested, I was supposed to be represented by Attorney Troubh, but then I found out Troubh was going to represent Herb if he was arrested!"

"So, why did everybody want this guy dead?"

"He was a dirty son of a bitch. We tried to do him in a couple of other times. Schwartz bought some 'H' [heroin] for $60, and it turned out to be fake—baking powder or sugar or something." He laughed, remembering about Herb's failed attempt. He sneered, "What a waste of money!" He paused. "Another time, Herb told me to let the air out of one of his tires, and when Jon was on his knee, I was supposed to hit him over the head with the tire iron. But I ended up changing the tire." There were too many witnesses.

"Can you put the finger on Schwartz?"

"If I get off, he'll get off. No direct way to blame him."

Dongo also said that he was concerned that the police talked to a girl named Jan.

Dube asked, "Can she hurt you?"

"She may or may not have information on this hit. I don't know what she told the cops."

Another friend of Truman's came up in conversations—Peter O'Donovan. Peter had put an apartment house in Truman's name to hide his asset, and Truman then turned it over to his attorney, leaving O'Donovan angry enough to call Mrs. Dongo. Schwartz told Truman not to worry about O'Donovan; he was going to send him to the Virgin Islands.

Truman was also worried that Pete had information on him concerning some "breaking and entering" and cheating at poker games. "But I don't think he has enough information about this hit; not enough to hurt me."

"What can hurt you?" Dube asked, attempting to get more information out of him.

"The gun. Ain't that a son-of-a-bitch of a thing? A fisherman found the gun. The ballistic test showed three shots but only one shot was identified. How can they prove anything? It must be all rusty!"

At one point during their incarceration together, Dongo was retrieved by the jail guards to take a lie-detector test. He returned very upset because he didn't pass. He told Dube that he demanded the test operator return his $500. He grumbled, "If I passed the test, I would have been released from jail," leaving Schwartz holding the bag. Dube knew Truman was bitter.

The next day, Truman told him, "The cops made my wife take a lie-detector test and she failed it!" He was very agitated.

"Did you go home after the murder and go to bed?"

"Yeah."

"Does your wife know about the murder?"

"If she does, she would stick with me to the end."

"What if you're put away for a long time?"

"She wouldn't *dare* divorce me."

On another occasion, prior to Schwartz' arrest, Dube asked Dongo if he had a good alibi for the night of the murder.

"Schwartz was waiting for me when I left Planet 3. I was advised to say that I had gone to the drive-in to see *Last Tango in Paris* with my wife. I have a friend, Minnie Tevanian, who works there. He will say I was there." Truman went on to say that Schwartz went to the drive-in with him, not necessarily to watch the movie, and they left together.

After Schwartz was arrested and held at the Cumberland County Jail (his cell was on a different level), he would often come down and talk to Dongo. He asked Truman, "Is this Dube 'okay'?"

"Yeah, I trust him, and he knows all about the case."

Every time Schwartz, Dongo, and Dube were together they talked about the case. At one time, Truman asked Schwartz, "What about the keys?" Schwartz said, "Don't worry. The keys were placed on him. They can't trace them to us."

They also discussed Truman's gun. "They know I paid the man for the gun."

Schwartz tried to reassure him. "The gun was under the seat of the car. The gun was taken. The man was paid. They can't trace it to us."

The three were discussing the lie-detector test that Truman failed. Schwartz asked, "Why didn't you take three Valiums like Castellucci and pass the test?" (As if Truman had access to Valium and knew when to take the pills ahead of time.) It wasn't funny to Dongo.

Dube told the investigators that both men wanted to get a gun. In the event of a conviction, the three men planned to make a jailbreak with the gun. Schwartz put $60 into the kitty, Dube $14, and Dongo $1. A man at the county jail named "Brady" was supposed to get the gun for them; however, Brady returned the money to Dube and said the deal was off. Dube refused to return money to Schwartz and Dongo, so Schwartz made a complaint to the administrator of the jail.

Dube also told the investigators that when this was all over, Schwartz was going to sell all three properties and Truman and his family, and Schwartz and his family, would go to a foreign country.

The investigators thanked Dube and concluded the interview.

On May 3, 1975, in a daring escape, Dube and one other inmate, Stanley Osnoe, shot their way out of the County Jail with a .25 caliber pistol, striking a deputy sheriff in the chest. Osnoe was apprehended hours after the break. Dube, who had been scheduled to testify as a material witness in the Dongo-Schwartz trial, was finally captured with two companions on May 11, 1975, at a roadblock in Canton, Maine. Officials said they "had no idea how the inmates had obtained a weapon." The deputy sheriff had emergency surgery and recovered.

Dube was not brought to court to testify. Instead, U.S. Marshalls took Dube to the Federal Penitentiary.

"Mortui non mordent"—a Latin phrase meaning *"Dead men don't bite"* — *Treasure Island,* Robert Louis Stevenson

Detectives connect the dots

Herb Schwartz had asked Truman Dongo to join Planet 3 Films as an "investor"...or was there a different, more specific reason for his "timed" presence? He never invested in the film, nor did he bring in any investors. Truman wasn't just a car-fender salesman, he was a convicted felon and known to police. The purpose of his presence at Planet 3 was unclear to Jon Pownall, other than he was a friend of Herb's, but he made Jon—and Joe—uncomfortable.

Castellucci told police how Dongo admitted to roughing up some people, describing exactly what he did to them, and how he let the air out of Jon's tire. Detectives already had the statement from Dongo's cellmate, Roland Dube, that Truman had planned to use the tire iron on Jon.

This is *what the evidence indicated* to the detectives, partially corroborated by Dube, and partially by the sworn deposition by Castellucci:

It was supposed to look like a robbery.

Truman Dongo and Herb Schwartz watched from Truman's car as Joe Castellucci left the Maine Bank wearing a white hat and placing a matchbook in the door, as Herb directed. Dongo waited for Joe to get into his car and drive off to establish an alibi. They may have held their breath as they observed Jon's student, David Joy, unexpectedly approaching the bank's door but not entering. When Joy walked away, Dongo—and possibly Schwartz—exited the car and went inside the bank. They took the elevator up, pushing a button to lock it open and ready for their departure.

When they opened the unlocked Planet 3 office door, Jon Pownall wasn't in the reception area.

They headed down the hallway to Jon's office (knowing exactly where it was located) and barged in.

According to the evidence, Jon was sitting at his desk, typing a release form and planning his trip.

Jon pushed his chair away from the desk when he heard the rush of footfalls coming down the hallway to his office. Although he had expected someone earlier to pick up the books, he wasn't expecting anyone in a hurry. He stood up to face the uninvited guest or guests.

A second or two later, Jon saw the office door open, and when he recognized Truman, he knew that he was in imminent danger, and there appeared to be no escape. Jon may have protested, "How did you get in? Who let you in? What do you want? Get out of here!" He may have swung his left fist and hit Schwartz in the face. (The next day Schwartz had a black eye, and, when Jean Pownall viewed the body, she noticed Jon's left hand appeared swollen.)

Truman's gun fired in the fracas and the bullet ricocheted off the wall above the window, landing on the carpet by the door. Jon turned his back, perhaps from being hit or shoved. The gun was pointed directly at the back of Jon's head when it was fired a second time, the bullet striking just above Jon's neck. The bullet traveled into his brain, killing him instantly, and he began to fall, face first. Jon was shot again, this time in the upper spine, perhaps by a different .38 caliber *gun since only two bullets were from Truman's 5-shot Chief's Special.*

*At autopsy, **neither** of the bullets that struck Jon could be proven to match to Truman's gun due to the **damage to the bullets** in Jon's body. Only the wild shot matched to Truman's gun.*

The perpetrators weren't sure if Jon was injured or dead, but they wanted to make sure he was dead. The killer picked up Jon's letter opener (or a blade brought to the scene), grabbed Jon's hair, lifted his head, and stabbed him in the throat to make sure he'd never talk.

The killers were in a panic and forgot to make it look like a robbery. They ran out of the Planet 3 offices to the elevator, dripping blood from the blade. They couldn't get the elevator to work so they scrambled down the stairs and ran out the bank door to their getaway car.

From Congress Street, they drove to Long Wharf and hurled the gun, with its three remaining bullets, into the ocean at high tide. Truman's gun. And most likely the letter opener and the second gun. The fog had rolled in, and no one was observed.

Long Wharf, Portland, Maine.

Photo ©Google Earth, 2022

Truman told his jail cellmate that he had gone to the drive-in with Schwartz.

Both Truman and Geraldine Dongo had failed the Police Department's lie-detector test, but the tests were not admissible in court.

Detectives then had to work with Deputy District Attorney Cohen to help him build the case against Dongo and Schwartz. The jury would expect eyewitness testimony and solid evidence; what the D.A. had was Dongo's gun and the testimony of Joe Castellucci.

GOODBYE, FAT LARRY

Author's note:

When I researched the weather the night of August 30, 1973, (and whether conditions were favorable to view an outdoor movie), Chief Meteorologist WMTW Channel 8 Portland, Roger Griswold reported the facts:
 "There was patchy fog reported at 10 p.m. and 11 p.m. and this makes sense given the high dew points, warm temperatures, and scattered clouds overhead. The reliable observations do show haze, and I suspect that haze became drizzle somewhere in the data gathering by the unreliable source."

The Trials

(May 12, 1975 – July 22, 1976)

"Up against a lion."

The judge and trial lawyers

Superior Court Judge, Harry P. Glassman

Maine superior court judge, the Honorable Harry P. Glassman, presided over the Pownall murder trial, which began on May 5, 1975.

Glassman's background included a tour of duty in Japan after enlisting in the United States Army and receiving both an undergraduate and law degree from the University of California at Berkeley. He later earned a master's degree in law and accepted a position as a professor of law at the University of Maine School of Law. Glassman was appointed as a superior court justice for the State of Maine in January 1972.

Interestingly, Judge Glassman, Planet 3 Attorney Norman Reef, and defendant Herbert Schwartz all worked on George Mitchell's gubernatorial election and were acquaintances. This went unrevealed. Some feel Glassman should have recused himself from this case or that it was sufficient for a mistrial. He did recuse himself from the conspiracy trial.

The Prosecution team

Deputy Attorney General Richard S. Cohen was a Republican and career prosecutor. He grew up in Brookline, Massachusetts, and graduated from the

University of Georgia and Boston University School of Law.

Assistant Prosecutor Vernon I. Arey graduated in 1971 (two years before this case) from the University of Maine School of Law and is still practicing as of this writing. Lynda remembers that Arey had a fiery personality, which was apparent in the courtroom.

Lynda Pownall described Cohen as a very well-mannered, quiet-spoken man, watchful and intelligent when they discussed the upcoming trial. He assured the Pownalls that they had the case in the bag, even though Dongo and Schwartz were to be tried together.

"We had no doubt who the murderers were," Lynda asserted.

The Defense team

After the Maine Supreme Court ruled in July that the income of Truman Dongo's spouse must not be considered, Dongo was now allowed to be appointed a free trial lawyer. Instead, the car-fender salesman Truman Dongo chose to hire Attorney Daniel G. Lilley for his defense. This trial made Lilley's name well known in the legal field, later known as "a lion of the bar." He had attended the University of Maine in Orono and furthered his education at Boston University School of Law.

Defender Lilley and Prosecutor Richard Cohen had worked together starting the Criminal Division in Maine, and each knew how the other would respond in court, a tactic Lilley used against Cohen in the Pownall case.

GOODBYE, FAT LARRY

Paul Weiner, Esq., assisted Lilley.

Jack H. Simmons, Esq., was hired by Herbert Schwartz for his defense. He attended Bates College and graduated from the Boston University School of Law and had been practicing law since 1964 and is still practicing as of this writing.

Gary Goldberg, Esq., assisted Simmons.

The Defense made sure that Dongo and Schwartz were in business suits every day for court instead of jail garb. A barber was also sent to style their hair and give them a close shave.

The jury

Twelve prospective jurors were chosen from a field of 21: Helen H. Brownell, Portland, housewife; Norman P. Charrier, Gorham, a warehouse worker; June E. Cook, Cumberland Foreside, a life insurance company employee; Jane G. Everett, South Portland, housewife; Diane C. Ferreira, Gray, an insurance company claims rep; John L. Mygatt, Freeport, print machine operator; Fernande E. Poliquin, Brunswick, housewife; Ellen R. Reidman, Portland, housewife; Clifford Stockford, Brunswick, shipyard worker; David A. Webster, Portland, radio station employee; Gladys E. Wilson, Brunswick, a retired school teacher; and Gene A. Moulton, Gorham, writer of science textbooks.

"Innocent until proven guilty." — The Universal Declaration of Human Rights

Jury considerations in the murder trial

Truman Dongo was the first to be indicted in the murder of Jon Pownall. He was refused bail based on his felony conviction a few years earlier.

Then, in a secret indictment, Herbert Schwartz was charged with conspiracy to commit murder. Deputy Attorney General Richard S. Cohen charged that Schwartz hired Dongo to kill Pownall when it appeared that he could not fulfill his part of the original option agreement (for 50 percent interest in the company) without cashing in the "key-man" life insurance policy on the director, Pownall. He was also charged with being an accessory before the fact in the slaying of Pownall.

Even though Dongo was the most culpable, having owned the gun that killed Pownall, the State decided to have Schwartz and Dongo tried together. If the jury was convinced that Dongo was the murderer and thereby convicted, Schwartz could also be convicted and sentenced to prison for murder.

Ralph Lancaster, attorney for Transamerica Life Insurance, was taking the formal depositions of all those who were required to testify, but Jean Pownall was not included, and therefore, was not on the list to testify for the murder trial. Neither was David Joy who saw the matchbook in the door at 465 Congress St.

GOODBYE, FAT LARRY

Police escort Schwartz and Dongo to court.

Photograph courtesy of Tammy Bonneau Walter.

As the trial began, several people had to be turned away from the courtroom door by deputy sheriffs, due to overcrowding. Every day that the trial was in session, there were at least 50 prospective witnesses, relatives of the victim and the accused, and spectators in the courtroom.

Court trial artist Donald Ross Thayer illustrated scenes from the trial every day. (Unfortunately, those illustrations have been either lost or ruined.)

During the first week of the trial, the police testified about their investigations. Defense Attorney Lilley carefully phrased his questions to raise doubt, especially about the condition of the gun and whether the ballistics results were conclusive. Some of the police officers had poor memories two years after the murder and became confused about the facts during Lilley's rigorous interrogation in court, contradicting their own testimony. Lilley also attacked the credibility of Castellucci, and Prosecutor Cohen seldom objected.

Deputy Sheriff Willard Stuart

Both Cohen and Lilley questioned part-time York Deputy Sheriff Willard Stuart about the sale of his gun to Dongo.

Cohen began by asking how he obtained the gun in question, and if he owned any other guns, which he did, including his service weapon.

Stuart testified how he met Dongo at Edna's Restaurant and that Dongo went to his car to look at the gun. The price of $75 was mentioned.

He was asked by Defense Attorney Daniel Lilley if he had been a Deputy Sheriff at the time that he sold the gun to Dongo and he said, "Yes, I was."

"Didn't you know that Mr. Dongo had gotten into trouble and had a conviction?"

"No, I didn't know."

"He didn't tell you about an incident involving breaking and entering?"

"No, he never told me that."

"When you discussed the sale of the gun, did Mr. Dongo inform you that he had a record, and in fact, was not permitted to own a firearm? That it's a violation of Federal law?"

Willard Stuart admitted, now deflated, "Well, yes, after he already had the gun."

"As a Deputy Sheriff, you were aware of that anyway, weren't you?"

Stuart submitted to the questioning. "Yes." He exhaled now that the truth was out.

"Did you ever tell him that he couldn't purchase the gun?"

Stuart understood the possible consequences of withholding that information. He didn't know what Dongo already told the police, and he didn't want to be caught lying.

"His exact words were, 'Don't tell anybody I've got the gun because I'm a felon and I can't buy a gun.'"

The questioning continued. "Didn't he also tell you that somebody else was interested in the gun or he might know someone else who was interested in the gun?"

"No, never."

"Did he tell you that he was a felon before he paid you the $75?"

"Well, it was before he paid me the money, right."

When Cohen asked Stuart to identify the man to whom he sold the gun, Stuart pointed at the defendants' table and said, "The man in the middle with the red pants and blue tie."

"For the record, your Honor," Cohen said, "the witness is pointing to the defendant Dongo." It was so noted.

Sergeant Peterson

Jack Simmons, Defense Attorney for Herbert Schwartz, asked Sergeant Peterson, who was first to arrive at the crime scene, "In looking at the total Planet 3 office area, did you find any hats?" He was referring to the white fedora and the leather hat Castellucci received from Pownall.

Peterson said he did not.

"Any hat boxes?"

"No."

Joe Emerton

Joe Emerton, the wormdigger, also testified about finding a gun in the mudflat by Long Wharf and turning it into police. When asked if he found any other guns or weapons, he said no.

Sergeant Eccles

Questioned by Lilley, Sergeant Eccles did not remember the date he turned over both bullets to the ballistics specialist, Corporal Manduca, at first stating that he remanded both bullets *before* he went to the autopsy, and that they were in the same condition. In fact, he had no memory of the fragments at all, just the bullet that had been removed from the head of the deceased and the slug he found on the Planet 3 floor.

However, it would have been impossible for him to have traveled to Headquarters to deliver the bullets and follow the morgue vehicle to the Maine Medical Center to attend the autopsy. Dr. Branch confirmed that Eccles was at the autopsy the entire time.

Eccles later contradicted his own testimony by saying that he gave the bullets to Cpl. Manduca that same day (August 31) and only placed other physical evidence in his locker, such as fingerprint material, lists, charts, clothing, and articles dusted for fingerprints.

And even later in his testimony, he stated that he didn't give the slugs to Manduca that day because Manduca was not in, and he was the State's only firearms examiner. So, he could not have remanded the bullets to Manduca that same day.

When Lilley questioned ballistics specialist Corporal Manduca regarding the condition of the newly found gun and how it was tested, he asked, "Did the pitting and rusting on the weapon affect the tooling marks?"

On the witness stand, Manduca defended his testing, saying that, since he could read the markings, it was a successful test.

Corporal Manduca also testified how he matched the carpet slug to the gun found by Emerton.

Lilley asked, "Was the damage to the mushroomed slug (found on the carpet), too damaged to be compared?"

Manduca testified that there were still three visible lands and grooves, enough to match it to the test bullet.

Lilley continued, "Why did you test *four* bullets from the wormdigger's gun?"

Manduca responded, "It was due to the condition of the gun."

However, Corporal Manduca said that, while he fired four test bullets, he only compared two. It was all he needed to confirm a match.

Lilley inquired, "If you did the same test today, would you come to a different conclusion?"

Manduca said yes, due to the continued rusting of the gun over time.

Richard Spencer

Jon's attorney, Richard Spencer, witnessed that Schwartz was "very abusive of Mr. Pownall" and himself, and Schwartz "refused to discuss the problems we saw in Reef's contract." Spencer had told Jon Pownall that he had never seen such a "one-sided" contract, and Jon would not sign it as written. Castellucci told Spencer that Reef demanded an apology for that statement because he was insulted, but Spencer refused.

Joseph Castellucci

When Joe Castellucci took the stand, he testified against Schwartz and Dongo and implied there was a conspiracy to murder Jon Pownall for the insurance money. He also had seen Herb Schwartz put unknown substances in Jon's drinks on two occasions. He claimed to be threatened by Schwartz and Dongo after the murder.

The Defense was quick to point the finger at Castellucci, saying he was the one who needed the money from the insurance policy to pay off his Planet 3 Films bank loans and other personal debts.

He continued to deny any involvement in the murder.

Joe admitted to wedging a matchbook in the door of the bank so that "the person Schwartz was sending to procure the books" from Planet 3 could get in. He also admitted that he lied to police about the matchbook in his first sworn deposition because he didn't want to implicate himself. He added that he made no effort to correct his statement because he feared for his life after being threatened by Herb Schwartz. (See testimony by Joe's attorney, Alex MacNichol later in this chapter.)

Joe's omissions and coverups made him look guilty. After naming Joe as the State's star witness in this murder trial, the Prosecution's case started to weaken and fall apart.

"The Prosecution's case essentially is based on Castellucci's testimony and the gun," wrote journalist John S. Day. Dongo and Schwartz did not take the stand to refute any of the testimony, but Joe Castellucci testified for five days as the State's star witness. And to the six-woman, six-man jury, he appeared "shifty." John Day went on to write, "In true Perry Mason tradition, Schwartz's defense attorney contends that Castellucci is the 'real murderer.' Simmons repeatedly interrupted Castellucci during cross-examination to exclaim, 'You really did it, didn't you?'" To which Castellucci said no; he did not murder Pownall.

Joe did admit that he never warned Pownall of the danger if he did not sign the Director's Contract since Joe assumed it was another one of Reef's tactics to put pressure on him and manipulate Jon into signing. As he witnessed beforehand, Reef took pleasure in pressuring recalcitrant subjects.

"Defense attorneys portrayed Castellucci as a liar, a forger, and an adulterer in their attempt to discredit the Prosecution's star witness," Day concluded.

The jury had to consider if *Castellucci made the whole thing up.*

Compared to Castellucci, Herb Schwartz was a clean-cut man with strong ties to the Democratic Party and the Jewish community, and he owned a thriving local business of interior design. *How could he possibly be wrapped up in a ruthless murder?* Unfortunately, well-known politicians declined to testify on Herb's behalf, as his possible murder conviction would damage their political standing, especially George J. Mitchell, who felt he could lose the election for governor if he was linked to Schwartz.

Geraldine Dongo

Geraldine Dongo, a registered nurse and phlebotomist, testified that she and her husband were at the Pride's Corner Drive-in to watch *Last Tango in Paris* the night of August 30, then went home and made love. The next morning, she called Donna Schwartz (Herb's wife). Without identifying herself, she carefully spoke these words: "I hated the movie." But it was not Donna who answered the phone; it was Jan, Herb's daughter. When Donna got on the phone, she told Geraldine that Jon Pownall had been murdered.

Attorney Daniel Lilley asked Mrs. Dongo, "What was the weather that evening?"

Mrs. Dongo replied, "A fine, clear, nice August evening."

GOODBYE, FAT LARRY

Donna Thomas

On the stand, Donna Thomas was asked by Simmons to tell the court about her husband's (Joe Thomas) business arrangement with Planet 3. She testified that her husband was to receive 50 percent of whatever Herbert Schwartz was to gain from the film company. When asked if it was a written agreement or oral, she said it was a verbal agreement.

Nancy Payne Alexander

The State began to call its witnesses. First up was Nancy (Payne) Alexander. Nancy testified that, on the night of August 30, Castellucci came to her place and asked her to go to the office with him. She described how they found the body of Jon Pownall and called the police.

When prosecuting Attorney Arey asked her about the relationship between Pownall and Schwartz, she said, "Mr. Pownall became fearful of Mr. Schwartz." Schwartz' attorney, Jack Simmons, objected. The Court ordered the last remark to be stricken and the jury to disregard it. Arey asked the Court if it could be included it as part of *voir dire*. The Court agreed. With *the jury removed from the room,* Nancy described Pownall as "physically afraid of Mr. Schwartz," and that Jon had told her that he "didn't like being worth more dead than alive."

James Craig, Daryl Hourihan, John Lane

The next witnesses were James Craig, Daryl Hourihan, and John Lane, who were all involved in the drug deal for Schwartz. Daryl testified that Herb Schwartz called him over to his table at the Tavern Lounge and asked about obtaining hard drugs to stir into the drink of a large man to render him unconscious. Daryl said he wasn't familiar with hard drugs, but Jimmy Craig, who was sitting at the next table, would know.

James Craig testified that Schwartz wanted to purchase heroin through him, for the right price. About 90 minutes later that night, Craig returned to the lounge with a small package. Craig thought Schwartz was a "narc," so he had filled the bag with powdered sugar. At the time, Schwartz said he didn't have the money to pay him. He agreed to wait.

After using "the dope," Schwartz told Craig that it "wasn't any good." Craig didn't care; he just wanted his $225.

The next day, Schwartz told Hourihan to come back later for the money. He was paid in the form of a check made out to Lane's Variety Store from Planet 3 Films signed by Joe Castellucci. (Joe admitted writing this check for Schwartz.) The check was delivered by Hourihan to John Lane at his apartment. Lane kept $25 for cashing the check and gave $200 to Hourihan for Jimmy Craig. Two or three days later, the check bounced due to insufficient funds.

Hourihan saw Herb Schwartz again, this time at Schwartz' business. Herb wanted "something else" to knock out a person. Hourihan "got him some free pills" and handed them to Herb. Hourihan was told that they were Quaaludes and would work in a drink.

John Lane now wanted $225 cash for the bounced check. Herb eventually paid him in cash, and the bad check was returned to Schwartz at the Tavern Lounge in the company of Dongo and Stanley Howard. Hourihan said Dongo told him not to mention the check to anyone.

Peter O'Donovan

When Peter O'Donovan, Dongo's acquaintance since high school, took the stand, he stated that he drove Truman around to view "ocean dumping sites deep enough to cover a Volkswagen van and a body." Truman's plan was to knock the person over the head, open all the windows so he'd drown, and push the van into deep water.

Cohen asked O'Donovan, "Now this was two weeks before the death of Jon Pownall?"

"Correct."

Asked if he had notified the police, O'Donovan replied that he did not—until a feud erupted between himself and Lilley over legal fees.

When cross-examined by Lilley, O'Donovan did not cooperate with the defense attorney and answered his questions by turning the tables back at him.

Lilley: Did you get into an argument with him (Dongo) over property?

O'Donovan: No. I never argued with Truman about property.

Lilley: You didn't?

O'Donovan: No. I have been arguing with you! You're the one that's got the second mortgage in your name, not Truman!

Lilley: If you would just answer my questions.

Judge Glassman: Now, Mr. O'Donovan, answer the questions asked of you, sir.

O'Donovan: Sorry.

Lilley: There is a piece of property, is there not, on Ashmont Street...

O'Donovan: You've got the second mortgage on it.

Lilley: That property has Truman Dongo's name on the deed and you claim some interest in it, right?

O'Donovan: I own it.

Lilley: He indicated to you that he wanted to sell the property...

O'Donovan: He asked if he could sell the property to pay your fee.

Lilley: Okay. He indicated that he would pay you back. Was that the understanding?

O'Donovan: Basically, the understanding was that I sell the property and give him $7500 to pay you.

Lilley: In any event, you discovered that Mr. Dongo's property was listed with Peterson Realty without your participation...You did not care for that situation, did you?

O'Donovan: No, I didn't care for it.

Lilley: You were pretty mad at Truman.

O'Donovan: I wasn't mad at Truman; I was upset with you!

Lilley: There is a lawsuit now pending between the two of you, is that correct?

O'Donovan: I don't know if it's between him or you.

Lilley: Doesn't it say Truman Dongo versus Peter O'Donovan? It is the question of ownership of the property.

O'Donovan: There is a second mortgage in your name. Why don't you bring that up?

Lilley: Did you not run to the police and tell them the story of taking Dongo around to find a place with deep water?

O'Donovan: That could be possible. I didn't run to the police.

Lilley: Every time they had you in for an interview, you never once disclosed that Truman asked you to find a place to dispose of a body until you discovered that the property was to be sold without your involvement?

O'Donovan: You'll have to ask the police.

Lilley: You never once told the police that Truman had a gun in his possession. Is that correct?

O'Donovan: That is correct. You're the one who asked me that.

Marie Ann Roy

Cohen called hairdresser Marie Ann Roy to the stand next. He asked whether she had occasion to see Truman Dongo. She testified that, yes, around December 1974, Truman came in for a haircut and asked her to cut it shorter than usual. She asked him why, to which he simply said, "Never mind." After he paid her, he left but came back in, looking for a parking stamp. Still curious, she asked again, "So what was that all about?" This time Truman asked, "Do you remember that director who got shot?" She said, "Yeah." Truman replied, "Oh, I murdered someone." She told him to get out.

(Before the trial, Truman had also confessed to his cellmate Dube, but the jury never heard it.)

Herbert "Minnie" Tevanian

The Prosecution called the Pride's Corner Drive-in owner, Minnie Tevanian, to the stand.

Cohen: Didn't you indicate at the time of Pownall's murder that you recalled seeing Mr. Dongo at one of the major features at Pride's Corner Drive-In, but you couldn't remember which feature?

Tevanian: Exactly, yes, I did say that.

Cohen: And you remember indicating that it could have been *Poseidon Adventure, Dirty Harry,* or *Last Tango in Paris*?

Tevanian: That's exactly what I said.

Cohen: And you remember talking to me at the bail hearing in January 1975?

Tevanian: Yes.

Cohen: And you indicated that you didn't remember anything more at that time?

Tevanian: No. I recall...I don't know, I'm so confused exactly who I have been speaking to. I was asked a lot of questions, but I recall saying it was *Last Tango in Paris* because it was X-rated.

Cohen: Was that your only X-rated movie...?

Tevanian: I think we played one other that summer.

Cohen: What was that?

Tevanian: *Swinging Models.*

Cohen: Did you see Mr. Dongo at the movie?

Tevanian: It had to be when the cartoons were over...when it quiets down. That would be probably ten after 8, right in there.

Cohen: Did you see him again that evening?

Tevanian: No.

Cohen: Did you see the car?

GOODBYE, FAT LARRY

Tevanian: I never looked.

Cohen: So, whenever you say you saw Mr. Dongo during that movie, you saw him at ten past eight and that was it?

Tevanian: Yes.

Cohen: And was there any small talk that you remember?

Tevanian: I'm sure the man didn't come up to talk to me.

Cohen: I have no further questions. Thank you.

Schwartz' attorney, Jack Simmons cross-examined Tevanian.

Simmons: (sic) As I understand it, this week, the last night he wasn't there. That you know?

Tevanian: Yes.

Simmons: And you know it was a nice night?

Tevanian: I beg pardon?

Simmons: You know for sure it was a nice night?

Tevanian: Yes.

Simmons: And didn't you also at one point tell someone that it was your impression that it couldn't have been the first night?

Cohen: Objection, Your Honor.

Simmons: This is cross-examination.

The Court: Objection overruled. Go ahead.

Simmons: Didn't you tell one of the people who asked you questions that it couldn't have been the first night because it was awfully busy, and you wouldn't have time to chit-chat?

Tevanian: No. I didn't say that. The only thing I said was that it very likely could possibly have not been the first night.

Cohen: I'm going to object, your Honor.

The Court: Sustained.

Simmons: Would you tell us what you said in regard to the first night?

Tevanian: Now what?

Simmons: Tell us what you said in regard to the first night.

Tevanian: You want me to repeat what I just said? I'm a little confused.

Lilley: Nothing further, your Honor.

Mr. Tevanian couldn't say for sure which night he saw Truman Dongo.

Detective Peter Conley

As the number of witnesses were winding down, Detective Peter Conley was called to testify.

Deputy Attorney General Richard Cohen asked Conley about his first interview with Truman Dongo at the police station. Conley testified that, in Dongo's initial statement a few days after Pownall's murder, Truman told him that he was at home, watching TV, at the time of the murder.

Conley also stated that, when Dongo was brought in for further questioning, he was read his Miranda rights. Truman had changed his story, claiming that he had been at a drive-in movie with his wife at the time of the murder.

When the prosecutor asked Conley if Truman confessed, Conley stated that Truman, in fact, told Joe Castellucci that he "did it;" however, Truman also said to Joe that, but he "was only kidding."

Cohen continued his examination. "Did you see Mr. Dongo again?"

"Yes, sir."

"And when was that?"

"On December 20, 1974."

"Where did you see him and just what were the circumstances?"

"At his house, 90 Chesley Street, and I had a warrant of arrest on him."

"For what, sir?"

"Murder."

Attorney Lilley then cross-examined Conley. Lilley stated that his questions were only for evidence in the case of State against Dongo, and not evidence in the case of State against Schwartz.

Lilley began by questioning Conley's credentials. "At the time of the Pownall death, you had only become a detective in the Portland Police Department. Is that true?"

Conley responded, "I had been a detective approximately seven months."

"Prior to that, you had been a regular police officer, is that correct?"

"Yes, sir, a police officer."

"Now, the fact of the matter is, this was the first murder case you ever worked on, is that not true?"

"As a detective, yes, sir."

Linda Jordan

The next witness was Joe Castellucci's neighbor, Linda Jordan, who testified that Joe greeted her shortly after 11 pm on the night of August 30.

Alexander MacNichol

Alexander MacNichol, Joe's attorney, took the stand. He told the Court how Joe came to his office and said that threats had been made on his life and the lives of his wife and child. Joe also explained that Schwartz had asked him to go to Florida and borrow a large amount of money from his relatives to pay the hit man. "I asked him point blank if he was a part of the murder, and he said no." MacNichol called the police, who came and took Castellucci's statement.

*****

At the end of the trial's third week, after all slated witnesses had given testimony, the Court addressed the jury.

"Ladies and Gentlemen of the Jury, the defendant Dongo has now rested his case. The defendant Schwartz has rested his case, as well. And the State has rested. You have heard all the evidence in this case.

"There are some matters of law which the Court must take up with counsel that must be done outside the presence of the jury. For that reason, I am going to excuse the jury until tomorrow morning at 9 o'clock."

After the jurors were warned not to discuss the case with anyone, they were asked to leave the courtroom.

Judge Glassman turned to Attorney Lilley. "Do I understand that the defendants have certain motions to address to the Court?"

Lilley replied, "Yes, Your Honor."

GOODBYE, FAT LARRY

"You may proceed."

Lilley began, "May it please the Court, at this time the defendant Truman Dongo through his attorney makes a motion for judgment of acquittal.

"There are two factors that the Court ought to consider. First is where the defendant was during the week up to and including the death of Mr. Pownall, when it has been sufficiently established that Mr. Dongo was at a movie. I don't recall anybody testifying that Mr. Dongo was not where he claims he was."

Knowing that Dongo never took the stand, the judge remarked, "He hasn't claimed anything, Mr. Lilley."

"Well, he claims he was at a movie through his witnesses, your Honor."

"All right."

Lilley continued, "Mr. Dongo claims to have been to a drive-in that particular evening. I think if the Court adds up the times from when Mr. Dongo arrived, the cartoons, the length of the movie, the length of intermission, and a half hour into the second feature, it would mean he was there..."

Judge Glassman completed Lilley's sentence, "Until 10:33."

"Well, if it started at 8 o'clock, I disagree, your Honor. Maybe I better do some computations..."

"One hundred fifty-three minutes, by my estimate, Mr. Lilley."

Lilley spoke up. "A hundred twenty-nine..."

Getting a little agitated, the judge addressed counsel, "Seven minutes for the cartoon, a hundred twenty-nine minutes for the feature, and seventeen minutes for the intermission is 153 minutes, or two hours and 33 minutes, 10:33 p.m."

"That's right, you Honor. Then they stayed a half hour into the second feature."

"Right."

"Which I compute to be around 11:03," said Lilley. "At that time, or conceivably even as early as thirteen minutes earlier, Miss Nancy Payne, who is now Mrs. Nancy Alexander, called the Planet 3 offices and got no answer. There is no corroborating evidence that Pownall may have stepped out for a candy bar, as testified by Castellucci.

"Mr. Castellucci was home at 11:15, according to his neighbor Mrs. Jordan. Mr. Dongo left the drive-in at 11:03, as we computed. He could not have committed the crime."

Lilley continued, "The second point is the large sum of money promised to a so-called hit man, supposedly Mr. Dongo. $20,000 was mentioned or $35,000. But that was based on Mr. Castellucci saying that's what Schwartz said to him.

"Through the entire 1974, the checks and vouchers and the bookkeeping entries verify that from August through January 1st, there were continuous payments of twenty-five and fifty dollars to Mr. Schwartz by Dongo, rather than the reverse."

He went on to say, "The Court will recall the testimony that the night of the drive-in movie, the weather was clear and there was no rain."

Judge Glassman responded, "Do I misinterpret the (weather) chart, Mr. Lilley, or does it show that on August 30 climatological data indicates that it was foggy and hazy?"

GOODBYE, FAT LARRY

"We don't know whether that's morning, afternoon, or evening. If the entire chart is read, it indicates that there was *no precipitation*. At the worst, it could have been foggy.

"In addition, there has been no rebuttal on Mrs. Dongo's corroboration for that evening and each and every day that week. Mr. Dongo could not have done the killing."

There was a pause, then Judge Glassman turned to the prosecutor, Deputy Attorney General Richard Cohen.

"Mr. Cohen, do you wish to be heard?"

"The State, without reviewing its argument as to the denial of the motion for acquittal after the State's case was over, I feel, of course, there is more than sufficient evidence wherein a jury could find Defendant Dongo guilty of murder beyond a reasonable doubt.

"The State realizes that the credibility of the witnesses is not for the Court to make any determination. It is ultimately and solely for the Jury to determine as to what weight to give the evidence. However, as far as the *alleged* alibi evidence is concerned, it does come solely from Mrs. Dongo as to the night of the alleged death. There is no corroboration in that regard. Mrs. Dongo indicated that it was a clear night when they went to the movies, and she reiterated this. The evidence that's been introduced through the climatological charts indicate, in the specified hours, that was not the case at all. In fact, just the opposite during the contested hours of August 30."

Prosecutor Cohen continued. "As far as the other evidence that was induced on the defense case is concerned, we feel it is completely irrelevant and non-germane to the issues of this case as to whether Mr. Dongo could have committed the murder of Jon Pownall in the evening of August 30, 1973. The State feels clearly, even now after the case has been rested as far as Defendant Dongo is concerned and with the evidence induced as to establishing alibis, that a jury, acting in a reasonable manner on weighing the facts, could find that Truman Dongo is, in fact, guilty of murder. And they could unquestionably find this based on the evidence and weighing the evidence of the parties as they must do as to the witnesses.

"They could find this clearly beyond a reasonable doubt. And we would move for denial of the motion for acquittal at this time."

It was time for Judge Glassman to decide.

"Upon analysis, the one witness who purports to establish an alibi for Mr. Dongo is his wife, obviously not a disinterested witness. These are matters concerning credibility and the weight to be accorded her testimony are clearly matters for the Jury and not this Court. I express no opinion upon those matters whatsoever.

"However, it seems to me that the evidence is such that a jury could be convinced beyond a reasonable doubt that Mr. Dongo is guilty of the criminal homicide, felonious homicide, of Mr. Pownall. Therefore, the motion for the judgment of acquittal will be denied."

The judge looked to Jack Simmons, the Defense Attorney for Herbert Schwartz.

"Mr. Simmons, do you have anything further?"

"Thank you, your Honor. If your Honor pleases, it seems to me that the Court has properly ruled throughout this trial that various matters were for the Jury and not the Court—that they were questions of fact and not questions of law. I would suggest to the Court that, while credibility is usually a question of fact, at some point it passes that sphere and enters into the sphere of the incredible which then becomes a question of law.

"I would move this Court that, on the basis of evidence against Mr. Schwartz is totally incredible and comes from the mouth of a *perjurer,* it is not sufficient, credible evidence which raises a substantial question of fact for a jury to consider.

"And I would move for a judgment of acquittal."

Not surprised, Judge Glassman once again turned to the Prosecutor. "Mr. Cohen, do you wish to be heard?"

"No, your Honor. The State would stand on its argument at the end of the State's case as to Mr. Schwartz."

"Well, Mr. Simmons, I do not find the evidence against Mr. Schwartz at all incredible. Therefore, if that is the basis upon which you suggest a motion for judgment of acquittal should be granted, the motion is denied.

"Court will be in recess until 9 a.m. tomorrow morning."

The gavel came down. It was now in the hands of the Jury.

*****

The next day, summations were made by the Defense and Prosecution.

Then the jury members were given instructions to determine their verdict. They had to consider:

...if **Castellucci's** testimony was credible.

...if **Schwartz** introduced **Dongo** as "an investor" but was a known felon.

...that the gun proven to be discharged at the crime scene was last bought (illegally) by **Dongo**. However, there was no testifying witness placing Dongo at the crime scene.

...that, soon after that car ride to New York, **Schwartz** changed his mind about a life insurance policy for $400,000 on Jon's life. To collect all of it, the murder had to occur before actor contracts were signed in Los Angeles.

...if **Schwartz** hatched a careful murder plan that covered all the possible situations and told Joe that he paid someone to murder Jon.

...that **Schwartz** threatened to kill Jon in front of several people. He also told Castellucci that he found someone to kill Jon for $35,000, and twice altered Jon's drinks with drugs and wanted Truman to hit him on the head with a tire iron. Joe asked Schwartz to stay away from Jon for a week.

...that **Schwartz** used a Planet 3 check to buy heroin to drug Jon. This purchase was confirmed by a drug dealer who testified to the purchase at trial.

...that **Schwartz** and Planet 3's attorney Reef were edging Jon out of the company and the film. There were "explosive" confrontations among Schwartz, Reef, and Pownall, according to Jon's lawyer and

GOODBYE, FAT LARRY

secretary over the Director's Contract, which was drawn up by Reef *and altered after signatures, in favor of Schwartz.*

...if **Dongo** used his wife and Minnie Tevanian for an alibi, even though Tevanian was confused about the date.

...the testimony of hairdresser Marie Roy that **Dongo** told her that he had "murdered someone."

More than one person may have participated in the murder—one with a gun and one with a blade. Two people may have had guns because there were three live rounds still in Truman's 5-shot revolver and two spent rounds—yet there were three shots fired at the crime scene. One bullet went to Jon's brain, one to his spine (neither with exit wounds), plus one mushroomed bullet on the carpet that had ricocheted on the wall/window which matched 100 percent to Truman's gun. Where did the third bullet come from? A second gun held by Truman or a second shooter? No one would take the time to reload the revolver with one bullet during the fracas. It's possible that one of Truman's bullets hit Jon (confirmed .38 caliber), and a bullet from another .38 caliber gun hit Jon, and neither were traceable due to their destruction inside his body.

On the other hand, **Castellucci**...

...asked Stu Lamont and Nancy Phillips of Transamerica about double indemnity to cover murder and inquired about a $100,000 policy on Jean Pownall's life.

...as Planet 3 Films, was the sole beneficiary of the insurance policy (although that could be argued if the Option for Schwartz had foundation). And it would have been important to file an insurance claim before Schwartz exercised that option.

...asked Nancy Payne to duplicate the office keys for him.

...gave Schwartz an alibi by telling him to stay away from Jon and Planet 3 Films during the week of the murder.

...admitted to wearing a white hat as a signal to "someone" outside, and he left a matchbook in the door so that "someone" could get in, and "make" Jon sign the Director's Contract, "or else." Castellucci held back this information in his initial deposition to police but admitted it in court.

...created his own seemingly planned alibi by phoning businesses looking for Jon, calling Jon's wife, and stopping in two stores to make his appearance obvious at the time of the murder. But that alibi did not disprove his involvement.

...used Nancy Payne as an alibi and wanted her to discover the body.

...had organized crime connections from his past to whom he owed money.

...was broke and not paying back Planet 3's bank loans and his other debts.

...admitted that he had perjured himself in his sworn deposition to deflect his involvement in Schwartz' plan.

If the jury thought Joe Castellucci was the murderer, how did he get Truman's gun? Did Joe hire is own hitman with the promise of the insurance payoff?

Most importantly, *Castellucci was not on trial.*

GOODBYE, FAT LARRY

Was it always Herb Schwartz who called the shots and arranged to have Jon killed? Could Reef have been involved?

* * * * *

The Cumberland County Superior Court jury deliberated only six hours before coming to a decision regarding Dongo and Schwartz.

A decision reached

After deliberating for six hours, the six-man, six-woman jury found Truman Dongo and Herbert Schwartz *not guilty*.

Schwartz and Dongo leaped from their seats and hugged their wives and family members.

Even though Truman's gun was used at the murder, there were no witnesses putting him at the crime scene. The jury acquitted Dongo primarily on his wife's testimony that they attended the drive-in movie together. Likewise, there was no hard evidence that Schwartz hired Dongo to kill Jon.

Jurors said that the *Prosecution did not prove guilt beyond a reasonable doubt*.

The two men still had to face charges of conspiracy to commit murder, which meant a second trial.

After the murder acquittal, Judge Glassman set double surety of $5000 on each and they were released.

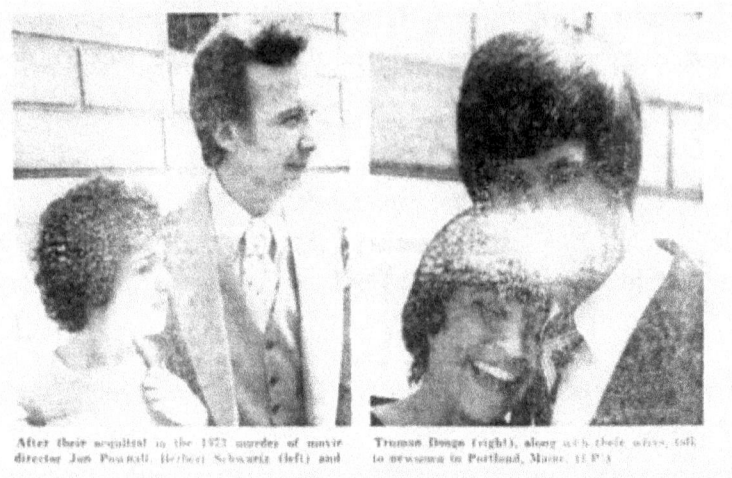

Photo UPI. *Boston Globe,* May 25, 1975, p19. No copyright infringement intended.

Jean Pownall commented that District Attorney Cohen had exhibited a look of "stage fright" during the trial. She explained in an after-trial document, "Cohen's performance was disastrous, and his conduct was incomprehensible." *Was he intimidated by Lilley? Was he threatened in any way or ordered by someone to back down?* It left her bewildered and angry that he let the case get away from him.

* * * * *

A special jury in Maine later found no cause to charge Castellucci with the murder. He would be involved in the civil suit regarding the Transamerica Life Insurance policy in the following months/years.

GOODBYE, FAT LARRY

* * * * *

November 20, 1975

Two years after the murder, Jon's brother, Richard Pownall of San Antonio, Texas, offered a $10,000 reward for "information leading to the final conviction" of Jon's killer(s). "I think there were three or four persons involved. I'm convinced it was a conspiracy," he told the *Portland Press Herald* staff writer John Lovell. "I feel I've got to do something."

Richard planned to forward any tips to the Maine Attorney General's office.

"Plots behind plots, plans behind plans. There was always another secret." — Brandon Sanderson

Preparation for the conspiracy trial

Herbert Schwartz, aged 46 in 1976, testified during an appeal hearing that he had been impoverished by the legal costs incurred for his defense on the murder charge in Jon Pownall's death, for which he was acquitted.

Schwartz said it had cost him $22,500 in legal fees, leaving him with major business debts and a yearly income of only $5,000. It wasn't enough to pay an attorney for the conspiracy trial.

Maine Supreme Court Justice Charles A. Pomeroy overturned the lower court ruling barring Schwartz from free counsel, and Schwartz was finally awarded public-paid counsel.

The Cumberland County Superior Court was directed to appoint a county-paid lawyer for Herbert R. Schwartz, who was now scheduled to stand trial on the murder conspiracy charge, along with 35-year-old Truman H. Dongo.

May 5, 1976

Truman Dongo also applied for public-paid counsel for the companion murder conspiracy trial. His application was denied.

Superior Court Justice Louis Scolnik ruled that the 35-year-old salesman and his wife, a registered nurse, had sufficient assets, including a combined $21,000 annual salary, to pay for a lawyer.

Daniel G. Lilley, who defended Dongo at his first trial, said he was "very disappointed" at Scolnik's ruling and would confer with his client before deciding whether to appeal.

Schwartz' lawyer planned to argue before Superior Court Justice Sumner Goffin that the conspiracy charge should be dismissed. If it was not, the pair would be tried in Cumberland County Superior Court, in the following month or so.

May 12

A Superior Court judge was asked to dismiss a murder conspiracy charge against interior designer Herbert Schwartz.

Schwartz' lawyer, Gary Goldberg, told Justice Sumner Goffin that "what we have is essentially a videotape replay of the first trial."

Goldberg argued that the Cumberland County jury which last year found Schwartz not guilty of murdering film director Jon Pownall also "rejected the fact that there was a conspiracy."

A conspiracy exists when two or more people join and form an agreement to violate the law, and then act on that agreement, but it is not necessary for all participants to know everything that is going on.

Opposing the dismissal motion was Assistant Attorney General Vernon Arey, who maintained that the question of whether Schwartz had engaged in a murder plot against Pownall had never been examined by a jury.

Charges *were not dismissed,* and the lawyers prepared for the conspiracy trial.

Goffin said briefs and replies on the motion would be filed during the following three weeks.

July 22

Deputy Attorney General Richard Cohen announced that there was a Superior Court decision to dismiss an appeal motion, clearing the way for the murder conspiracy trial of Schwartz and Dongo.

Superior Court Justice Sumner Goffin dismissed a motion by Schwartz to appeal his case to the Maine Supreme Court.

As a result of Goffin's action, Cohen predicted the joint trial concerning the 1973 slaying of movie director Jon R. Pownall, would start in September or October of 1976.

However, Gary Goldberg, an attorney for Schwartz, suggested that Goffin's ruling might be appealed.

Schwartz's lawyers maintained that the upcoming trial on conspiracy charges would be nothing more than a replay of the first trial. They argued that it would subject the defendants to *double jeopardy.* In criminal cases, the Fifth Amendment guarantees the right to a grand jury, forbids double jeopardy, and protects against self-incrimination.

"No justice for Jon."

The conspiracy trial

It had been nearly two years since Schwartz and Dongo were acquitted of murdering film director Jon Pownall.

January 5, 1977

The lengthy process of jury selection began for the conspiracy trial. The session was presided over by Justice Robert L. Browne, who introduced the eight attorneys to the pool of 50 prospective jurors.

The two defendants appeared relaxed as they sat through the seven hours of juror questioning. On the first day, the Defense and Prosecution took turns questioning a group of 20 prospective jurors and selected five, who were then sequestered at a nearby hotel.

A total of twelve regular jurors and two alternatives were chosen.

January 20

The Prosecution in the murder conspiracy trial of Schwartz and Dongo suffered a major setback when the court, in a surprising move, ruled *against admission of any evidence relating to the 1973 murder of film director Jon Pownall in the upcoming conspiracy trial.*

Justice Robert L. Browne ruled that any testimony or evidence, *including the gun,* relating to the earlier murder trial would be contrary to the prohibition against trial twice for the same offense; in other words, double jeopardy.

Browne said a conspiracy charge did "not necessarily depend on whether a crime was committed. It is something that went on before..."

He went on to say that an admission of any testimony or evidence relating to the earlier charge might result in the jury "concerning itself with evaluating the same evidence...and the judgment made by the previous jury."

January 26

During the conspiracy trial, Prosecution claimed that it was Schwartz' job to raise money to produce *The Salem Six* film, and he had hired Dongo to have Pownall killed because the director refused to sign a Director's Contract that Planet 3's lawyer, Reef, drew up. The state had charged Schwartz with planning the murder in the offices of Planet 3 Films and Dongo with carrying it out.

Jean Pownall was also called upon to testify.

After a 13-day trial, A Cumberland County jury took only two hours to acquit Herb Schwartz and Truman Dongo of conspiring in August 1973 to murder local film director Jon Pownall.

Muriel Trafford of Raymond, Maine, the jury forewoman, said after the verdict was announced, "We just didn't think the state proved the case beyond the shadow of a doubt."

Once again, Schwartz and Dongo walked free.

Sadly, the family felt there was no justice for Jon. No one held accountable.

The case was shelved, and the murder was never solved.

* * * * *

Preparation for the civil suits

January 31

The Superior Court jury's acquittal of Dongo and Schwartz put to rest criminal charges in the 1973 slaying of Jon Pownall. However, a seemingly endless web of civil suits awaited action in federal court that dealt largely with Pownall's life insurance policy, an issue which figured prominently in both Schwartz-Dongo trials.

Laying chief claim to $400,000 in proceeds from the policy was Joseph Castellucci, the State's star witness at both trials (and cleared of charges in the murder) and owner of Planet 3 Films. Also claiming part of the money was Jean Pownall. It was evident that Jon wanted her to be a beneficiary and that was shot down by the company attorneys and the type of policy (key-man). Herb Schwartz also made a claim, based upon the August 10, 1973, option agreement—the page that appeared to have been amended after Castellucci's signature—making Herb 50 percent liable for any losses and, therefore, considered owner of half the company and its profits, in his opinion.

"A small win."

Civil-suit deposition

The deposition by Joe Castellucci was taken, under oath, regarding a civil suit on behalf of Planet 3 Films against Transamerica Life Insurance for the $400,000 policy on Jon Pownall's life.

Ralph I. Lancaster, a graduate of Harvard Law School and the attorney for Transamerica, took Joe Castellucci's deposition. Here are some of the questions and responses:

Q. Would you name the beneficiary of the Transamerica Life Insurance policy?

A. Planet 3 Films.

Q. Please read the policy as written. Is it not marked Beneficiary: Joseph A. Castellucci, and signed by you?

A. I signed Joseph A. Castellucci as Planet 3 Films.

Q. (Castellucci was also asked under oath about his conversation with Nancy Phillips of Transamerica.) Did you ask Miss Phillips as to whether or not the policy would pay on murder?

A. We had a conversation about justification of the policy...and I went on to say that it covered murder, and she said yes, it did.

GOODBYE, FAT LARRY

Q. Do you deny that you also asked Mr. Stuart Lamont if his Horace Mann policy covered someone who was murdered?

A. I don't deny it.

Q. Do you deny any reference to $200,000 being held in escrow pending issuance of insurance?

A. I don't deny it. It's very possible. The way I understood the financial arrangements, let's say Mr. Dickerman had $200,000 put aside for the film upon completion of the package as we discussed it.

Q. Mr. Castellucci, that $200,000 in escrow pending the insurance. That's your definition of escrow?

A. Yes.

Q. And you understand that escrow is a firm commitment, right? That somebody is holding something and is bound by the terms of the commitment.

A. Um. No. I didn't understand it to be a legal escrow account.

Q. Did you tell Miss Phillips that, at the time, Planet 3 did not own anything?

A. No, not at that point.

Q. Did you ever sit down with Mr. Schwartz and ask why he objected to insurance when the investors were demanding it?

A. No.

Q. Mr. Castellucci, didn't you say that not only was Herb Schwartz against insurance, but when he found out you applied for insurance, he wanted to cancel it?

A. I don't recall that.

Q. Let me help you. Question: 'What did he say to you?' Speaking about Herb Schwartz. "The discussions we had with Norman Reef where Herb said maybe we should just cancel the insurance. He didn't like insurance companies. It was an unnecessary expense. And Norman felt we should have the policy..."

A. I don't recall making that statement during deposition.

Q. When did you come back to Maine?

A. Two weeks ago.

Q. Where are you staying?

A. The Holiday Inn in Portland.

Q. Do you expect the State of Maine to pay for it?

A. Yes.

Q. Who else is staying at that hotel?

A. Mr. Cohen, the prosecutor. And Mr. Arey, the Assistant District Attorney.

GOODBYE, FAT LARRY

Q. And have you been consulting with them on a regular basis?

A. Yes.

Q. Have they given you documents to study?

A. Yes.

Q. Was the civil deposition one of them?

A. Not that I recall.

Q. Have you been studying the documents a whole week before taking the stand?

A. Yes.

Q. And working on your recollections?

A. I've been going over my statements and trying to pinpoint the days and times.

Q. Is it true that Jon Pownall owned the concept to the movie?

A. Yes.

Q. So, Planet 3 *did* own something.

A. Yes.

Q. I assume that if Mr. Jean Shepherd did not deliver the script, you could hire someone else.

A. That is true.

Q. Similarly, if you didn't want Mr. Pownall to direct the movie anymore, you could hire someone else to direct.

A. That's true.

Q. There is nothing to indicate that the investors ever had any contact with Mr. Pownall or could care two hoots whether Mr. Pownall or anyone else directed the movie.

A. That probably is true.

Q. All right. I suggest to you that the important ingredients missing from the package when Mr. Schwartz starting objecting were the conceptual agreement, the script, and the budget.

A. Those are some of the things...

Q. Weren't you just as interested as Mr. Schwartz in getting this thing moving?

A. Of course.

Q. Wasn't it your job as the business head of this corporation to get it?

A. That's right.

Q. Now, tell me why any investor who didn't know Jon Pownall would be interested in key-man insurance on his life?

A. (Castellucci explained how it would delay the film and cost more money.)

GOODBYE, FAT LARRY

Q. All right, I'll buy that. But Mr. Pownall could have been replaced in early August.

A. We were locked into Jon Pownall at that point.

Q. Subsequently, others suggested that Mr. Pownall be discharged, isn't that correct?

A. I was told by Mr. Reef that I should fire Mr. Pownall, or he would drop me as a client.

Q. Wasn't Mr. Pownall concerned that he didn't have a contract, he wanted something in writing to protect him?

A. He became concerned when Mr. Schwartz entered the picture.

Q. That's when he lost his conceptual rights and 10 percent of the film, the profit of the film plus a fee?

A. It was August 22 when he was told his 10 percent was gone.

Author's note: It was August 15 when Jon was told about his 10 percent.

Q. And isn't it true, that in that caucus with you, Reef told you that it was a negotiation tool, that he was trying to deal from strength?

A. He only referred once to a contract tactic, and that was insulting Mrs. Pownall.

Q. You understood, did you not, all along that the decision—any decision—was the corporation's to make, not the attorneys'?

A. That's right.

Q. And whether Mr. Pownall was to be fired or not to be fired was not Mr. Reef's decision, it was your decision?

A. It wasn't as clear-cut as that.

Q. Who are the corporate officers?

A. I was the President of the company.

Q. Was Mr. Reef a voting corporate officer?

A. No.

Q. You were the controlling officer, weren't you?

A. Yes, I was.

Q. And you claimed to be a 100% stockholder.

A. Yes. May I explain? At the time, Reef had a great deal of influence on what was being done. He talked about dropping me as a client if Jon didn't sign his contract. That would put things in disarray. Mr. Schwartz was closely aligned with Mr. Reef on fundraising. It was not a simple matter of saying I had the final decision.

Q. And while you were talking to Schwartz about replacing Jon, you were also talking to Jon about replacing Herb—up until the August 10 option which you signed. The last sentence of page 2 talks about termination. "This agreement terminates ten years from the date hereof under the following

GOODBYE, FAT LARRY

circumstances (a) Mutual agreement in writing, or (b) upon the exercise of the option." Is that correct?

A. Um-hum.

Q. So, it's very clear...you have no power whatsoever to get rid of Mr. Herb Schwartz, even if you wanted to.

A. If Mr. Schwartz had raised the financing for this movie, he could have exercised his option. But if he did not raise the financing, and I got money from Churubusco, I would think that would be reason for termination.

Q. Now at some point, it was decided that Parent and Doyle be bought out, is that correct?

A. That's correct. There was a cash consideration for their 2 percent to be paid within 90 days.

Q. It was suggested that there ought not to be small investors in the corporation, is that right?

A. The discussion about the buy-out came from Mr. Schwartz relating to Mr. Dickerman. Mr. Dickerman wanted half of the company and didn't want one- or two-percenters.

Q. If Mr. Schwartz had 50 percent, and Mr. Dickerman had 50 percent, what was left for you?

A. When Dickerman came into the company, obviously we had to alter the documents so that Mr. Schwartz would receive half of what I had left. In essence, Mr. Dickerman would own 50 percent,

Mr. Schwartz would own 25 percent, and I would own 25 percent. I wasn't going to write myself out of the company!

Q. Or you would have ended up with nothing.

A. Absolutely.

Q. Were those documents ever altered?

A. No.

Q. I suggest to you, sir, that Mr. Dickerman was not a factor in your company at that time.

A. According to Mr. Schwartz, Mr. Dickerman was in on August 20, out on August 21, and back in again on August 29.

Q. The day before Mr. Pownall's death.

A. Yes.

June 23, 1977

Jean Pownall and her three children intervened in a suit between Transamerica and Planet 3 Films Ltd., for the $400,000 insurance policy on Pownall's life.

The following is a Portland, Maine, newspaper article published in regard to the final civil suit decision.

GOODBYE, FAT LARRY

* * * * *

June 28, 1977 / *Portland Press Herald*

Lawyers spar over Pownall insurance policy

By Miranda Spivack, *Press Herald* writer

PORTLAND—Joseph A. Castellucci and Portland lawyer Ralph I. Lancaster, Jr. sparred almost continually Monday in a federal civil trial over a disputer $400,000 life insurance policy, with Lancaster attempting to show that the policy had been obtained fraudulently.

The disputed policy, on the life of slain movie director Jon R. Pownall of Springvale, has been the focal point of most of five days of testimony in the trial, as Planet 3 Films, Pownall's employer, seeks to obtain the policy proceeds.

Castellucci, former president of the film company which was to have employed Pownall to make a movie, "The Salem Six," testified on the company's behalf Monday in U.S. District Court here, disagreeing with earlier testimony from an insurance company representative about the content of conversations regarding Planet 3's assets and contracts with movie stars.

Nancy Phillips, of Transamerica Life Insurance and Annuity Co., Lancaster's client, said in testimony last week that Castellucci had told her in August 1973 that the contracts had been signed with Jim Backus and Margaret Hamilton to star in the film and that other agreements had been signed for equipment.

She also said that Castellucci had discussed a previous insurance application on Pownall from the

Horace Mann Co., and Castellucci had told her he didn't know what had happened to the policy.

Later, Stuart Lamont, a Pownall insurance agent, said he discussed with Castellucci that the Horace Mann application had been turned down both on Castellucci's life and on Pownall.

Castellucci has maintained throughout the trial that he was never certain of the final disposition of the Horace Mann applications; that he thought the company might write a policy for an amount smaller than the $400,000 he requested on Pownall, but he was not interested in a smaller policy.

When he took the stand for the second time in the trial on Monday, Castellucci disputed Phillips' testimony, saying he "never told" Phillips that "we had signed contracts."

Castellucci also went over earlier testimony he had made when called as a witness by Lancaster, saying that he had not told police nor later Lancaster about propping a matchbook in Planet 3's Monument Square office door on the night Pownall was killed, until March 1974, several months after Pownall's slaying Aug. 30, 1973.

He had said he did not tell the police in early statements after the murder about leaving the door open to permit Herbert R. Schwartz to enter the offices to get Pownall to sign a Director's Contract. Schwartz and Truman H. Dongo were tried and twice acquitted on charges stemming from Pownall's death.

GOODBYE, FAT LARRY

The life insurance payout

Testimony ended on June 28, 1977, in the civil trial over the disputed $400,000 life insurance policy on the life of Jon Pownall.

After the closing arguments, the U.S. District Court jury began deliberations.

Joe Castellucci sought the proceeds of the "key-man" insurance policy on Pownall, the director of the movie, "The Salem Six." Joe was the sole beneficiary as president and owner of the company, and producer of the film.

Transamerica Life Insurance and Annuity Co. of Los Angeles flat out refused to pay out the funds from the policy which had been issued just 10 days before the murder. Ralph I. Lancaster Jr., the lawyer representing Transamerica, claimed that former Planet 3 Films Ltd. President Joseph A. Castellucci, Herbert R. Schwartz, and Truman H. Dongo were morally and legally responsible for Pownall's death, even though Schwartz and Dongo were tried and acquitted of criminal charges of murdering and conspiring to murder Pownall.

The key Prosecution witness at both trials was Castellucci, who testified that Schwartz, a financial backer of the film company, hired Dongo to kill the director for the insurance money. The Defense insisted that Castellucci, not Schwartz or Dongo, was the killer.

After more than a week of complex and often contradictory testimony, the jury decided that Castellucci had provided misinformation to Transamerica to obtain the policy on Pownall's life.

The jury also found that the insurance application (completed by Joe Castellucci) misrepresented the fact that Pownall, had been denied coverage by another company.

On a third issue, the jurors decided in favor of Castellucci. The verdict did not find that the former producer had conspired to kill Pownall.

The 6-member U.S. District Court jury deliberated more than nine hours before returning June 29 with its verdict in favor of Transamerica Life Insurance Co. of Los Angeles.

In other words, the jury found that the insurance company did not have to pay the proceeds of the $400,000 insurance policy to Planet 3 Films. However, Mrs. Pownall was awarded $35,000. No other payout was made.

Counsel for Planet 3 Films President Joe Castellucci did not know at that time whether his client planned to appeal.

* * * * *

But this is not the end of the story...

Whatever Happened to...?

Whatever happened to Herbert R. Schwartz?

Photograph of Herbert Schwartz courtesy of Tammy Bonneau Walter.

During the murder trial of Jon Pownall, 46-year-old Herbert Schwartz testified that he had been impoverished by the legal costs incurred for his defense. The court, therefore, directed to appoint a county-paid lawyer.

Herb Schwartz, the power-driven interior designer, had difficulty getting and retaining clients after his acquittal in the Jon Pownall murder case. Essentially broke, he was forced to close shop and look elsewhere for work, where, perhaps, people were less apt to associate his name with a murder.

For 20 years he operated the Sleepy Town Motel and The Captain's Table restaurant on Routes 1 and 9 in Wells, Maine. It's unknown to the Pownall family how he came up with the money for these businesses, but he eventually sold them for $600,000.

Herb remained active in the Maine Democratic Party and continued to be friends with Truman Dongo.

After a brief illness, he passed away on February 18, 2006, at age 76.

Whatever happened to Truman H. Dongo?

Photograph of Truman Dongo courtesy of Tammy Bonneau Walter.

Truman Dongo and Herbert Schwartz were friends since high school and the police knew they had committed juvenile crimes together. That information was not admissible in court. When Dongo was acquitted in Jon Pownall's murder in January 1977, he enjoyed a life of freedom for six more years, involving himself in cocaine distribution until his death.

Geraldine Dongo divorced him, although he was able to see his kids.

Dongo and Attorney Daniel Lilley remained friends.

Tammy Bonneau Walter

Author's note: The following narration may be hard for some to read. I contacted Tammy Bonneau Walter on Facebook after I found an online photo of Truman with her and one other person. She wanted to be interviewed and her story told, saying Truman had been her boyfriend and was the "scariest person" she had ever met in her life.

"Truman admitted to me that he did it," she said, referring to the Jon Pownall murder.

"I left him after five years because he almost killed me."

She went on to say, "I've been dying for someone to write a book about him."

January 1979

Tammy Bonneau was a 20-year-old, pretty, blonde girl, who tended bar at a racquetball club in Falmouth, Maine, and caught the eye of recently divorced Truman Dongo. He stopped into the bar often, playing gin rummy with her and always leaving a good tip. She found out who he was, and what he had been accused of doing to Jon Pownall, but Tammy found him "charming."

While working at the club and attending Southern Maine Community College, Tammy was also working at the Cape Elizabeth Police Department and had an "unfortunate" relationship with an officer. After she started dating Truman, one of her instructors said, "I heard you're dating Truman Dongo. You know, you're never going to be a police officer if you're dating him."

GOODBYE, FAT LARRY

She replied, "I don't care! At least he's not pretending to be good."

June 1979

Tammy graduated from SMCC with a degree in criminal justice in June and left her job at the police department. She knew it was also time to move out of her aunt's house and into her own apartment. A difficult relationship with her aunt made her want more freedom to do what she wanted.

She started going to the beach with Truman, still getting to know him. Truman had read the book *How to Win Friends and Influence People* by Dale Carnegie and used Carnegie's methods to get people to like him. He would remember their names, stock their favorite liquor, even buy toothbrushes with the names of his guests printed on them. It made him more endearing to Tammy.

By late summer 1979, Tammy and Truman had become closer and closer. After Truman gave her some prescription cough medicine with codeine when she was sick, Tammy's aunt and cousin saw his name on the bottle. Tammy's cousin said, "You are NOT dating TRUMAN DONGO, are you?" In a rebellious moment, it made her want to get more involved with Truman.

She genuinely cared about him and liked him a lot, and Tammy was enjoying the attention that came with seeing Truman.

"One night we went to Old Port for dinner with another couple. Everyone knew Truman and said 'Hi, Truman!' and bought us drinks, and it made me feel like I was with a celebrity."

That night she went home with Truman and slept with him for the first time. In the morning, she looked at sleeping Truman and asked herself, *Did I just sleep with a murderer?*

When Truman woke up, Tammy said, "I have to ask you a question."

"I know what you're going to ask me: if I murdered Jon Pownall."

"Yes. Did you?"

In response to her curiosity, Truman replied, "I didn't murder him."

"Really?"

"There's this thing called 'double jeopardy.' I could tell you that I did it right now, but they could never try me again. I could tell you the truth, but I didn't do it."

"Are you in the Mafia?"

"There's no such thing," he responded, and Tammy believed him.

At that time, Tammy was also in casual relationships with two other men, Ronnie and Johnny, and she wasn't ready to be in a committed relationship. She liked Truman but didn't "love" him.

On Wednesday and Friday nights, Truman held illegal poker games at his apartment on the top floor above Herb Schwartz' interior design office.[7]

Truman called the apartment with red walls and white carpet the "Attic Social Club." He would "rake"

---

[7] Tammy said that she and Truman often entertained Dan Lilley at Truman's place. And, according to Jean Pownall, Schwartz, Reef, Mooers, and Lilley were involved in Truman's high-stakes, illegal poker games (stated in depositions).

in cash by taking one dollar for every round of poker from each of the players. Truman also supplied everyone's brand of cigarettes, liquor, and beer. There was one occasion when Tammy was present that Truman became explosive, most likely from losing too many hands—throwing the card table and everything else in sight—in a total rage. Tammy said that she had never seen such a scary, angry person in her life. "I was terrified!" she recalled.

Around that time, Tammy knew that two narcotics officers, Russo and Pike, would often stake out the building, trying to get into Truman's apartment or find out information.

Although Tammy had her own apartment at the time, she'd borrow Truman's brown Suburban on poker nights and switch off seeing Ronnie and Johnny. However, Truman had a key to her apartment and showed up one morning when she was in bed with another man. She said, "Truman, you have to leave." He did so silently. Later, she went to his place and found him very upset and crying. She promised that she would never do that again. But she did—with Johnny.

One night about 5 a.m., Tammy parked Truman's Suburban on the street in front of Johnny's house, so it was easy for Truman to spot. While she was in bed with Johnny, they heard Truman banging on her door, ordering them to come out. They were both too scared to answer it and hoped he would just go away. Finally, he left. Later that day, she arrived back at her apartment and Truman was sitting there with two glasses of red wine. When she walked in, he threw the second glass at the wall. It shattered and the red wine went everywhere!

Truman warned her, "If you EVER see Johnny again, I'm going to do to him like I did to Jon Pownall. He can put his head between his legs and kiss his ass goodbye. I'm going to fucking blow him away, which is exactly what I did to Jon Pownall."

She knew he wasn't kidding. Johnny never saw Tammy again. Neither did Ronnie. Tammy knew Ronnie really cared about her so she couldn't understand why he just completely stopped calling her and answering her calls. Ten years later, Tammy ran into Ronnie, and she asked why he stopped seeing her. "Because Truman Dongo came to see me. He threatened me, saying, 'If you ever see her again, I will fucking kill you.'"

Tammy said that Herb Schwartz was creepy, and his relationship with Truman was extremely odd, as if he owed Truman something.

Interestingly, Attorney Dan Lilley remained close friends with Truman after the trials and would often get together with Tammy and Truman, along with Lilley's mistress. It was not unusual for them to do cocaine. Tammy heard Dan Lilley say that, at the time of the murder trial, he knew he could get Truman off; and even if he couldn't, there was a card he could have played. "There was one juror who was compromised. We could have declared a mistrial," he told Truman.

Summer 1980

Tammy moved in with Truman who was dealing and using cocaine and Tammy became addicted. Then things got really, really crazy. He beat her three or four times. She'd always leave him, but she was as addicted to him as much as she was addicted to cocaine, and she always went back.

One time, they both had six days of coke in their system without eating or barely sleeping, and Truman thought she had lost her mind. He drove her to Maine Med like a madman, even crashing into their gate, and told them to admit her into the P6 (psychiatric ward), but they let her go and admitted him there instead! Twenty minutes later, Tammy drove out of the hospital parking lot and hit a building. An ambulance took her back to Maine Med for stitches. She said that, even though she had coke in her pocket, they left it there. When Truman got home, despite her stitches, he beat her and pushed her down a flight of stairs.

Every time Truman would walk out of the room, Tammy would take some coke, put it in a piece of paper, then slip it into her back pocket until she had enough to fill a Noxzema jar, just in case she decided to leave Truman.

At one point, she did leave Truman and went to Florida with an old boyfriend and the stash of coke. When the coke was gone, she flew back to Boston and asked Truman to pick her up, which he did without complaint. She had no money, no coke, and nowhere else to go.

There was one night when Truman told Tammy that he was very angry with their friends—another couple—accusing them of stealing his coke. He grabbed his gun and wanted to go to the couple's house to confront them and get his coke back. He took Tammy along. Tammy realized that the couple was sound asleep and, if they had stolen the cocaine, they would have been using it, not sleeping. Everyone was soon awake and dealing with Truman's interrogations and threats. Tammy wrote on their kitchen chalkboard, "Be careful, he has a gun." Then she pointed out the chalkboard to the man. Instead of thanking her for the warning, he called out, "Hey, Truman! I want you to see this!" Truman ended up beating Tammy again that night.

The only way for Tammy to get out of this relationship was to tell Truman that she was stealing his coke. After she admitted it to him, she left, knowing that he'd never trust her again.

However, she did eventually call Truman and ask if she could come back, and he said yes. But after a couple of weeks, things were getting worse and worse. Truman and Tammy got into a huge argument in front of some friends, and he got on his motorcycle and crashed it into a dumpster.

He screamed at Tammy, "I'm done with you now. It's over!" Then he told everyone to leave. They didn't dare disobey Truman Dongo.

She cried out, "Please, somebody, call 911. He's got a gun!" Her plea fell on deaf ears, as they left without her.

Tammy knew Truman had the gun in a tissue box in the bedroom, and she also knew he'd use it on her. She went upstairs and lifted the waterbed mattress, pushing the gun into the middle. Sure enough, Truman came in and looked in the box for his gun. It wasn't there.

"Where's my gun?"

"Teresa took it," she said over and over again.

He didn't believe her and, in a frenzy, tore up the room, even lifting the waterbed mattress, but not far enough to see the gun.

A female roommate, who had been living with them for some time, was in another room. Truman went to her, proclaiming his love for her, loudly enough for Tammy to hear.

Tammy got down on her knees and prayed, "Please God, I will do anything if you get me out of this. I'll never do cocaine again."

Truman came back upstairs and threw $50 at Tammy. "Get out," he ordered. And she did.

A month later, Tammy went to see Truman, and he gave her two bouquets of flowers as a truce. "Come back in a couple days and I'll let you take your stuff," he offered.

A couple of days later, she called Truman, but a police officer answered his phone. They asked, "Tammy, do you know where Truman is?"

"No, I have no idea. He's probably off partying somewhere," she responded.

"The only things missing are Truman and his telephone cord," the police officer commented.

She thought that was a strange thing for him to say.

* * * * *

September 1983

A few days after her conversation with the police, Tammy was walking to work when she stopped for a newspaper. The headline stated that the badly decomposed body of Truman Dongo was found in

Stow, Maine. Murdered. She thought, "Oh my God, you did it now, buddy. You thought you could just get away with this forever, didn't you?" referring to the times he threatened people, tortured them.

She realized that she was just moments, days, weeks from being with Truman when he was shot. "My whole body just shook, and I cried and cried, knowing I could have been killed, too."

After Truman's murder, Tammy went to the police and talked to Detective Conley about how Truman confessed many crimes to her, including the burglary of a safe and arson of a Friendly's Ice Cream restaurant. He wasn't just a thief; he committed a litany of crimes, including murder.

Tammy started going to AA and got clean. She never did cocaine again. In fact, she ran for Maine House of Representatives/District 121 from Cape Elizabeth in 2022.

Lisa Morelli

Truman became heavily involved in dealing cocaine, and in September 1983 he was murdered (an "occupational hazard") in a bad drug deal.

* * * * *

According to The State of Maine v. Lisa Morelli—

September 21, 1983

"Truman Dongo, a reputed drug dealer, was shot and killed in Stow [Maine] where he had been taken by

GOODBYE, FAT LARRY

Michael Marshall, Michael's brother Robert Marshall, and defendant Lisa Morelli.

"Michael Marshall testified for the State at the defendant's (Lisa Morelli) trial. He admitted that he had dealings with Mr. Dongo in the cocaine distribution business. Michael Marshall also testified that he owed Mr. Dongo approximately $8,500, and that Mr. Dongo had begun to pressure him to pay the debt. At trial, Michael Marshall stated that about one and one-half weeks before the shooting, he went to Mr. Dongo's apartment and was kept there against his will with his hands and feet bound. Shortly after this incident, according to Michael Marshall, he developed a plan to take Mr. Dongo's money and drugs.

"On September 20, Michael Marshall, Robert Marshall, and defendant were at Mr. Dongo's apartment. Because, in his words, 'the situation looked right,' Michael Marshall threatened Mr. Dongo with a gun and then tied Mr. Dongo's hands and feet. At about 4:00-4:30 a.m. on September 21 after locating and taking Mr. Dongo's drugs and money, Michael Marshall, Robert Marshall, defendant, and Mr. Dongo left Mr. Dongo's apartment by car, eventually arriving in Stow after making several stops for soda, beer, and motor oil.

"After leaving the highway and driving onto a logging road, Michael Marshall parked the car. At trial, he agreed that he had a gun in his hand and control over Mr. Dongo. Michael Marshall testified that after a short walk with Mr. Dongo and defendant, he decided that he would 'just tie Truman up, leave, take his money and drugs, and leave the state.' According to Michael Marshall, he told defendant (Lisa) to go back to the car to get a telephone cord that had been used to tie up Mr. Dongo. Michael Marshall testified that defendant refused to get the cord, saying 'You can't leave him here,' and then she raised a gun and shot Mr. Dongo. According to Michael Marshall, Mr. Dongo, after being shot by defendant, began to move toward the defendant, lunging for the gun that defendant had discarded after the shooting. Michael Marshall testified that he then shot Mr. Dongo once.

"Lisa Morelli also gave testimony at her trial.

"In defendant's version of the events of September 21, after the car was parked on a woodsy road in Stow, Robert Marshall gave her a small handgun. Defendant testified that Michael Marshall asked her, about four times, 'Are you going to do it?' which defendant took to mean, 'Are you going to shoot the gun?' The defendant stated that she thought Michael Marshall was going to kill Mr. Dongo. She testified that she buried her head in Michael Marshall's chest and 'shot the gun in the general direction. I didn't know what I was shooting at.' Defendant testified that Mr. Dongo was about three or four feet away from her when she fired. According to defendant, after she fired, she heard Mr. Dongo call her name, 'Lisa!' and saw him running toward her. Defendant testified that she threw down her gun, which fired on impact, and ran toward the car. She stated that while on the way to the car, she heard three more shots.

"Dr. Ronald Roy, deputy chief medical examiner, testified that Mr. Dongo was struck by three or four bullets. One wound, made by a .22 caliber bullet, was in the lower right abdomen. In addition, there were several broken ribs on the left side and a severely fractured shoulder blade. Vertebrae in Mr. Dongo's neck were fractured, as was a bone in his upper right arm. Mr. Dongo's skull was also fractured. Dr. Roy testified that the level of fracture found in the upper body wounds indicated that a different weapon, capable of higher velocity, caused the upper body wounds as compared to the .22 caliber wound in the lower abdomen. Dr. Roy concluded that the cause of death was gunshot wounds of the head and trunk. He specifically included the wound in the 'right pelvic area near the groin' among the wounds to the trunk."

* * * * *

Essentially, Truman was shot by Miss Morelli, then finished off by Michael Marshall.

Whatever happened to Joseph A. Castellucci?

Joe Castellucci

©Photography by Tom Jones. *The Maine Times,* Sept. 7, 1973.

Courtesy of Lynda Pownall.

Joseph A. Castellucci, the State's star witness for the Prosecution in the trial of Herbert Schwartz and Truman Dongo for the murder of Jon Pownall, was never charged in the murder, despite that he admitted (in court) to following orders to leave a matchbook in the exterior door so that anyone, including the killer(s), could enter the building, and to wear his white hat as a signal that the coast was clear. And he had admittedly been involved in the discussions and scheming with the defendants for a month before the murder. The jurors called him "shifty," and did not believe that the Prosecution proved its case against

GOODBYE, FAT LARRY

Herbert Schwarz and Truman Dongo, deciding there was reasonable doubt.

Joe was never awarded the money from the $400,000 insurance policy. But Castellucci did not stop his quest for the fast buck, an easy mark, an opportunity to make money, even at the expense of his loved ones. He was used to the laid-back life on the coast of Maine, great seafood, satisfying cocktails, company of the influential and affluent, the good life of someone who earned it. But an honest day's work was never part of the plan to achieve his goal. Every job he had over the years since college graduation did not work out, and he was used to keeping company with big-time gamblers and drug dealers. "Unorganized crime."

And Joe's dubious cohorts often persuaded him that there was a "plum" ready for the picking. Make a plan. Prepare yourself for the unexpected. Then do it. Just be smart about it.

Joe was convinced that he could always outsmart the law, that he had all the answers and could talk his way out of any situation—even play dumb.

Castellucci thought he could get away with another murder, or murders, using a similar tactic to the murder of Jon Pownall: hire a professional assassin to kill his in-laws, Elliott and Yana Stern and their daughter Vicki, of Freeport, New York. His goal? With his wife's family dead, she would inherit Elliott's photography business! Disturbingly similar to his desire for Jon Pownall's business.

Then Joe made a mistake. A big mistake. His intention was to "pay a hit man $150,000 to commit the murders," said Lieutenant Joseph Kobus of the

New Jersey State Police. He didn't check out the credentials of the hit man. The assassin "turned out to be a state police detective" equipped with a tape recorder. Every word, every detail of how he wanted this abominable crime to play out was taped and submitted into evidence at his trial.

Superior Court Judge C. Judson Hamlin described Castellucci as "amoral." He also commented that "nearly everyone connected to him seemed to get into trouble." Judge Hamlin sentenced him to serve 30 years in the Trenton State Prison for the attempted murder of his family members.

But Joe's story doesn't end there.

Following his conviction on the attempted murder charges, but before sentencing, Castellucci was indicted again. This time, it was a charge of stealing $30,000 worth of silver from a female neighbor. He had posed as a "go-between" for the "thief," trying to sell the silver back to the neighbor for $10,000. It was the belief of the police that Joe planned to abscond with the money to avoid prison.

His escape plan didn't work. He was held on bail in Middlesex County Jail in lieu of $100,000 bail. After pleading guilty, he was handed a 5-year sentence to run concurrently with his 30-year sentence.

Joe never thought he would end up in prison, amongst hardened criminals, murderers, thugs, drug dealers, pushers, and users. It seemed to be terrifying for him. He came across as an everyday guy, trying to eke a living as an executive salesman in Piscataway Township, New Jersey, at the time of the attempted murder, even though his methods were hardly innocent.

GOODBYE, FAT LARRY

Or was it just another game for a "Get Out of Jail" card?

When he entered Middlesex County Adult Correction Center on January 8, 1981, to await trial, he stood five-foot seven inches and weighed 210 pounds. By April of that same year, he weighed 185 pounds. On October 26, 1984, "his pale, bony frame carried only 107 pounds," according to the Superior Court Judge Barnet Hoffman. The doctor at the prison reported he was "suffering from depression and an anorexic condition." Judge Hoffman agreed that private care would be beneficial, but he could not justify such an expense to taxpayers, as Castellucci would have to be under constant guard. And yet another doctor claimed he was "suffering from chronic depression, which creates psychosomatic gastro-intestinal disorders," caused by prison life. Another doctor recommended that Joe be placed in a private hospital for electric shock therapy.

Joe had also been taken to the prison infirmary of St. Francis Medical Center in Trenton where doctors tried to feed him.

Judge Hoffman reviewed Joe's medical reports, noting that he also suffered from gastroenteritis, colitis, and dental problems. However, he also read that Castellucci had maintained the same weight for the past two years and, therefore, he determined that his condition "was not life-threatening or deteriorating, as a result of his incarceration."

The judge said that he "was forced" to deny Castellucci's request for a change of sentence due to the "severity of the crimes."

However, after just six years, he was released from prison and settled in Boothbay, Maine.

In a 2024 Seacoast Oldies radio broadcast with Richard Stanley, Lynda Pownall said she had recorded an interview with Castellucci, asking him, "Why did you send Herb Schwartz to my dad's office the night of the murder?" He replied without hesitation, "Because I thought they could work things out." That was a direct admission that he was involved, and that Herb was there!

Eventually, Joe moved to California to live with family and died on February 18, 2020, from cancer.

Whatever happened to The Salem Six cast?

The Salem Six cast at a reunion August 25, 2019. Left to right, Top row: Luke Pickett, Charles Hall, Geoff Stump, Bottom row: Melanie McGorrill, Sam Patton, Diane Dee, and Billy Foster.

Photo ©Kim Chapman Photography, 2017

In 2019, Lynda Pownall-Carlson was working with Alix Lambert on a movie project and one of her questions was, "How did the murder affect the kids from *The Salem Six*?"

Lynda recalled, "Alix and I started a search to find them. My mom had been in touch with one of the kids,

Melanie McGorrill, over the years, so she was the first person we contacted.

"Alix surprised me by gathering everyone at Fort Williams Park in Cape Elizabeth, Maine. I can't describe the emotions! I wish my brother T.G. could have been there, but he had too many work responsibilities at the time."

It was the first time the kids had seen each other in 46 years. After everyone became reacquainted, they shared their personal memories and expressed how they reacted to Jon's death and cancellation of the movie.

Melanie recalled that, shortly after Jon's death, her family had invited Jean Pownall for dinner. She handed Jean the paycheck she received for her part in the film. Jean didn't want to accept it, but Melanie's parents insisted, since Mel remembered what Jon had said about his family not receiving any money if he died. Jean was very touched by her generosity.

Billy Foster, who played the lead role of "Rick," wrote poetry about the moment when time seemed to stand still as the news of Jon's death was delivered to the cast.

Sam Patton, who played "Sam," wondered if anyone had an inkling of "the doom and gloom that was to come."

Luke Pickett shared that his dad was told by the FBI that Planet 3 Films had a $150,000 life insurance policy on each of the kids.

Geoff Stump and Charles Hall had bonded during the film rehearsals as they were both musicians even at an early age, so reuniting was special. Charles passed away in August 2020, but he stood out in the

GOODBYE, FAT LARRY

cast by being different—always wearing a hat and having the only kayak with a bold design.

Author's note: I felt very honored to receive a call from Charles Hall's mother in March 2023. She said that, even as a child, Charles was very independent and a go-getter. He took it upon himself to travel to Portland by bus to audition for The Salem Six during the time she was having a baby. Of course, when Jon was shot and killed, it was quite a shock for him.

* * * * *

It was sad for everyone to say goodbye that weekend, but now they plan to stay in touch.

Whatever happened to the gun?

After the murder trial, the .38 caliber 5-shot Smith & Wesson Chief's Special was borrowed from Evidence by Attorney Ralph Lancaster for use in the civil trial, but never returned.

After confronting Lancaster at his Portland, Maine, office about it, Lynda, her cousin Todd, and husband Larry Cieslinski were told by Lancaster that it was secure in his office safe.

When Lynda asked that he return the gun to State's Evidence, Lancaster rudely responded, "Stop picking at an old scab!"

Despite the rudeness that he exhibited to them, Lynda said that Lancaster was a sophisticated, intelligent, and highly skilled attorney, and the best attorney associated with her father's case.

"I remember looking at the family photos in his office. Would he not want his children to seek the truth if he had been murdered?" she wondered. "Why would he even want the murder weapon? What right would he have to keep it? Were the police aware that

GOODBYE, FAT LARRY

he had never returned it? And why did he feel the need to treat us that way?"

It is unknown if Lancaster ever returned the gun.

Whatever happened to the Pownall family?

Jean Pownall, Family photo.

After the murder trial, the conspiracy trial, and the civil trial regarding the $400,000 Transamerica insurance policy, Jean Pownall decided to move back to her hometown of Rochester, New York, with two of her children. In an interview with Jon Lovell, senior writer for the *Casco Bay Weekly,* Jean told him, "One of the reasons I left Maine was that I didn't want my children ever to walk down a street in Portland and run into their father's murderer."

With her insurance payout of $35,000 (with a third going to an attorney), Jean bought a Dutch Colonial house in the suburbs.

Jean was hired at Pennwalt Pharmaceuticals in Henrietta, New York, and worked there for 14 years. Co-workers remember her as a hardworking, sophisticated lady who had a Rubenesque figure, dressed well, and wore nicely applied makeup.

Jean passed away on September 13, 2012, at the age of 77.

Jon and Jean's eldest son Jon (Richard) Pownall passed away in 2011. Their daughter Lynda started her own artisan glassworks company. The younger son, Thomas, still lives in New York with his family.

Jon's mother, Germaine Mailhot Pownall, a devout Jehovah Witness, died in 1989 and is buried in Springvale, Maine, awaiting the Resurrection. Her gravestone is next to Jon's.

Jon Pownall's stone is clearly engraved "MURDERED" at the quiet spot in Springvale's Riverside Cemetery. The burial plot that sits in front of his stone remains empty, with no promise of resting in peace for its unfortunate future occupant.

Photo ©Elly Stevens, 2021

ELLY STEVENS

Memoriam posted by Lynda Pownall on the 50th anniversary of Jon's death in 2023.

IN MEMORIAM
In Loving Memory Of

JON POWNALL
Aug. 12, 1934 - Aug. 30, 1973

Once upon a time in 1973,
I saw my father kiss my mother goodbye.
I never saw him again.

My Dad, Jon Pownall, was the center of our family and kept us all together with his charisma, love, and incredible talent.

In 1973 he was making a movie called, "The Salem 6." That creation ended in August of that same year when he was murdered.

Jon is missed by us, his family, and by all the lives he touched in his 39 years. Thirty nine years was too short. Murder has many victims.

A book will be released by Elly Stevens in the near future and a movie about Jon Pownall is planned.

Author's thoughts

By Elly Stevens

In retrospect I must ask, what could have been done differently or better in the Jon Pownall murder case?

The trial may have ended in one or two convictions if the State had tried Truman Dongo and Herbert Schwartz separately. They did consider it. However, it probably cost the state less to try them together. I am sure that the D.A. felt it also made a stronger case to try Schwartz with Dongo, but it unequivocally backfired.

The District Attorney should have put Jean Pownall and David Joy on the stand on the murder trial, as they both had valuable information.

Dongo may have been convicted if it hadn't been for his wife's testimony that they were at a drive-in movie that night. If the jury had been able to learn that Mrs. Dongo failed the polygraph test, and also heard the testimony of the jailhouse snitch who said that Dongo and Schwartz went to the drive-in to create an alibi, it may have changed their decision.

Schwartz was not kind to Jon Pownall. In fact, he was filled with anger and rage, and he was not open to negotiation. He also threatened to kill him. Herb was an intelligent, clever man but was capable of planning every detail of the murder. That doesn't necessarily mean that he shot Jon, but he may have been the brains behind it. However, the Prosecution failed to prove his participation in the crime or that he was a conspirator. Herb also viewed Castellucci as a lackey, but Joe proved to be calculating enough to cover his tracks, more than even Schwartz himself.

In my opinion, Joe Castellucci should have been indicted and tried (separately) for his participation in Jon Pownall's murder, as well as Dongo and Schwartz. He may not have pulled the trigger, but he did pay close attention to the time that night, peer out at the parking lot before he left Planet 3 under the guise of checking the time, and place the matchbook cover in the door after his meeting with Jon. He had the police and his own attorney hoodwinked, and they underestimated his cunning. No one saw through his lies or realized that he had a carefully constructed alibi and his own agenda. Joe failed to get the insurance payout, but he didn't spend one day in jail for his involvement in this crime.

In court, two narratives were presented, and each side selected the evidence to support their narrative. Without question, the Defense Team of Lilley and Simmons blew away the Prosecution. Lilley also keyed in on Cohen's approach and dismantled his case. They had even skillfully broken down the police on the stand and made them look incompetent. The Defense used all the tactics, evidence, and narrative that persuaded the jury to believe there was reasonable doubt. The D.A.'s case disintegrated with only one proven piece of evidence: it was Truman's gun that was used at the scene. Everything else was circumstantial and based on Joe Castellucci's testimony. His story was often incredible.

Perhaps Judge Glassman should have recused himself since he knew Herb Schwartz. It was sufficient for a mistrial, but it was never revealed. Lilley had personal connections to Cohen, Reef, Mooers, and Dongo.

Some of the police officers could have handled the evidence better. Many were lacking recall of important information and should have reviewed their own reports before testifying. The State never accounted for the extra bullet, which added even more doubt.

The only mistake Jon Pownall made was trusting his associates. He needed someone to handle his movie's finances, but never checked out the people he trusted with his money, his film, or his film company. More than one person had connections to the underworld, and it's not known if those connections were tied to Jon's death. And one bad mistake (hiring Castellucci) led to another and another and another.

It's obvious that insurance money was the motive for Jon's murder, no matter which possible suspect we look at. First, there was Joe Thomas who mentioned bumping off Jon for the money; then Herb Schwartz who saw it as the means to get control of the company, the movie, and the insurance money; Truman Dongo who would do anything for cash; and Attorney Reef who had private conversations with Schwartz to remove Jon from the picture permanently. After the murder, Reef assured them saying, "It's a case that will never be solved." Why was he so confident? What did he know? Attorney Lilley had a plan up his sleeve to declare a mistrial to protect his friend Dongo. Lastly, there was Joe Castellucci who was submersed in debt through his own spending, bank loans for Planet 3 Films, and what he owed to Sal Cataldo. Joe also inquired if the policies covered murder.

The timing of Jon's death was paramount. Once the Hollywood contracts were signed, they'd have to pay off the stars. If Jon had signed Reef's Director's Contract, he might have lived, although he would have lost control of his own movie and been kicked to the curb. Joe might have been next.

The next question is, who stabbed Jon in the throat? Did the police assume that Dongo, Schwartz, or even Castellucci had done it? Truman wasn't talking, leaving some to think he acted alone.

Could there have been another man present, perhaps a stranger to Jon, a pig farmer or a butcher, at the crime scene with the sole duty of stabbing Jon "like a fat pig"? Sending a message is a classic maneuver of a mob hit.

This "accomplice" may have also carried a second .38 revolver—accounting for the third bullet. Or did the assassin carry a second gun? There was no solid evidence for a second weapon, but the police confirmed it was indeed Dongo's gun that was fired at the crime scene. Lt. Dodd said it looked like a "professional hit." So much hate, disgust, and revenge in that one action.

All Jon wanted to do was make his movie. It might possibly have made him a "household name." The six kids might have even gone on to become well-known child actors in Hollywood.

It was Jon's time to be famous. After all the screaming matches with Reef and Schwartz, he still believed his movie would be made and he'd be blessed with good press and accolades from his peers.

GOODBYE, FAT LARRY

He was certainly taken advantage of.

I am very sad for his family, who never found justice. To read in the court transcripts that Castellucci was contemplating a life insurance policy on Jean just a day or two before the murder sends chills down my spine. It could have been at Jon's insistence, or just another way to get his hands on money.

Jean Pownall had to start life all over again as a single parent, while protecting her children from the murderers who were never punished for their crime. Lynda, her brother Tom, and their cousin Todd Pownall continue to be haunted by Jon's murder since the acquittal. They don't want him to be forgotten for the husband, father, and creative filmmaker he was.

I know there is no resolution. There will never be justice. No one will ever be held accountable in this life for the death of Jon Pownall, even if they test for DNA. The truth will never be revealed.

Jon Pownall, I hope you will rest in peace now that your story has been shared with the world.

And Larry...you, too, have been obsessed with Jon's story of injustice for decades. Telling your own story made this book interesting. You accomplished what you set out to do. It's time to move on to different things in your life, such as your children, grandchildren, and other loved ones. God bless you, Larry, and thank you for finding me to work on this story.

Epilogue

By Larry Cieslinski

Coincidences? Hardly.

Was it coincidence that Jon's parked Volkswagen bus was captured in a Portland Historical Photo of Monument Square during its reconstruction just before his death? Not a chance.

Was it coincidence that his daughter walked into my shop? What was the possibility that I would take interest in her? I already had a "full dance card" with two little girls at home and their mom. Then I discovered that Lynda lived down the street from me. When she opened up about her father's untimely demise, the adrenalin of talking to a person on the other side lit a fire inside me. There was also the adventure of going to the crime scene on the anniversary of his death. The first time I met Jon, as a ghost, was in the light of a full moon in the cemetery where he's buried.

Then there was the psychic who told me to wait until everyone was dead before telling my story. And there were threats I never understood till recently.

I had read the court transcripts and learned how the gun was sold to a felon, discarded, then found by accident, and about the trial and the jury's conclusion.

Forty-seven years later, when everyone directly involved in the crime was dead, I met up with my old classmate, Elly Stevens, at a grammar school reunion.

GOODBYE, FAT LARRY

I never went to reunions, but I felt compelled to attend this one. Elly, who had authored two books and was working on her third, said she would write the book so that Jon could rest—and so I could rest, too. I had never thought about that, but she was right. It was time.

Interestingly, Elly said that Jean Pownall had worked in the same company as her sister. Another coincidence?

With so many coincidences, I knew that everything I was experiencing was happening exactly the way Jon planned it.

My marriage to Lynda wasn't going to last forever. Only a fool would think so.

Was I afraid that something would happen to me? Hell, yes. When you're sniffing around a murder, they know who you are.

What did it cost me, anyway? A good woman, a beautiful daughter, a house, a car business I worked so hard to build, money, my reputation, and a heart that was broken. It was a rude awakening. I was half ashamed for my failure and half ashamed for the people who tried to warn me. I had ignored them. Yes, I was blinded by love. It cost me something so deep inside, but it made me the man I am today.

Now, don't get me wrong. I'm not a little bitter. I'm a LOT bitter, and I was a little hurt. But you know, obviously, that you can't be "a little hurt" or "a little pregnant." At least I didn't take out a large life insurance policy on myself.

Goodbye, Fat Larry.

Acknowledgements

This book would not have been possible if Larry Cieslinski had not approached me and insisted this would be possible. Thank you, Larry, for chronicling your side of the story and keeping Jon's memory alive all these years. Our connection was not a coincidence.

Thanks to Irene Knights for holding the class reunions in 2013 and 2015 after which Larry and I connected.

To Retired Detective Peter Conley, I extend my sincerest appreciation for reviewing the crime scene copy.

My gratitude to the Portland Police Department, especially Detective Robert Martin and Attorney Jen Thompson, for allowing us to review and copy case files, and to Julie Sherman, the Executive Assistant to the Chief of Police, for getting some of the files scanned and sent to me. Without these files, I would never have known many of the details. And Ray Saba, thank you for accommodating us in the PD's parking garage and making sure we didn't get lost.

I am grateful to Tricia Gesner, the Associated Press researcher, who provided the photo of *The Salem Six* for this book. It's one of the most important images for the story.

A tremendous thank you to Abraham Schechter, the Special Collections Librarian and Archivist in the Portland Room of the Portland Public Library, for working relentlessly to obtain the historical photo of Monument Square for this book.

It was an honor to speak with each of *The Salem Six* cast members who shared their memories from that summer in 1973. This is their story, too.

I was not able to reach Tom Jones of Tom Jones Photography, Brunswick, Maine, regarding four photos. However, they had been purchased by the McGorrill family who provided them for this book.

I appreciate all the journalists who have kindly allowed me to quote from their articles: John Lovell, John S. Day, and Miranda Spivack; and Larry Postaer for the backstory on "Son of Helicopter" (and for Britt McColl's help reaching Larry).

Thanks to Roger Griswold, Meteorologist for WMTW Channel 8, Portland, for taking the time to research the weather on the night of August 30, 1973.

Larry and I express our gratitude to Attorney Tyson Blue for thoroughly editing the manuscript and reviewing it for legal issues.

My friend Retired Lieutenant Fred Lisanby, Lexington Kentucky Police Department, reviewed the ballistics-testing content and I value his expertise and comments.

Tammy Bonneau Walter, thank you for sharing this part of your life story and photos with us. We know it was an intense time, and you held nothing back. We are amazed at all your accomplishments since then, and you should be proud.

To authors Michael Benson and Joe Janowicz who read my first draft and gave me positive feedback, I am so appreciative.

Thanks to the owner of Old Port Tavern in Portland, Maine, for the use of a photo from their website.

Even though some sources were unable to find images, I appreciate the research efforts of Lori Thayer whose father was the courtroom artist during the trial; Douglas Rooks, former owner of *The Maine Times;* Sara Duke of the Library of Congress; John Kyros of General Motors Media Archive; Colby Cotter of *The Boston Globe;* Michele McDonald of the *Portland Press;* Sofia Yalouris of the Maine Historical Society; Emily Arbuckle of the Portland Museum; Carmen Greenlee, Humanities and Media Librarian, Bowdoin College; the Photographic Society of America; the Art Institute of Chicago; and the *Chicago Tribune.*

With my good friend Suzanne Blessing's layout skills, this book turned out masterfully! Thank you for your time and patience, as well.

To Kate Rawlins of Fiverr, I am very pleased with the creative cover and video book trailer.

A shout out to all my book fans. I couldn't do this without you.

And thanks to my patient husband who wondered why this book had taken so long to research, write, and publish.

Finally, thank you, Lynda and Thomas Pownall, for supporting this effort, not only with content and photos, but providing me with insight into the family's perspective during the most heartbreaking and frightening time of your lives. You wanted your father to be remembered as a brilliant and creative man who

GOODBYE, FAT LARRY

loved his family and who had great aspirations and big dreams. I hope I have accomplished that goal and pray that your family will find some peace.

Elly

About Elly Stevens

Elly Stevens was born and raised in Rochester, New York, in a family of storytellers. Her mother, Helen Fedyk, was an avid reader and owned a collection of pulp fiction where there was always a detective, a dame, and a dead body. Elly developed the same love of pulp and started writing detective stories as early as age 6.

Following her dream of writing, she joined the Publications group at Eastman Kodak Company as a proofreader, writer, editor, and project manager. She retired in 2004.

When Larry Cieslinski told her about the chilling murder of his father-in-law, Jon Pownall, she read the court transcripts and felt compelled to write this book.

For more information on Elly, see her website at **https://www.authorellystevens.com**.

About Larry Cieslinski

Larry Cieslinski was born into a Polish-Italian family and has been communicating with the dead since he was four. After learning of his father-in-law's murder, he was obsessed to have the story told.

Larry and Elly Stevens have known each other since kindergarten. In 2020, he asked Elly to write the book and include his story, too.

When Larry was 19, he was recruited by Ford Motor Company and was later asked by General Motors to discuss fuel injection with their engineers. An enthusiast of "imperfect classic cars," Larry started his own foreign-car repair and parts business, Access Auto, that was written up nationally before he turned 21.

He also plays guitar and harmonica and jammed with countless rock and country stars for ten years, working onstage and backstage with them.

He has a son, four daughters and several grandchildren.

Sources

Court Transcripts

State of Maine, Cumberland, Maine, Superior Court, Docket Nos. 74-2013, I-75-309, May 1975

Newspapers

Asbury Park Press, Asbury Park, New Jersey
   Thu. Jan. 29, 1981, p.62, *Accused Jerseyman had role in murder trial*
   Thu. Nov. 19, 1981, p.35, *Suspect was 'set up,' lawyer claims*
Biddeford-Saco Journal, Biddeford, Maine
   Fri. Aug. 31, 1973, p.2, *Portland Movie Director Found Dead at Office*
   Sat. Sep. 1, 1973, p.2, *Slain Director Met With Producer Before Shot*
   Mon. Oct. 8, 1973, p.5, *No Arrests Made in Recent Slayings*
   Wed. Jan. 8, 1975, p.10, *Dongo Refused Bail*
   Sat. Feb. 15, 1975, p.3, *Decorator Named in Pownall Killing*
   Thu. Sep. 25, 1975, p.10, *Schwartz Gets Court Attorney*
   Wed. May 5, 1976, p.5, *No Court-appointed Dongo Counsel, Judge Says*
   Wed. Jan. 26, 1977, p.2, *Doubting jury frees Dongo and Schwartz*
Casco Bay Weekly, Portland, Maine
   Thu. Sep. 16, 1993, p.9, *A Murder Remembered* by Jon Lovell

GOODBYE, FAT LARRY

Chicago Tribune, Chicago, Illinois
Tue. Sep. 5, 1967, p.67, *Pownall & Veinat Cinematography*
Tue. Apr. 21, 1970, p. 52, *'Son' Has Happy Ending* by Allan Jaklich
Evening Express, Portland, Maine
Fri. Aug. 31, 1973, p.1, *Movie Director Slain in Monument Sq. Office* by Joseph Coyne
Sat. May 17, 1975, p.1 & 10, *Castellucci Wavers on Previous Testimony* by John Lovell
Express News, San Antonio, Texas
Sat. Sep. 1, 1973, p.6-B, *Movie Director Found Slain, Shot in Head*
Kennebec Journal, Augusta, Maine
Thu. Sep. 25, 1975, p.23, *High court allows Schwartz free counsel*
Wed. Jun. 2, 1976, p.5, *Dongo files appeal*
Wed. Jan. 5, 1977, p.2, *Dongo-Schwartz jury selection is under way*
Tue. Jan. 11, 1977, p.10, *Trial begins*
Wed. Jan. 12, 1977, p.10, *Witness relates threat to Pownall*
Thu. Jan. 13, 1977, p.3, *Dongo-Schwartz trial continues in Portland*
Wed. Jan. 19, 1977, p.2, *Murder trial continues*
Thu. Jan. 20, 1977, p.20, *Court rules previous evidence not usable*
Mon. Jan. 31, 1977, p.5, *Pownall case suits expected*
Wed. Jun. 22, 1977, p.17, *Castellucci denies motivation*
Thu. Jun. 23, 1977, p.4, *Ex-film producer testifies in court*
Sat. Jun. 25, 1977, p.2, *Intervenor settles in slain director's case*
Tue. Jun. 28, 1977, p.3, *Lawyers spar over Pownall insurance policy,* by Miranda Spivack, Press Herald writer

ELLY STEVENS

Wed. Jun. 29, 1977, p.18, *Testimony ends*
Fri. Jul. 1, 1977, p.3, *Pownall: Jury says firm not liable*
Maine Sunday Telegram, Portland, Maine
   Sun. May 25, 1975, p.1A & 12A, *Time Stressed By Castellucci, Witness Says*
Maine Times, Portland, Maine
   Fri. Sep. 7, 1973, p.8-11, *Murder at Planet Three* by John N. Cole
Nashua Telegraph, Nashua, New Hampshire
   Tue. Dec. 23, 1974, p.2, *Hearing Is Set on Dongo Bail*
   Tue. Dec. 23, 1974, p.21, *Portland man indicted for Pownall killing*
Naugatuck Daily News, Naugatuck, Connecticut
   Wed. Oct. 31, 1973, p.7, *Film Co. Demands Payment*
Portland Press Herald, Portland, Maine
   Fri. Apr. 6, 1973, *You Ought to be in Pictures. Casting to Start Here in May,* provided by Portland Police Dept.
   Tue. Sep. 11, 1973, p.1 & 12, *Jon Pownall: He Had A Dream Murder Destroyed*
   Thu. Nov. 20, 1975, p.1 & 11, *Pownall's Brother Offers $10,000 For Conviction Evidence*
Press Courier, Oxnard, California
   Sat. Sep. 1, 1973, p.3, *Film Director Slain; No Weapon Found*
Rutland Daily Herald, Rutland, Vermont
   Tue. Dec. 24, 1974, p.5, *Portland Man Held in Director Slaying*
The Argus, Fremont, California
   Sun. May 25, 1975, p.34, *Murder suspects found innocent*
The Bangor Daily News, Bangor, Maine
   Fri. May 16, 1975, p.19, *Murder trial witness admits financial woes*

GOODBYE, FAT LARRY

Sat. May 17, 1975, p.25, *Castellucci denies he killed filmmaker*
Mon. May 19, 1975, p.5, *Castellucci admits gap in testimony*
Tue. May 20, 1975, p.13, *Testimony resumes in murder case*
Wed. May 21, 1975, p.21, *Pownall lawyer gives testimony*
Thu. May 22, 1975, p.5, *Defense to begin presentation*
Sat. May 24, 1975, p.22, *Future Shock: Portland* by John S. Day
Tue. Oct. 18, 1983, p.21, *Bullet wound killed Dongo*
Sat. Jul. 14, 1984, p.33, *Killer testifies that Morelli shot Truman Dongo*

The Boston Globe, Boston, Massachusetts
Mon. Sep. 3, 1973, p.24, *Police continue probe into director's murder*
Mon. Dec. 23, 1974, p.4, *Maine man indicted in film director death*
Sun. May 25, 1975, p.19, *2 Maine men found innocent in '73 murder of film director*
Wed. Oct. 19, 1983, p.68, *3 in Maine accused in slaying*

The Brattleboro Reformer, Brattleboro, Vermont
Wed. May 30, 1984, p.2, *Maine brothers found guilty of murder*

The Central New Jersey Home News, New Brunswick, New Jersey
Fri. Jan. 9, 1981, p.1, *Piscataway exec charged in plot to murder 3 in-laws*
Thu. Jan. 29, 1981, p.8, *Murder-for-insurance plot a rerun?*
Sat. Sep. 26, 1981, p.3, *Accused in death plot, he faces new counts*
Wed. Nov. 18, 1981, p.46, *Castellucci called cold-blooded killer and 'set-up' victim*

The Courier News, Bridgewater, New Jersey
  Mon. Jan. 12, 1981, p.15, *Entrapment to be drug case plea*
  Thu. May 21, 1981, p.2, *I never tried to kill my in-laws, suspect claims*
  Mon. Dec. 14, 1981, p.11, *Castellucci pleads innocent to burglary*
  Sat. Oct. 27, 1984, p.11, *'Anorexic' felon must stay in jail.*
The Daily Review, Hayward, California
  Sun. Sep. 2, 1973, p.24, *Slain producer insured $400,000*
The Portsmouth Herald, Portsmouth, New Hampshire
  Sat. Sep. 1, 1973, p.1, *Movie Man Shot Down From Rear*
  Mon. Dec. 8, 1975, p.10, *Double jeopardy claimed in murder case*
  Fri. Mar. 12, 1976, p.2, *Murder Trial on May 10*
  Wed. May 12, 1976, p.2, *Charge dismissed*
  Wed. Jun. 2, 1976, p.10, *Dongo wants free lawyer*
  Fri. Jul. 2, 1976, p.2, *Court rules to appoint trial lawyer*
  Thu. Jul. 22, 1976, p.23, *Conspiracy trial in murder case*
  Wed. Jan. 5, 1977, p.2, *Jury selection resumes*
  Wed. Jan. 12, 1977, p.2, *Murder trial*
  Mon. Jan. 31, 1977, p.2, *Criminal charges apparently ended*
Star News, Pasadena, California
  Sat. Sep. 1, 1973, p.A-6Z, *Director Jon Pownall Murdered*

Police Case Files, Portland Police Department

GOODBYE, FAT LARRY

Websites

https://zingmagazine.com/issues/zingmagazine24/?modal=alix-lambert

https://www.leagle.com/decision/1985829493a2d3361826, State v. Morelli

https://law.justia.com/cases/maine/supreme-court/1985/491-a-2d-554-0.html, State v. Marshall

https://www.pressherald.com/2023/09/01/filmmaker-killed-in-brutal-slaying-50-years-ago-remembered-at-vigil/

https://www.newscentermaine.com/article/news/local/portland/family-honors-man-killed-in-portland-50-years-ago-jon-pownall-maine/97-36741bb5-7796-411c-bde2-8cc532410675

Podcast/Interview

https://www.darkdowneast.com/episodes/jonpownall

https://seacoast oldies.com Richard Stanley with Lynda Pownall, Jun. 30, 2024

MURDER ON THE ERIE CANAL
By Elly Stevens

Do you know a killer when you see one?

Sue Gainer starts her career as a private investigator in a Rochester, NY, detective agency. When a missing person's case is dropped in her lap that ends in murder, Sue faces unusual and desperate suspects and unlocks the clues that lead to the surprising truth—and soon finds herself in deep water with a killer.

Available on Amazon.
https://www.AuthorEllyStevens.com

DANGEROUS PASSION
By Elly Stevens

When obsession turns to murder!

It started with a seemingly innocent goodnight kiss... Innocent, until one person's desire ignited a firestorm of passions leading to a disastrous chain of events.

When a prostitute is murdered, the police think they have their man. But do they? Will the evidence reveal the real killer? Or will the killer remain at large? Love, lust, jealousy, hatred, revenge, and greed. All part of everyday life. And all motives for murder. You won't want to put down this fast-paced book until the very end.

Available on Amazon.
https://www.AuthorEllyStevens.com

www.ingramcontent.com/pod-product-compliance
Lightning Source LLC
Chambersburg PA
CBHW060450030426
42337CB00015B/1540